CAMBRIDGE LIBRARY COLLECTION

Books of enduring scholarly value

Religion

For centuries, scripture and theology were the focus of prodigious amounts of scholarship and publishing, dominated in the English-speaking world by the work of Protestant Christians. Enlightenment philosophy and science, anthropology, ethnology and the colonial experience all brought new perspectives, lively debates and heated controversies to the study of religion and its role in the world, many of which continue to this day. This series explores the editing and interpretation of religious texts, the history of religious ideas and institutions, and not least the encounter between religion and science.

The Catechism of Positive Religion

This English edition of The Catechism of Positive Religion was published in 1891, thirty-four years after the death of Comte, the French philosopher of science and politics and founder of positivism, whose work was widely read in the later nineteenth century. Comte's self-published French original of 1852, translated here, outlines his progressive ideal of 'sociocracy', which would provide a systematic basis, free of metaphysics, for intellectual and moral transactions among humans. Congreve's edition, in common with other, divides the book into five parts. The introduction contains two dialogues, entitled General Theory of Religion and Theory of Humanity. Parts 1-3 respectively consider the Positivist's private and public 'worship'; 'doctrine', including the external world and human society and ethics; and 'regime' or way of life, private and public. The final two dialogues cover polytheism, monotheism and theocracy. This book remains of interest as an early precursor of secular humanist ethics.

T0381823

Cambridge University Press has long been a pioneer in the reissuing of out-of-print titles from its own backlist, producing digital reprints of books that are still sought after by scholars and students but could not be reprinted economically using traditional technology. The Cambridge Library Collection extends this activity to a wider range of books which are still of importance to researchers and professionals, either for the source material they contain, or as landmarks in the history of their academic discipline.

Drawing from the world-renowned collections in the Cambridge University Library, and guided by the advice of experts in each subject area, Cambridge University Press is using state-of-the-art scanning machines in its own Printing House to capture the content of each book selected for inclusion. The files are processed to give a consistently clear, crisp image, and the books finished to the high quality standard for which the Press is recognised around the world. The latest print-on-demand technology ensures that the books will remain available indefinitely, and that orders for single or multiple copies can quickly be supplied.

The Cambridge Library Collection will bring back to life books of enduring scholarly value across a wide range of disciplines in the humanities and social sciences and in science and technology.

The Catechism of
Positive Religion

*Or Summary Exposition of the Universal
Religion in Thirteen Systematic Conversations
Between a Woman and a Priest of Humanity*

AUGUSTE COMTE

CAMBRIDGE
UNIVERSITY PRESS

CAMBRIDGE UNIVERSITY PRESS

Cambridge New York Melbourne Madrid Cape Town Singapore São Paolo Delhi

Published in the United States of America by Cambridge University Press, New York

www.cambridge.org
Information on this title: www.cambridge.org/9781108000871

© in this compilation Cambridge University Press 2009

This edition first published 1891
This digitally printed version 2009

ISBN 978-1-108-00087-1

This book reproduces the text of the original edition. The content and language reflect the beliefs, practices and terminology of their time, and have not been updated.

THE

CATECHISM OF POSITIVE RELIGION

THE CATECHISM

OF

POSITIVE RELIGION

*TRANSLATED FROM THE FRENCH OF
AUGUSTE COMTE*

BY

RICHARD CONGREVE

𝔗𝔥𝔦𝔯𝔡 𝔈𝔡𝔦𝔱𝔦𝔬𝔫

REVISED AND CORRECTED

LONDON
KEGAN PAUL, TRENCH, TRÜBNER, & CO. LTD.
PATERNOSTER HOUSE, CHARING CROSS ROAD
1891

REPUBLIC OF THE WEST
ORDER AND PROGRESS—LIVE FOR OTHERS

———

THE

CATECHISM OF POSITIVISM

OR

SUMMARY EXPOSITION

OF

THE UNIVERSAL RELIGION

IN THIRTEEN SYSTEMATIC CONVERSATIONS BETWEEN A WOMAN AND A PRIEST OF HUMANITY;

By AUGUSTE COMTE

AUTHOR OF "THE SYSTEM OF POSITIVE PHILOSOPHY," AND OF "THE SYSTEM OF POSITIVE POLITICS"

LOVE FOR PRINCIPLE
AND ORDER FOR BASIS;
PROGRESS FOR END.

PREFATORY NOTE TO THIRD EDITION.

——+——

In the preface to the fourth volume of his *System of Positive Politics* (Treatise of Sociology instituting the Religion of Humanity), Auguste Comte says :—

"Taking the volume as a whole, the general constitution of the religion has become at once more systematic, more moral, and more practical, by definitively placing the worship before the doctrine. I regret that this correction is subsequent to the composition of the *Positivist Catechism*, the purpose of which it would have aided. Without waiting, however, for a second edition of that short work, the improvement may be effected by dividing into two the long conversation on the doctrine as a whole. The first half, bearing directly on the theory of the Great Being (Humanity), should for the future form a separate chapter and follow on the Introduction. Then we may pass at once to the study of the worship and after it to that of the doctrine, the general conversation on which will thus be limited to its second half, the half which alone relates to the encyclopedic constitution.

"This division of a long chapter allows the adoption of the definitive arrangement, the transposition being easy, and involving no change in the exposition as it stands. I take the opportunity to urge the readers of my Catechism also to divide the last chapter, studying first the Fetichist and Theocratic part common to all nations, then the three-fold transition peculiar to the West. By these two changes, the small work which is the organ of propagation should for the future be considered as consisting of thirteen chapters instead of eleven."

In obedience to this formal injunction, the change recommended was introduced into the English translation in 1858. It has been adopted by the later French editions of the work, by the Italian and Portuguese translations, and will doubtless be adopted by any other translations.

The only change I have made in this new issue, rendered necessary by the accidental destruction by fire at the printers of the unsold copies of the second edition, is the suppression of the Appendix; I think it better that all such additional matter should appear in a separate form as a supplement to the Catechism. I have added from the Positivist Tables the sketch of the treatises on theoretical and practical morals, and I have added also an index of the proper names—any other index should be the work of each diligent student for himself. The text has been revised throughout.

RICHARD CONGREVE.

55 Palace Gardens Terrace,
London, W.
24 Gutenberg 103 (5th September 1891).

CONTENTS.

—•—

Third Part.

EXPLANATION OF THE REGIME, OR SYSTEM OF LIFE.

CONCLUSION.

GENERAL HISTORY OF RELIGION.

TABLES.

PREFACE.

" IN the name of the Past and of the Future, the servants
of Humanity—theoricians and practicians—come forward to claim as their due the general direction of this
world, in order to construct at length the true Providence,
moral, intellectual, and material ; excluding once for all
from political supremacy all the different servants of
God—Catholic, Protestant, or Deist—as at once belated
and a source of trouble." With this uncompromising
announcement, on Sunday, 19th October 1851, in the
Palais Cardinal, after a summary of five hours, I ended
my third *Course of Philosophical Lectures on the General
History of Humanity.* Since that memorable conclusion,
the publication of the second volume of my *System of
Positive Politics* has lately manifested directly how appropriate is such a social destination to the philosophy
which is able to suggest the most systematic theory of
the human order.

We come forward then, avowedly, to deliver the West
from an anarchical democracy and from a retrograde
aristocracy, so to constitute, as far as practicable, a true
Sociocracy, one combining wisely, in furtherance of the
common regeneration, all the powers of man, each in
every case brought to bear according to its nature. In
fact, we Sociocrats are no more democrats than aristo-
crats. In our eyes the respectable mass of these two
opposite parties represents, though on no system, on

A

ACE.

the one hand solidarity, and on the other continuity, between which Positivism establishes on a deep foundation a necessary subordination, the substitute at last for their deplorable antagonism. But whilst our policy rises equally above these two incomplete and incoherent tendencies, we are far from equally condemning in the present the two parties which represent them. During the thirty years of my philosophical and social career, I have ever felt a profound contempt for that which, under our different governments, bore the name of *the Opposition*, and a secret affinity for all constructive statesmen. Even those who would build with materials evidently worn out seemed to me constantly preferable to the mere destructives, in a century in which general reconstruction is everywhere the chief want. Our official conservatives are behindhand, it is true, but our mere revolutionists seem to me still more alien to the true spirit of our time. They continue blindly, in the middle of the nineteenth century, the negative direction which could only suit the eighteenth, without redeeming this stagnation by those generous aspirations after a universal renovation which distinguished their predecessors.

Hence it is that, though the popular sympathies are instinctively with them, power constantly passes to their opponents, who at least have recognised the impotence for organising of the metaphysical doctrines, and seek elsewhere for principles of reconstruction. With the majority of these last, their retrográde attitude is, at bottom, but a provisional choice of the least evil as against an impending anarchy, without any real theological convictions. Though all statesmen seem for the moment to belong to this school, we may assert confidently that it only supplies the formulas indispensable for the co-ordination of their empirical views, whilst waiting for the more real and stable connection to spring from a new doctrine of universal applicability.

Such is certainly the only temporal governor of real

eminence of whom up to the present time our century
can boast, the noble Czar who, whilst he gives his
immense empire all the progress compatible with its
actual condition, preserves it by his energy and prudence
from useless ferment. His sagacity, however empirical,
leads him to see that the West alone is charged with the
glorious and difficult mission of laying the foundations of
human regeneration, which the East has subsequently
and peaceably to appropriate as it shall rise. He seems
to me to be even conscious that this immense elaboration was reserved specially for the great Western
centre, the spontaneous action of which, though of necessity disorderly, is the only one which should always be
respected, as absolutely indispensable to the common
solution. The habitual agitation of all the remainder of
the West, though more difficult to restrain than that of
the East, is in reality almost equally prejudicial to the
natural course of the final regeneration, for it tends
without ground to displace its principal centre, which
the whole of the past fixes in France.

Our situation in the West so excludes the simply revolutionary point of view that it reserves for the opposite
camp the production of the maxims which best express
it. Not forgetting the memorable practical formula,*
the author of which was a democrat fortunately without
literary training, it is among pure conservatives that the
most profound political sentence of the nineteenth century had its birth—*To destroy you must replace.* The
author of this admirable sentence, equally excellent in
expression and thought, presents, however, nothing remarkable in point of intellect. His only real recommendation is a rare combination of the three practical
qualities—energy, prudence, and perseverance. But the
constructive point of view so tends at present to enlarge

---

* *Il faut faire de l'ordre avec du désordre*—Your materials are
disorder, with them you must organise order.—M. Caussidière.

conceptions, that, given a favourable situation, it can
by itself suggest to an intellect of small depth a really
profound principle, which is adopted and systematically
developed by Positivism.

Be this as it may, the retrograde nature of the worn-
out doctrines which our conservatives provisionally employ, must disqualify them absolutely for directing
political action in the midst of an anarchy which had its
origin in the irremediable weakness of the old beliefs.
The West can no longer submit its reason to the guidance
of opinions which evidently admit of no demonstration ;
nay, which are radically chimerical, as are all opinions
derived from theology, even if reduced to its fundamental
dogma.   All now recognise that our practical activity
must cease to waste itself on mutual hostilities, in order
peaceably to develop our drawing out in common the
resources of man's planet.   But still less can we persist
in the state of intellectual and moral childhood in which
our conduct rests only on motives which are absurd and
degrading.   Without ever repeating the eighteenth century, the nineteenth must always continue its work,
realising at length the noble aspiration of a demonstrated
religion directing pacific activity.

Now that our circumstances set aside every simply
negative tendency, the only ones of the philosophical
schools of the last century really discredited are the
illogical sects whose predominance was necessarily very
short.   The incomplete destructives, such as Voltaire and
Rousseau, who thought that they could overthrow the
altar and preserve the throne, or the converse, are fallen
without possibility of rising, after ruling, such was the
destiny allotted them, the two generations which prepared and achieved the revolutionary explosion.   But,
ever since reconstruction has been the order of the day,
the attention of men reverts more and more to the great
and immortal school of Diderot and Hume, which will
really give its stamp to the eighteenth century, connecting

it with the seventeenth through Fontenelle, and with the nineteenth through Condorcet. Equally emancipated in religion and politics, these powerful thinkers necessarily tended towards a total and direct reorganisation, confused though its conception must then be. All of them would now rally in support of the only doctrine which, basing the future on the past, at length lays a perfectly firm foundation for the regeneration of the West. It is from this school that I shall always consider it an honour to be descended in a direct line through my leading precursor, the eminent Condorcet. On the other hand, I never expected anything but hindrances, intentional or not, from the belated relics of the superficial and immoral sects sprung from Voltaire and Rousseau.

But with this great historical stock I have always connected whatever of real eminence came from our latest adversaries, whether theological or metaphysical. Whilst Hume is my principal precursor in philosophy, Kant comes in as an accessory; his fundamental conception was never really systematised and developed but by Positivism. So, under the political aspect, Condorcet required, for me, to be completed by De Maistre, from whom, at the commencement of my career, I appropriated all his leading principles, which now find no adequate appreciation except in the Positive school. These, with Bichat and Gall as my precursors in science, are the six immediate predecessors who will ever connect me with the three fathers of the true modern philosophy—Bacon, Descartes, and Leibnitz. Carrying on this noble genealogy, the Middle Ages, intellectually condensed in St. Thomas Aquinas, Roger Bacon, and Dante, place me in direct subordination to the eternal prince of true thinkers, the incomparable Aristotle.

Retracing our steps as far as this true fountain-head, we feel deeply that, since the adequate extension of Rome's dominion, the more advanced populations are vainly seeking for an universal religion. Experience

has made it quite clear that no supernatural belief can
satisfy this ultimate longing. Two incompatible Monotheisms equally aimed at this necessary universality,
without which Humanity could not follow her natural
destiny. But their opposed efforts only resulted in their
mutually neutralising each other, so as to reserve this
attribute for doctrines susceptible of demonstration and
admitting discussion. For more than five centuries, Islam
renounces the conquest of the West, and Catholicism
abandons to its eternal rival even the tomb of its pretended founder. These vain spiritual aspirations have
not even been able to extend over the whole terri-
tory of the old temporal rule, divided with an almost
equal division between the two irreconcilable Monotheisms.

The East and the West, then, must seek, apart from
all theology or metaphysics, the systematic bases of their
intellectual and moral communion. This long-expected
fusion, which must afterwards gradually embrace the
whole of mankind, can evidently only come from Positivism, that is, from a doctrine whose invariable characteristic is the combination of the real with the useful.
Long limited to the simplest phenomena, its theories have
there produced the only really universal convictions
which as yet exist. But this natural privilege of the
Positive methods and doctrines cannot for ever be confined to the domain of mathematics and physics. First
developed in the sphere of natural order, it thence
passed naturally to the vital order, whence it has lately
extended finally to the human order, collective or individual. This decisive completeness of the Positive
spirit now does away with every pretext for preserving,
by artificial means, the theological spirit, which has come
to be, in modern Europe, as disturbing as the metaphysical, of which it is both historically and dogmatically
the source. Besides, the moral and political degradation of the theological priesthood had long precluded any

hope of restraining, as in the Middle Ages, the vices of
the doctrine by the instinctive sagacity of its best in-
terpreters.

Instinctively abandoned henceforward to its natural
decay, the monotheistic belief, Christian or Musulman,
deserves more and more the unfavourable judgment
which, during the three centuries of its rise to power,
it elicited from the noblest statesmen and philosophers
of the Roman world. Not able at that time to judge
the system but by the doctrine, they hesitated not to
reject, as the enemy of the human race, a provisional
religion which placed perfection in detachment from
earth. Modern instinct reprobates still more strongly
a morality which proclaims that the benevolent sentiments are foreign to our nature, which so misunderstands
the dignity of labour as to refer its origin to a divine
curse, and which makes woman the source of all evil.
Tacitus and Trajan could not foresee that, for some centuries, the wisdom of the priesthood, aided by favourable circumstances, would so far check the natural defects
of such doctrines, as to draw from them, provisionally,
admirable results for society. But now that the Western
priesthood has become hopelessly retrograde, its belief,
left to itself, tends to give free scope to the immoral
character which is inherent in its anti-social nature.
It deserved the respectful treatment of prudent conservatives only so far as it was impossible to substitute
for it a better conception of the world and of man—a
conception entirely dependent on the slow rise of the
Positive spirit. But this laborious initiation being now
complete, Positivism definitively eliminates Catholicism,
as every other form of theologism, by virtue even of the
admirable social maxim above quoted.

After fully satisfying the intelligence and the activity,
the Positive religion, ever impelled by the reality which
characterises it, has extended in due form even to feeling,
which is henceforth its principal domain and becomes the

basis of its unity. We see no reason to fear then that
any true thinkers, theoretical or practical, can at the
present day, as in the early days of Catholicism, fail to
see the superiority of a real and complete faith, which,
far from being social by accident, shows itself such by
its inherent nature. For the rest, it is for the nascent
priesthood of Positivism and for all its true disciples, by
their conduct as men and citizens, to secure on grounds
of experience a due appreciation of its excellence, even
from those who cannot directly judge its principles. A
doctrine which shall always develop all the human
virtues, personal, domestic, and civic, will soon be respected by all its honest opponents, whatever may be
their ungrounded predilection for an absolute and egoistic
synthesis, as opposed to a relative and altruistic one.

But, to establish this crucial competition, it was
necessary first to so condense Positivism that it may
become really popular. This is the particular object of
this small exceptional work, for which I interrupt, for
some weeks, my great religious construction, of which
the first half only is as yet accomplished. I had
thought at first that this valuable episode should be
postponed until the entire completion of that immense
work. But after writing, in January 1851, the Positive
theory of human unity, I felt sufficiently forward to
allow me to introduce such an interlude after the volume
in which that theory forms the first and most important
chapter. Growing, as I worked out that capital volume,
this hope became mature when I wrote its final preface.
I realise it to-day, before I begin the construction of
Dynamical Sociology, which will be the special subject of
the third volume of my *System of Positive Politics*, to be
published next year.

Due to the unexpected ripeness of my principal conceptions, this resolution was greatly strengthened by the
fortunate crisis which has just abolished the parliamentary regime and instituted a dictatorial republic, the

two preliminary conditions of any true regeneration. It is quite true that this dictatorship by no means wears as yet the character set forth as essential in my Positivist Lectures of 1847. What it most wants is to be compatible with full freedom of exposition and even of discussion—a freedom absolutely indispensable for spiritual reorganisation, not to say that it alone can reassure us against all retrograde tyranny. But under one form or other, this necessary complement will before long be attained, which seems to me to involve, as the preceding phases, one last violent crisis. Once attained, its advent on empirical grounds will soon determine the peaceful creation of the systematic triumvirate which gives its form and expression to the temporal dictatorship put forward, in the Lectures above mentioned, as the government adapted to the organic transition. Without, however, waiting for these two new phases of our revolutionary experiment, the actual dictatorship already permits the direct propagation of renovating thought. The freedom of exposition which as a natural consequence it brings to all really constructive thinkers by breaking at length the sterile sway of the talkers, naturally acted as a special invitation to me to direct the thoughts of women and proletaries towards the basis of thorough renovation.

This work, then—an episode—by furnishing a systematic basis for the active propagation of Positivism, necessarily forwards my principal construction, for it brings the new religion to its true social audience. However solid the logical and scientific bases of the intellectual discipline instituted by Positive Philosophy, its severe regime is too antipathetic to our present mental state for it ever to prevail without the irresistible support of women and the proletaries. The urgent need of it can only be soundly appreciated by these two social masses, which, alien to all pretension to teaching, can alone enforce on their systematic chiefs the encyclopedic

conditions demanded by their social office. This is why
I was bound not to shrink from introducing into the
popular language philosophical terms which are absolutely indispensable, terms not created by Positivism, but
of which it has systematised the meaning and fostered
the use. Such are, in particular, two pairs of essential
value as characteristic formulas, first *Static* and *Dynamic*,
then *Objective* and *Subjective*, without which my exposition would remain inadequate. Once properly defined,
especially by their uniform use, their judicious employment greatly facilitates instead of obscuring philosophical explanations. I do not scruple in this work to
consecrate expressions which the Positive religion must
at once pass into universal circulation, considering the
high importance of their use from the intellectual and
even the moral point of view.

Thus led to compose a true Catechism for the Religion
of Humanity, I had first to examine, on rational principles, the form always adopted for such expositions, the
dialogue. I soon found in it a fresh instance of the
happy instinct by which practical wisdom often anticipates the conclusions of sound theory. Fresh from the
special work of constructing the Positive theory of
human language, I felt at once that since expression
should always issue in communication, its natural form
is the dialogue. Further, as all combinations, even
physical, and still more logical, are binary, the dialogue
admits, under pain of confusion, only one interlocutor.
The monologue is in reality adapted only to conception,
limiting itself to the formal expression of its process,
as if one were thinking aloud, without reference to any
hearer. When language is used not merely to assist the
investigations of the reason, but to direct the communication of its results, then it requires a fresh shape,
specially adapted to this transfer of ideas. Then we
must take into account the peculiar state of the listener,
and foresee the modifications which the natural course

of such exposition will call for. In a word, the simple statement must thus become a real conversation. Nor can its essential conditions be satisfactorily met except by assuming one single and clearly determined interlocutor. But if this type is judiciously chosen, it may, for ordinary use, adequately represent every reader; since indeed it were not possible to vary the mode of exposition to meet the exigencies of each individual, as may be done in actual conversation.

A discourse, then, which is in the full sense didactic, ought to differ essentially from one simply logical, in which the thinker freely follows his own course, paying no attention to the natural conditions of all communication. Still, to avoid the great labour of recasting one's thoughts, in general we limit ourselves to laying them before others as we originally thought them ; though this rough method of exposition largely contributes to the scanty efficacy of most of our reading. The dialogue, the proper form for all real communication, is reserved for the setting forth of such conceptions as are at once important enough and ripe enough to demand it. This is why, in all times, religious instruction is given in the form of conversation and not of simple statement. Far from betraying a negligence excusable only in cases of secondary importance, this form, rightly managed, is, on the contrary, the only mode of exposition which is really didactic : it suits equally every intelligence. But the difficulties attendant on the new elaboration which it requires justify our not adopting it for ordinary communications. It would be childish to aim at such perfection for any instruction not of fundamental interest. On the other hand, this transformation for the purposes of teaching is only practicable where the doctrines are sufficiently worked out for us to be able to distinctly compare the different methods of expounding them as a whole, and to easily foresee the objections which they will naturally elicit.

Were I bound here to point out all the general principles applicable to the art of communication, I should
dwell on the improvements admissible in regard to style.
Especially devoted to the expression of feelings, poets
have always felt how superior is verse to prose for that
expression, to render artificial language more esthetic, by
bringing it nearer to natural language. Now, the same
reasons would equally apply to the communication of
thoughts, if we had to attach as much importance to it.
Conciseness of language and the aid of imagery, the two
essential characteristics of true versification, would be as
appropriate for perfecting the exposition of thought as
the expansion of feeling. So, perfect communication
would require not merely the substitution of dialogue
for monologue, but also that of verse for prose. This
second improvement in teaching, however, must be still
more of an exception than the first, because of the additional labour it requires. It presupposes even a greater
maturity in the conceptions to be expressed, not only in
their interpreter but also in the audience, which has, by
an effort of its own, to fill up at once the gaps left by
poetical concision. This is why several admirable poems
are still only in prose, the imperfection of the form being
at the time excusable, where the subject was not generally familiar. An analogous motive acted more strongly
against putting into verse any religious catechism. But
the reality and spontaneity which distinguish the Positive belief will enable it in time to introduce this last
improvement into its popular exposition, when that
belief shall begin to spread sufficiently to admit of conciseness and imagery. Only provisionally, then, need we
feel limited in it to the substitution of the dialogue for
the monologue.

In accordance with this special theory as to the didactic form, I was led not only to justify previous practice, but even to improve upon it, so far as concerns the
interlocutor. By leaving the hearer completely unde-

termined, the dialogue became extremely vague, and as such even almost illusory. Having placed on rational grounds the empirical adoption of the dialogue, I soon felt that it would remain incomplete, and if incomplete, inadequate, so long as it was not clear who the second person was, at least to the author. Unless you set before you a real, although in the immediate instance, an ideal communication, you cannot draw out to the full all the inherent advantages of such a form. Then you institute a real conversation, as distinct from a statement thrown into dialogue.

Applying at once this clear principle, I naturally chose the angelic interlocutress who, after only one year of direct living influence, has been now for more than six years subjectively associated with all my thoughts as with all my feelings. It is through her that I have at length become for Humanity an organ in the strictest sense twofold, as may any one who has worthily submitted to woman's influence. Without her I should never have been able practically to make the career of St. Paul follow on that of Aristotle, by founding the universal religion on true philosophy, after I had extracted the latter from real science. The constant purity of our exceptional connection, and even the admirable superiority of the angel who never received due recognition, are moreover already fully appreciated by nobler minds. When, four years ago, I revealed this incomparable inspiration by the publication of my *Discourse on the System of Positivism*, she could at first only be judged by its intellectual and moral results, thenceforward appreciable by the sympathetic heart as by the synthetic mind. But last year the three introductory pieces, which will ever be the distinctive feature of the first volume of my *System of Positive Politics*, enabled all to directly appreciate this eminent nature. Hence, when I recently published the second volume of the same treatise, I was already able to openly congratulate myself on the touching unanimity of marked sympathy which both sexes feel towards the new Beatrice. These three public antecedents dispel at once all doubt as to my sainted hearer, with whom the duly prepared reader is sufficiently acquainted for our conversations to possess their own peculiar and immediate interest.

Such a catechumen meets perfectly all the essential conditions of the best form of teaching. Superior though she was, Madame Clotilde de Vaux was yet so early snatched from me that it was impossible sufficiently to initiate her in Positivism, the point to which her own wishes and efforts tended. Before death broke off finally this affectionate instruction, pain and grief had seriously impeded it. When I now accomplish subjectively the systematic preparation which I could hardly enter upon during her life, my angelic disciple brings with her nothing beyond the primary dispositions to be found in most women, and even in many proletaries. In all those souls which Positivism has not yet reached, I presuppose solely, as in my eternal companion, a profound desire to know the religion which can overcome the modern anarchy, and a sincere veneration for its priest. I should even prefer for readers those in whom no scholastic training interferes with the spontaneous fulfilment in fair degree of these two previous conditions.

All who know my general institution of the true guardian angels, already sufficiently explained in my *Positive Politics*, are aware, moreover, that the principal female type becomes in it habitually inseparable from the two others. This sweet connection holds good, even in the exceptional case which presents to me in combination, in my pure and immortal companion, the subjective mother my second life presupposes, and the objective daughter who should have added grace to my transient existence. From the time that her invariable reserve had so purified my affection as to raise it to the level of her own, all I aspired to was the openly avowed union which should follow on a legal adoption, suitable to our disparity in age. When I shall publish our noble correspondence, my last letter will give direct evidence of this holy project, the only one which, under our respective destinies, was compatible with repose and happiness.

It is then without effort that I proceed to use in this catechism the personal designations habitually used in religious instruction. More even than the priesthood of theology does the priesthood of Positivism require in its priests complete maturity, most particularly by virtue of its immense encyclopedic preparation. This is why I have fixed the ordination of the priests of Humanity at forty-two, the age at which the development of the body and the brain is completely ended, as is also the first social life. The names of *father* and *daughter* become then peculiarly appropriate as between the teacher and the catechumen, in conformity with the old etymology of the word priest. By using them here, I naturally approximate to the personal relations amid which I should have lived had it not been for our fatal catastrophe.

But this concentration of the holy conversation on the presiding angel ought not to conceal from the reader, any more than from myself, that my two other patronesses take constantly an appropriate though silent part in it. The venerable mother and the noble adopted daughter, whose subjective influence and objective service I have elsewhere explained, will always here be present to my heart when my intellect shall be duly feeling the dominant impulse. For the future become inseparable, these three angels are so my own that their constant co-operation has lately suggested to the eminent artist, whom Positivism now claims with pride, an admirable esthetic inspiration, which converts a mere portrait into a picture of profound meaning.

A didactic conversation on this plan renders my own

labour easier as well as that of my reader.   For such a
public exposition comes very near the private explanations for which my sainted companion would have naturally asked me had our objective union lasted longer, as is
already clear from my philosophical letter on Marriage.
The very period of the year at which I accomplish this
pleasant task recalls with peculiar force her own un-
suggested wishes, during our incomparable year, for a
methodical initiation.   I have only then to carry myself
back seven years to conceive, as actually spoken, that
which I must now develop subjectively, by placing myself, in 1852, in the situation of 1845.   But this effort
of transposition brings with it the precious compensation
that I am able to give a better idea of the angelic ascendency which I can only adequately characterise by
combining two admirable verses, respectively meant for
Beatrice and Laura—

> Quella che imparadisa la mia mente *
> Ogni basso pensier dal cor m'avulse. †
>
> She who doth imparadise my soul (*Cary*)
> Tore from my heart every low thought.

This tardy accomplishment of an initiation prompted by
affection brings it moreover into fuller agreement with
the paternal feelings which finally prevailed towards her
who will always be associated with me as at once disciple
and colleague.   Her age having become fixed, in obedience to the general law of the subjective life, mine exceeds it more and more, so as even now to allow only
filial images.   This more perfect continuity of our two
lives perfects also the whole harmony of my own nature.
In thus explaining the Positive constitution of human
unity, I am developing and consolidating the fundamental connection between my private and my public
life.   The philosophical influence of the angel who in-

---

* Dante, *Par.* xxviii. 3.   † Petrarch, Sonnet lxxxvi. 8.

spires me becomes then as complete and as direct as it ever can be, and consequently beyond dispute in the eyes of all. I venture then to hope that, to enable me to testify my just gratitude, the nobler minds will soon by their due aid supply the deficiency of which I am profoundly conscious in the midst of my best daily prayers, as was Dante in regard to his sweet patroness—

> Non è l' affezion mia tanto profonda
> Che basti a render voi grazia per grazia.
> —*Par.* iv. 121.
>
> Affection fails me to requite thy grace
> With equal sum of gratitude.—CARY'S *Translation.*

But this gratitude of the public must, equally with my own, embrace the two other guardian angels who complete the presiding female influence over me. However distant, alas! the imposing memory of the perfect Catholicism which swayed my noble and tender mother, it will always be an incitement to me to give precedence, more than in my youth, to the constant cultivation of feeling over that of intellect and even of activity. On the other hand, were a too exclusive sense of the necessity of basing all real public virtue on private goodness to lead me to undervalue the importance of civic morality, an importance inherent in it and directly its own, I should soon correct myself by the admirable sociability of my third patroness. I undertake this episodic work, then, under the especial assistance of all my angels, although two of them can only co-operate silently, without prejudice to their personal claims to the veneration of all.

Looked at from a more general point of view, this form of teaching tends directly to convey a strong impression of the character of the religion to be taught. For, of itself, it brings out the fundamental nature of the Positive system which, aiming above all at the systematic dis-

B

cipline of all the powers of man, rests principally on the
constant concurrence of feeling with reason to regulate
activity. Now, this series of conversations always represents the heart and the intellect as combining in religious
union to moralise the material power to which the world
of action is necessarily subjected. In that world the
woman and the priest are, in fact, the two indispensable
elements of the true moderating power, which is at once
domestic and civic. In organising this holy coalition
in the interests of society, each constituent proceeds
here in conformity with its true nature: the heart
states the questions, the intellect answers them. Thus
the very form of this Catechism points at once to the
great central idea of Positivism : man thinking under
the inspiration of woman, to bring synthesis into constant harmony with sympathy in order to regularise
synergy.

The adoption of this method for the new religious instruction shows that it addresses by preference the sex in
which affection predominates. This preference, quite in
accordance with the true spirit of the final regime, is in
an especial manner adapted to the last transition, in which
every influence recognised by the normal state must
always work with greater strength, if with less regularity.
The better proletaries are likely, it seems to me, ere long
to welcome heartily this short but decisive work ; yet it
is more suited to women, especially to women without
instruction. They alone can fully understand the preponderance that ought to be given to the habitual cultivation of the heart, so borne down by the coarse activity,
both in speculation and action, which prevails in the
modern Western world. It is solely in this sanctuary
that, at the present day, we can find the noble submis-
siveness of spirit required for a systematic regeneration.
During the last four years, the reason of the people has
suffered profoundly from the unfortunate exercise of universal suffrage ; it had previously been preserved from

the constitutional sophisms and Parliamentary intrigues
of which the rich and the literary class had had the
monopoly. Developing a blind pride, our proletaries
have thought themselves able to settle the highest social
questions without submitting to any serious study.
Though this deterioration is much less in the southern
populations of the West, the resistance of Catholicism
sheltering them against the metaphysics of Protestantism
or Deism, the reading negative books is beginning to
spread it too much even there. I see none anywhere
but women, who, as a consequence of their wholesome
exclusion from political action, can give me the support
required to secure the free ascendency of the principles
which shall in the end qualify the proletaries to place
their confidence aright on points of theory as well as on
points of practice.

Besides, the deep-seated mental anarchy justifies this
special appeal of the Positive religion to the affective sex,
as it renders more necessary than ever the predominance
of feeling, the sole existing preservative of Western
society from a complete and irreparable dissolution.
Since the close of the Middle Ages, the influence of
women has been the sole though unacknowledged check
on the moral evils attaching to the mental alienation towards which the West more and more tended, especially
its centre—France. This chronic unreason being henceforth at its height, since there is no social maxim but
succumbs to a corrosive discussion, feeling alone main-
tains order in the West. But feeling even is seriously
weakened already by the reaction of the sophisms of the
intellect, these being always favourable to the personal
instincts which are, moreover, the more energetic.

Of the three sympathetic instincts which belong to
our true cerebral constitution, the first and last are
much weakened, and the intermediate nearly extinct, in
the majority of the men who take an active part at present in Western agitation. Penetrate to the interior

of existing families, and you find how little strength attachment has left, in the intercourse which should foster it most. As for the general kindness, so much vaunted at present, it is more an indication of hatred of the rich than of love of the poor. For modern philanthropy too often expresses its pretended benevolence in forms appropriate to anger or envy. But the social instinct of most constant use, as affording the only immediate basis of all true discipline of man, has suffered even more than the two others. The deterioration in this respect, most traceable in the rich and educated, spreads even among proletaries, unless a wise indifference divert them from the political movement.

Still, veneration can continue to exist in the midst of the wildest revolutionary aberrations; it is indeed their best natural corrective. I learnt this formerly by personal experience during the profoundly negative phase which necessarily preceded my systematic development. At that time enthusiasm alone preserved me from a sophistical demoralisation, though it laid me peculiarly open for a time to the seductions of a shallow and depraved juggler. Veneration, at the present day, is the decisive mark which distinguishes the revolutionists susceptible of a real regeneration, however behind they may be in point of intelligence, especially among the Communists who are without instruction.

But, though in the immense majority of those who are negative we may still discern this valuable symptom, in the majority of their chiefs it is certainly not found, the existing anarchy giving everywhere a temporary predominance to bad natures. These men, absolutely insusceptible of discipline, despite their small number wield a vast influence, which infects with the ferment of subversive ideas the heads of all who are without firmly-rooted convictions. There is no general remedy at present for this plague of the West except the contempt of the people or the severity of the governments. But the doctrine which alone will secure the regular action of these two safeguards can at the outset find no commanding support but in the feeling of women, soon to be aided by the reason of the proletariate.

Without the due intervention of women, the discipline of Positivism would not succeed in driving back to the last ranks these pretended thinkers who speak with decision on sociological questions though ignorant of arithmetic. For the people, still sharing in many respects their worst faults, is incapable as yet of supporting the new priesthood against these dangerous talkers. At least, I can, for the moment, hope for no collective assistance except from the proletaries who, standing aloof hitherto from our political discussions, are not the less instinctively attached, as women are, to the social aim of the great revolution. These two classes form the milieu prepared for this Catechism.

Over and above the general reasons which should in this place direct my attention chiefly to women, I was long ago led to look principally to them for the triumphant advent of the solution of the Western problem indicated by the whole Past.

In the first place, it would be absurd to propose to end without them the most thorough of all human revolutions, whilst in all previous revolutions they took a very large share. Were their instinctive repugnance to the modern movement really invincible, that would be enough to ensure its failure. It is the true source of the strange and fatal anomaly which forces retrograde chiefs on progressive populations, as though idiocy and hypocrisy were to supply the official securities for Western order. Till Positive religion has sufficiently overcome this resistance of women it will not be able, in its treatment of the leading partisans of the different belated systems, to give free scope to its decided and just reprobation of their mental and moral inferiority.

Those who at the present day deny the innate existence

of the disinterested affections lay themselves open to the
just suspicion of rejecting on this point the demonstrations of modern science only because of the radical imperfection of their own feelings. As they pursue no
good, however trifling, but from the lure of an infinite
reward or from the fear of an eternal punishment, they
prove their heart to be as degraded as their intellect
evidently is, considering the absurdity of their beliefs.
And yet, by the tacit adhesion of women, the direction
of the West is still intrusted to those whom such characteristics will exclude, and wisely, from all the higher
functions, when Positivism shall have duly systematised
the reason of mankind.

But the Religion of Humanity will soon strip the
retrograde party of this august support, which it retains
solely from a just horror of anarchy. For in spite of
adverse conceptions resting on previous associations,
women are well disposed to value aright the only doctrine
which in the present day can thoroughly combine order
with progress. Above all, they will recognise the fact
that this final synthesis, while it comprehends every
phase of our existence, better secures the supremacy of
feeling than did the provisional synthesis which sacrificed to it the intellect and the activity. Our philosophy
comes into perfect agreement with the tendencies of
women by ending the encyclopedic scale with morals,
which, as science and as art, are necessarily the most
important and the most difficult study, condensing and
controlling all the others. Giving at length full scope
to the feelings of chivalry, which in earlier times were
compressed by the conflicts with theology, Positive worship makes the affective sex the moral providence of our
species. In that worship every true woman supplies
us in daily life with the best representative of the true
Great Being. The Positive regime constituting, on
systematic principles, the family as the normal basis of ·
society, ensures the due prevalence therein of the influence

of women, at length become the supreme private authority
on the common education. On all these grounds, the
true religion will be fully appreciated by women, as soon
as they grasp adequately its leading characteristics.
Even those who at first should regret the loss of chimerical hopes will not be slow to feel the moral superiority
of our subjective immortality, so thoroughly altruistic
in its nature, as compared with the old objective immortality, which could never be other than radically egoistic.
The law of eternal widowhood, the distinctive feature
of Positivist marriage, would be enough to form, on this
point, a decisive contrast.

The better to incorporate women into the Western
revolution, its last phase must be looked on as having
naturally for them a deep and special interest, in direct
relation with their own peculiar destiny.

The four great classes which substantially constitute
modern society, were destined to experience in succession
the radical convulsion required at first for its final regeneration. It began, in the last century, with the
intellectual element, which rose in successful insurrection against the whole system based on theology and
war. The political explosion which was its natural
result took its rise soon after in the middle classes, who
had long been growing more eager to take the place of
the nobility. But the resistance of the nobility throughout Europe could only be overcome by calling in the
French proletariate to the aid of its new temporal chiefs.
Thus introduced into the great political struggle, the
proletariate of the West put forward irresistible claims
to its just incorporation into the modern order, as soon
as peace allowed it to make its own wishes sufficiently
clear. Still this revolutionary chain does not yet
include the most fundamental element of the true
human order. The revolution in regard to women must
now complete the revolution which concerned the proletariate, just as this last consolidated the revolution of the

middle classes, sprung originally from the philosophical revolution.

Then only will the modern convulsion have really prepared all the essential bases of the final regeneration. Till it takes in women, it can only result in prolonging our lamentable oscillations between retrogression and anarchy. But this final complement is a more natural outcome of the whole of the antecedent phases than any one of them is of its predecessor. It connects most closely with the popular phase, as the social incorporation of the proletariate is evidently bound up with and dependent on, the due enfranchisement of woman from all labour away from home. Without this universal emancipation, the indispensable complement of the abolition of serfage, the proletary family cannot be in a true sense constituted, since in it women remain habitually exposed to the horrible alternative of want or prostitution.

The best practical summary of the whole modern programme will soon be this indisputable principle—*Man ought to maintain woman,* in order that she may be able to discharge properly her holy function. This Catechism will, I hope, make sensible the intimate connection of such a condition with the whole of the great renovation, not merely moral, but also mental, and even material. Influenced by the holy reaction of this revolution in the position of women, the revolution of the proletariate will by itself clear itself of the subversive tendencies which as yet neutralise it. Woman's object being everywhere to secure the legitimate supremacy of moral force, she visits with especial reprobation all collective violence : she is less tolerant of the yoke of numbers than of that of wealth. But her latent social influence will soon introduce into the Western revolution, under its two other aspects, modifications less directly traceable to it, but not less valuable. It will facilitate the advent to political power of the industrial patriciate and of the Positive priesthood, by leading both to dissociate themselves once for all from the heterogeneous and ephemeral classes which directed the transition in its negative phase. So completed, and so purified, the revolution of the West will proceed firmly and systematically towards its peaceful termination, under the general direction of the true servants of Humanity. Their organic and progressive guidance will completely set aside the retrograde and anarchical parties, all persistence in the theological or metaphysical state being treated as a weakness of brain incapacitating for government.

Such are the essential conditions which represent the composition of this Catechism as fully adapted to its most important office, in the present or for the future. When the Positive religion shall have gained sufficient acceptance, it will be the best summary for constant use. For the present it must serve, as a general view, to prepare the way for its free acceptance, by a successful propagation, for which hitherto there was no systematic guidance available.

Taken as a whole, this episodic construction expresses, even by its form and conduct, all the great intellectual and moral attributes of the new faith. There will be felt in it throughout a worthy subordination of the reason of man to the feeling of woman, in order that the heart may bring all the powers of the intellect to the most difficult and important teaching. Its ultimate reaction should then secure respect for, and even the extension to others of, my own private worship of the incomparable angel from whom I derive at once the chief inspirations and their best exposition. Such services will soon render my sainted interlocutress dear to all truly regenerated spirits. Henceforward inseparable from mine, her glorification will constitute my most precious reward. Irrevocably incorporated into the true Supreme Being, her tender image supplies me, in the eyes of all, with its best impersonation. In each of my three daily prayers, the adoration of the two condenses all my wishes for inward perfection in the admirable form in which the sublimest of Mystics foreshadowed in his own way the moral motto of Positivism—(*Live for others*) :—

May I love Thee more than myself, nor love myself save for Thee.

Amem te plus quam me, nec me nisi propter te !

　　—*Imitatio Christi*, iii. 5, 82, 83—(ed. Hirsche.)

AUGUSTE COMTE,

Founder of the Religion of Humanity.

PARIS, 25*th* CHARLEMAGNE 64
(SUNDAY, 11*th July* 1852).

P.S.—To increase the usefulness of this Catechism, I add to its preface an improved edition of the short catalogue which I published, 8th October 1851, with the view of guiding the more thoughtful minds among the people in their choice of books for constant use. It is a service which at the present time could only originate with the Positive priesthood, by virtue of its encyclopedic character, thus brought into distinct light. The damage both to intellect and morals everywhere resulting from irregular reading, should sufficiently indicate at the present time the increasing importance of this short synthetical work. Though the collection has not yet been formed, each can without difficulty even now collect in one shape or other its separate parts.

THE POSITIVIST LIBRARY

FOR THE

NINETEENTH CENTURY.

150 VOLUMES.

———••———

I.—POETRY. (30 VOLUMES.)

The Iliad and the Odyssey, without any notes.
Æschylus, the King Œdipus of Sophocles, Aristophanes, do.
Pindar, Theocritus, Daphnis and Chloe, do.
Plautus and Terence, do.
Virgil, Horace (Selections), Lucan, do.
Ovid, Tibullus, Juvenal, do.
Fabliaux du Moyen Age, par Legrand d'Aussy.
Dante, Ariosto, Tasso, Petrarca (Selections).
Opere Scelte di Metastasio è d'Alfieri.
I Promessi Sposi di Manzoni.
Cervantes, Don Quijote y Las Novelas.
Teatro Español Escojido (Edn. J. S. Florez).
El Romancero Español Selecto y el Cid.
Théatre choisi de Pierre Corneille.
Molière.
Théatre choisi de Racine et de Voltaire.
Fables de la Fontaine, suivies de quelques Fables de Lamotte et
 de Florian.
Gil Blas, par Le Sage.
La Princesse de Clèves, Paul et Virginie, le Dernier Abencerrage
Les Martyrs, par Chateaubriand.
Shakespeare (select plays).
Milton, Paradise Lost and Lyrical Poems.
Robinson Crusoe, the Vicar of Wakefield.
Tom Jones (if French translation, that by Chéron).

The Seven Masterpieces of Walter Scott:—Waverley, Ivanhoe, The Fair Maid of Perth, The Legend of Montrose, Old Mortality, The Heart of Midlothian, The Antiquary.
Byron (without Don Juan).
Goethe (Selections).
The Arabian Nights.

II.—SCIENCE. (30 Volumes.)

L'Arithmétique de Condorcet, l'Algèbre et la Géométrie de Clairaut, la Trigonométrie de Lacroix ou de Legendre.

La Géométrie Analytique d'Auguste Comte, précédée de la Géométrie de Descartes.

La Statique de Poinsot, suivie de tous ses Mémoires sur la Mécanique.

Le Cours d'Analyse de Navier, précédée des Réflexions sur le Calcul Infinitésimal, par Carnot.

Le Cours de Mécanique de Navier, suivi de l'Essai sur l'Équilibre et le Mouvement, par Carnot.

La Théorie des Fonctions, par Lagrange.

L'Astronomie Populaire d'Auguste Comte, suivie des Mondes de Fontenelle.

La Physique Mécanique de Fischer, traduite et annotée par Biot.

Alphabetical Manual of Practical Philosophy, by John Carr (Weale's Series).

La Chimie de Lavoisier.

La Statique Chimique. par Berthollet.

Elements of Chemistry, by James Graham.

Le Manuel d'Anatomie, par Meckel.

L'Anatomie Générale de Bichat, précédée de son Traité sur la vie et sur la mort.

Blainville sur l'Organisation des Animaux.

La Physiologie de Richerand, annotée par Bérard.

L'Essai Systématique sur la Biologie, par Segond, et son Traité d'anatomie générale.

Les Nouveaux Eléments de la Science de l'Homme, par Barthez (2nd edition, 1806).

La Philosophie Zoologique, par Lamarck.

L'Histoire Naturelle de Duméril.

Guglielmini sulla Natura de' Fiumi.

Les Discours sur la Nature des Animaux, par Buffon.

The Art of Prolonging Human Life, by Hufeland. preceded by Hippocrates on Air. Water. and Places, and followed by Cornaro sur la Sobriété.

L'Histoire des Phlegmasies Chroniques, par Broussais, précédée
de ses Propositions de Médecine, et d'abord des aphorismes
d'Hippocrate, en Latin, without any commentary.
Les Éloges des Savants, par Fontenelle et Condorcet.

III.—HISTORY. (60 Volumes.)

Abrégé de Géographie Universelle, par Malte-Brun.
Le Dictionnaire Géographique de Rienzi,
Cook's Voyages. Les Voyages de Chardin.
L'Histoire de la Révolution Française, par Mignet.
Heeren's Manual of Modern History.
Le Siècle de Louis Quatorze, par Voltaire.
Les Mémoires de Mme. de Motteville.
Le Testament Politique de Richelieu. The Life of Cromwell.
Davila, Storia delle Guerre Civile di Francia.
Vita di Benvenuto Cellini.
Les Mémoires de Commines.
L'Abrégé de l'Histoire de France, par Bossuet.
Denina, Rivoluzioni d'Italia.
Istoria di España, par Ascargorta.
Robertson's Charles V.
Hume's History of England.
Hallam's Middle Ages.
L'Histoire Ecclésiastique, par Fleury.
Gibbon's Decline and Fall of the Roman Empire.
Heeren's Manual of Ancient History.
Tacitus (the French translation recommended is that of Dureau
de la Malle).
Herodotus, Thucydides.
Plutarch's Lives.
Cæsar's Commentaries and Arrian's Alexander.
Le Voyage d'Anacharsis, par Barthélemy.
Winckelmann's History of Ancient Art.
Trattato della Pittura da Leonardo da Vinci.
Les Mémoires sur la Musique, par Grétry.

IV.—SYNTHESIS. (30 Volumes.)

The Politics and Ethics of Aristotle.
The Bible.
The Koran.
The City of God, by St. Augustine.

The Confessions of St. Augustine. St. Bernard On the Love of God.

The Imitation of Jesus Christ (the original and Corneille's verse translation).

Le Catéchisme de Montpellier, l'Exposition de la Doctrine Catholique, par Bossuet, le Commentaire sur le Sermon de Jésus-Christ, par St. Augustine.

L'Histoire des Variations Protestantes, par Bossuet.

The Novum Organum of Bacon. Le Discours sur la Méthode, par Descartes. L'Interprétation de la Nature, par Diderot.

Select Thoughts of Cicero, Epictetus, Marcus Aurelius, Pascal, and Vauvenargues. Les Conseils d'une Mère, par Mme. de Lambert. Les Considérations sur les Mœurs, par Duclos.

Le Discours sur l'Histoire Universelle, par Bossuet. L'Esquisse Historique, par Condorcet.

La Politique Sacrée, par Bossuet. Le Traité du Pape, par De Maistre.

Les Dissertations sur les Sourds et les Aveugles, par Diderot. Hume's Philosophical Essays. Adam Smith's Essay on the History of Astronomy.

L'Essai sur le Beau, par Diderot. La Théorie du Beau, par Barthez.

Les Rapports du Physique et du Moral de l'Homme. par Cabanis.

Lettres sur les Animaux, par George Leroy. Le Traité sur les Fonctions du Cerveau, par Gall.

Le Traité sur l'Irritation et la Folie, par Broussais (1ère édition, 1828).

The Positive Philosophy of Auguste Comte (condensed by Miss Martineau), The Positive Politics, the Positivist Catechism, the Appeal to Conservatives, la Synthèse Subjective, Vol. 1.

HINT TO THE READER.

———✦———

To facilitate the study of this Catechism, the author advises the reader to devote at first two weeks to it, allowing a day for each conversation. Two hours a day will suffice for reading in the morning, and reading again in the evening, each of the fourteen chapters, the Preface included. After this general introduction, the reader will be able to go back upon the several dialogues at his pleasure, till he has made them his own.

INTRODUCTION.[1]

GENERAL THEORY OF RELIGION.

CONVERSATION I.

The Woman.—I have often asked myself, my dear father, why you persist in designating as a religion your universal doctrine, though it rejects all supernatural belief. But on reflection I considered that this term is given in common use to many different and even incompatible systems, each of which claims it exclusively, whilst no one of them has at any time been able, taking the whole of our species, to reckon up as many adherents as opponents. This led me to think that this fundamental term must have a general acceptation, radically independent of every special faith. If so, I conjectured that, keeping close to this essential meaning, you might so denominate Positivism, in spite of the greater contrast that exists between it and the previous doctrines, which openly avow that their mutual differences are as serious as the points in which they agree. Still, as this explanation seems to me yet far from clear, I ask you to

---

[1] The Roman numerals attached to the headings indicate the series of the thirteen conversations, the Arabic the divisions of each part of the work.

begin your exposition by explaining, in direct and precise language, the radical sense of the word *Religion*.

The Priest.—This name, my dear daughter, has, in fact, by its etymology no necessary connection with any of the opinions that may be used for attaining the end to which it points. In itself, it expresses the state of perfect *unity*, which is distinctive of our existence, both individual and social, when all its parts, moral as well as physical, habitually converge towards a common purpose. Thus the term would be equivalent to the word *synthesis*, were it not that this last, not by force of its composition, but by nearly universal custom, is now limited entirely to the domain of the intellect, whilst the other embraces all the attributes of man. Religion, then, consists in *regulating* each individual nature, and in *rallying* all the separate individuals ; which are but two distinct cases of one problem. For every man, in the successive periods of his life, differs from himself not less than at any one time he differs from others ; so that the laws of permanence and participation are identical.

Such harmony, for the individual or society, not being ever fully attainable, so complicated is our existence, this definition of religion delineates, then, the unchanging type to which tends more and more the totality of human effort. Our happiness and our merit consist, above all, in drawing as near as possible to this unity, the gradual development of which is the best measure of real progress towards individual or social perfection. As the various attributes of man come into freer play, the more important becomes their habitual concert, but at the same time the more difficult, were it not that their evolution tended of itself to make us more susceptible of discipline, as I will explain to you shortly.

The value always set on this synthetical state naturally concentrated attention on the method of attaining it. Thus men were led, taking the means for the end, to transfer the name of *religion* to whatever system of opinions it represented. But however irreconcilable these numerous beliefs at first sight appear, Positivism brings them into essential agreement, by referring each to the purpose it answered in its own time and country. There is, at bottom, but one religion, at once universal and final, to which all the partial and provisional syntheses more and more pointed, so far as their respective conditions allowed. These several empirical efforts are now succeeded by the systematic development of human unity; for it has at length become possible to constitute this unity, immediately and completely, by virtue of the sum total of our unsystematic preparations. Thus it is that Positivism naturally removes the mutual antagonism of the different antecedent religions, by taking as its own peculiar domain that common ground on which they all instinctively rested. Its doctrine could never be universally received were it not that, despite its anti-theological principles, its relative spirit secures it, by the nature of the case, strong affinities with every form of belief that has been able for a time to guide any part whatever of Humanity.

The Woman.—Your definition of religion will satisfy me completely, my father, if you can succeed in clearing up the serious difficulty which seems to me to arise from its too great comprehensiveness. For, in defining our unity, you take in the physical as well as the moral nature. They are, in fact, so bound up together that no true harmony is possible if one tries to separate them. And yet I cannot accustom myself to include health under religion, so as to make moral science, in its full conception, extend to medicine.

The Priest.—And yet, my daughter, the arbitrary separation which you wish to perpetuate would be directly contrary to our unity. It is due solely to the inadequacy of the last provisional religion, which could not discipline the soul save by giving into profane hands the management of the body. In the ancient theocracies, the most complete and most durable forms of the supernatural regime, this groundless division did not exist; the art of hygiene and of medicine was in them always a mere adjunct of the priesthood.

Such is really the natural order which Posivitism comes forward to restore and to consolidate, by virtue of the completeness which characterises it. The art of man and the science of man are each of them indivisible, as are the several aspects of their common object, all parts of which are in unbroken connection. No sound treatment of either body or mind is possible, now that the physician and the priest study exclusively the physical or the moral nature; not to speak of the philosopher, who, in our modern anarchy, wrests from the priesthood the domain of the intellect, leaving it that of the heart.

The diseases of the brain, and even many others, daily prove the powerlessness of all medical treatment limited to the lowest organs. It is quite as easy to see the inadequacy of every priesthood which aims at guiding the soul whilst taking no account of its subordination to the body. This separation, which is in two ways anarchical, must then cease, once for all, by a wise reincorporation of medicine into the domain of the priesthood, when the Positive clergy shall have adequately fulfilled its encyclopedic conditions. In fact, the moral point of view is alone able to secure active obedience for hygienic injunctions, alike whether they concern the individual or society. This is easily verified by the fruitlessness of the efforts made by Western physicians to regulate our diet, now that it is no longer under the control of the old religious precepts. Men will not generally submit to any practical inconvenience solely on the ground of their personal health, where each is left to judge for himself; for we are often more sensible of actual and certain annoyance than of distant and doubtful advantages. We must appeal to an authority higher than any individual, to establish, even on the most unimportant points, rules of real efficacy, resting then on a social judgment which never admits uncertainty.

The Woman.—Now that I have thus surveyed, in all its extent, the natural province of religion, I would know, my father, what are its general conditions. It has often been represented to me as depending solely on the heart. But I have always thought that the intellect has also its part in it. Could I gain a clear idea of the parts respectively assigned the two?

The Priest.—A right judgment on this point, my daughter, follows from a searching examination of the word *religion*, perhaps the best in point of composition of all the terms used by man. It is so constructed as to express a twofold connection which, if justly conceived, is sufficient to summarise the whole abstract theory of our unity. To constitute a complete and durable harmony, what is really wanted is to *bind together* the within by love and to *bind it again* to the without by faith. Such, generally stated, is the necessary participation of the heart and the intellect as regards the synthetical state, individual or collective.

Unity implies, before all, a feeling to which all our different inclinations can be subordinated. For our actions and our thoughts being always swayed by our affections, harmony would be unattainable by man if these last were not co-ordinated under one paramount instinct.

But this internal condition of unity would be inadequate, did not our intelligence make us recognise, outside of us, a superior power, to which our existence must always submit, even whilst modifying it. It is in order that we may be the better subjects of this supreme rule, that our moral harmony, as individuals or as societies, is especially indispensable. And conversely, this predominance of the without tends to regulate the within, by favouring the ascendency of the instinct most easily reconciled with such necessity. Thus, the two general conditions on which religion depends are naturally

connected, especially when the external order can become
the object of the internal feeling.

The Woman.—In this abstract theory of our unity I
find, my father, a radical difficulty, in regard to the moral
influence. In considering the internal harmony, you
seem to me to forget that our personal instincts have un-
fortunately greater energy than our sympathetic tendencies. Now, their preponderance, which seems calculated
to make them the natural centre of our whole moral
existence, would on the other hand make personal unity
almost incompatible with social unity. Yet the two uni-
ties not having been found irreconcilable, I need fresh
explanation to show that they are in themselves entirely
compatible.

The Priest.—Herein you have, my daughter, directly
raised the grand problem of man's existence, which is,
in fact, to secure the gradual predominance of sociability
over personality, whereas personality is naturally pre-
dominant. The better to understand the possibility of
this, we must begin by comparing the two opposite
forms which our moral unity seems naturally to admit,
according as its internal basis is egoistic or altruistic.

You just now used the plural in speaking of our personality, and by so doing involuntarily bore witness to
its radical inability to constitute any real and lasting
harmony, even in a being cut off from society. For this
monstrous unity would require not merely the absence
of every sympathetic impulse, but also the preponderance of one single selfish instinct. Now this is only
found in the lowest animals, where all is referred to the
instinct of nutrition, especially when there is no distinction of sex. But everywhere else, and particularly in
man, this primary want once supplied, there is scope
for the prevalence in succession of several other personal
instincts, the nearly equal energy of which would neutralise their conflicting claims to the entire command
of our whole moral existence. Unless all submitted to

affections resting on outward objects, the heart would be
for ever agitated by internal conflicts between the impulses of the senses and the incitements of pride or of
vanity, etc., supposing that cupidity proper should cease
to reign, together with the purely bodily wants. Moral
unity, then, is impossible, even in a solitary existence,
for every being under the exclusive dominion of personal
affections, which prevent his living for others. Such are
many wild beasts, whom we see, allowing for times of
temporary union, usually oscillating between a disorderly
activity and an ignoble torpor, from their not finding
outside of themselves the chief motors of their conduct.

The Woman.—I understand now, my father, the
natural coincidence between the true moral conditions
on which the individual and those on which the collective harmony depends. Still, however, I have the
same difficulty in conceiving of the strongest instincts
as habitually yielding.

The Priest.—Your difficulty, my daughter, will easily
disappear if you observe that altruistic unity does not, as
egoistic unity, require the entire sacrifice of the inclinations which are contrary to it in principle, but merely
their wise subordination to the predominant affection.
When it condenses all sound morality in the law of *Live
for others,* Positivism allows and sanctions the constant
satisfaction in just degree of the several personal instincts, as being indispensable to our material existence,
which is always the foundation for our higher attributes.
Consequently it blames, however estimable the motives
may often be, any austerities which, by lessening our
strength, make us less fit for the service of others. The
social purpose in the name of which it recommends attention to ourselves should at once ennoble and regulate
such attention, whilst we avoid equally excessive care
and culpable negligence.

The Woman.—But, my father, this very sanction of
the egoistic inclinations, constantly stimulated as they

moreover are by our bodily wants, seems to me still incompatible with an habitual supremacy of our weak sympathetic feelings.

The Priest.—And therefore, my daughter, this moral improvement will always form the principal object of the art of man, the constant efforts of which, both individual and collective, bring us nearer and nearer to it, but never attain it completely. This progressive solution of your difficulty depends entirely on social existence, in accordance with the natural law which develops or restrains our functions and our organs in proportion to their exercise or disuse. In fact, domestic and civic relations tend to compress the personal instincts, from the struggles which they occasion between individuals. On the contrary, they favour the growth of our benevolent feelings, the only ones that admit of a simultaneous development in all — a development by its nature continuous, as the mutual stimulus is continuous, although necessarily limited by the aggregate material conditions of our existence.

This is why the true moral unity can only satisfactorily exist in our species, social progress appertaining exclusively to the best organised of the races capable of society, except so far as others join it as free auxiliaries. Still, though such a harmony cannot be developed elsewhere, it is easy to trace its principle in many higher animals, which even furnished the first scientific proofs of the natural existence of the disinterested affections. If this great conception, at all times a presentiment of universal experience, had not been so long in taking a systematic form, no one would at the present day tax with sentimental affectation a doctrine which may be directly verified in so many species inferior to our own.

The Woman.—This satisfactory explanation leaves me, my father, only one last general elucidation to wish for, as regards the intellectual conditions of religion. Athwart the incoherence of the various special beliefs,

I do not clearly apprehend what constitutes the essential province of faith; yet faith must admit of a sense common to all systems.

The Priest.—Practically, my daughter, our faith never had but one and the same main object : namely, to form a conception of the whole order under which man lives, so as to determine our relation generally to it. Whether we assigned it to fictitious causes or studied its real laws, our object was always to understand this order which is independent of us, so the better to submit to it and the more to modify it. Every system of religious doctrine necessarily rests on some explanation or other of the world and of man, the twofold object at all times of our thoughts, whether speculative or practical.

The Positive faith sets forth directly the real *laws* of the different phenomena observable, whether internal cr external ; *i.e.*, their unvarying relations of succession and resemblance, which enable us to foresee some as a consequence of others. It puts aside, as absolutely beyond our reach and essentially idle, all inquiry into *causes* properly so called, first or final, of any events whatever. In its theoretical conceptions it always explains the *how*, never the *why*. But when it is pointing out the means of guiding our activity, it on the contrary makes consideration of the end constantly paramount ; as the practical result is then certainly due to an intelligent will.

Yet though vain in its direct results, the search after causes was at the outset no less indispensable than inevitable, as I will explain to you more particularly, as a substitute and preparation for the knowledge of laws, a knowledge which presupposes a long introduction. In the search for the *why*, which could not be found, men ended by discovering the *how*, which had not been the immediate object of inquiry. Nothing is to be really blamed but the childish persistence, so common still with our literary men, in the attempt to penetrate to causes when laws are known. For as these last alone have any relation to our conduct, the search after the others becomes as useless as it is chimerical.

The fundamental dogma, then, of the universal religion is the proved existence of an unchangeable order to which all events of every kind are subject. This order is at once *objective* and *subjective :* in other words, it concerns equally the *object* contemplated and the *subject* contemplating. Physical laws in fact imply logical laws, and the converse. If our understanding did not of itself obey any rule, it would never be able to appreciate the external harmony. The world being simpler and more powerful than man, order in man would be still less compatible with disorder in the world. All positive belief, then, rests on this twofold harmony between the object and the subject.

Such an order can be shown to exist, but it can never be explained. On the contrary, it supplies the only possible source of all rational explanation, the essence of which is the bringing under general laws each particular event, which thus comes within the sphere of systematic prevision, the only distinctive aim of all true science. And therefore the universal order was not recognised so long as arbitrary wills were in the ascendant, for to them men naturally at first attributed all the most important phenomena. But it was recognised at last in reference to the simplest events, in defiance of contrary opinions, on the evidence of experience constantly recurring and never belied, and from the simpler the recognition gradually extended to the more complex. Not till our own time has this extension reached its last domain, by representing as always subject to invariable laws the highest phenomena, those of the intelligence and of society—a point still denied by many cultivated minds. Positivism was the direct result of this final discovery, the completion of our long initiation and, as such, necessarily closing the preliminary era of human reason.

The Woman.—My father, the Positive faith on this

first glimpse seems to me very satisfactory for the intelligence, but scarcely favourable enough to the activity,
which it seems to place under the control of inflexible
destinies. And yet, since you often say that the Positive
spirit had its origin, in all cases, in practical life, it can
hardly be in contradiction with it. I wish a clear conception of their agreement in general.

The Priest.—To attain it, my daughter, all you have
to do is to correct the instinctive judgment which leads
you to look on natural laws as not susceptible of modification. Whilst phenomena were attributed to arbitrary
wills, an absolute fate was a conception necessary to
rectify an hypothesis directly incompatible with any
efficient order. Later, the discovery of natural laws
tended to uphold this general disposition, because it re-
lated first to astronomical phenomena, which are entirely
out of the reach of man's interference. But in proportion as the knowledge of the natural order extended,
it was regarded as essentially modifiable, even by man.
It becomes the more so as its phenomena become more
complicated, as I will explain to you shortly. At present
this idea extends even to the order of the heavens, its
greater simplicity allowing us more easily to conceive
improvements, with a view to correcting a spirit of blind
respect, though our weakness in regard to physical means
for ever precludes our effecting them.

In all events equally, even the most complex, the
fundamental conditions admit of no change; but in all
cases also, even the most simple, the secondary arrangements may be modified, and most often by our intervention. These modifications in no way interfere with the
invariability of the laws of nature, because they never
can be arbitrary. Their nature and degree are always
determined by appropriate rules, which complete the
domain of science. Entire immutability would be so
contrary to the very idea of *law*, that it in all cases
expresses constancy perceived in the midst of variety.

Thus the natural order always amounts to a fatality admitting modifications, which becomes the indispensable basis of the order we create. Our true destiny is then a compound of resignation and action. This second condition, far from being incompatible with the first, rests directly upon it. A judicious submission to the fundamental laws is the only means of preventing all our purposes, of whatever nature, from becoming vague and uncertain ; the only means, therefore, of enabling us to introduce a wise interference, in accordance with the secondary rules. This is how the dogmatic system of Positivism directly sanctions our activity, which no theological synthesis could include. The development of activity even becomes the chief regulator of our scientific labours in regard to the order of the world and its various modifications.

The Woman.—After such an explanation I have yet, my father, to apprehend how the Positive faith can be brought into full harmony with feeling, to which it seems to me by nature diametrically opposed. I understand, however, that its fundamental dogma supplies a strong basis for moral discipline in two ways ; first, by bringing our personal inclinations under the control of an external power; secondly, by awakening our instincts of sympathy to make us more wisely submit to or modify the necessity which presses on us all alike. But allowing these valuable attributes, Positivism still does not as yet offer me enough of direct stimulus to the holy affections, which, it would seem, should constitute the chief province of religion.

The Priest.—I confess, my daughter, that hitherto the Positive spirit has offered the two moral disadvantages attendant on science, the puffing up and withering, by encouraging pride and by turning from love. These two tendencies will always be sufficiently strong in it to habitually require systematic precautions, of which I will speak later. Still in the main, on this point, your reproach is the result of an inadequate judgment of

Positivism, which you look at solely in the state of incompleteness it still exhibits in the greater number of its
adherents. They limit themselves to the philosophical
conception which is the offspring of the scientific preparation, not going on to the religious conclusion which
alone summarises this philosophy as a whole. But complete the study of the real order of nature, and we see the
Positive doctrine finally concentrate around a synthetic
conception, as favourable to the heart as to the intellect.

The imaginary beings whom religion provisionally
made use of inspired lively affections in man, affections
which were even more powerful under the least elaborate
fictions. This valuable aptitude could not but seem for
a long period alien to Positivism, from the immense
scientific introduction it required. So long as the philosophical initiation only extended to the inorganic order,
nay, even to the vital order, it could only reveal laws
which were indispensable for our action, without furnishing us with any direct object for enduring and common
affection. But it is no longer so since the completion at
length of this gradual preparation by the special study of
the human order, both individual and collective.

This last step condenses the whole of Positive conceptions in the one single idea of an immense and eternal
Being, Humanity, whose sociological destinies are in
constant development under the necessary preponderance
of biological and cosmological fatalities. Around this
real Great Being, the prime mover of each individual
or collective existence, our affections centre by as
spontaneous an impulse as do our thoughts and our
actions. Its mere idea suggests at once the sacred
formula of Positivism—*Love for principle, and Order
for basis ; Progress for end.* Always founded on the
free concurrence of independent wills, its compound
existence, which all discord tends to dissolve, sanctions
by its very notion the constant predominance of the
heart over the intellect, as the sole basis of our true

unity. Thus it is that henceforth the whole order of
things is summed up in the being who studies it and
is ever perfecting it. The growing struggle of Humanity
against the sum of the necessities under which it exists
offers to the heart no less than to the intellect a better
object of contemplation than the necessarily capricious
omnipotence of its theological precursor.·ʹ More within
the reach of our feelings and our conceptions, by virtue
of an identity of nature which does not at all preclude
its superiority to all its servants, such a Supreme Being
powerfully arouses them to an activity the aim of which
is its preservation and amelioration.

The Woman.—Still, my father, the constant physical
labour necessitated by our bodily wants seems to me
directly in opposition with this tendency to affection in
the Positive religion. For such activity it seems to me
must always, in the main, wear a character of egoism,
extending even to the scientific efforts it evokes. Now
this would be enough to prevent the predominance in
fact of an all-pervading love.

The Priest.—I hope, my daughter, soon to make you
see that it is possible to radically transform this egoism
originally attaching to human labour. In proportion
as man's industrial action becomes more and more collective, it tends more and more to the altruistic character,
though the impulse of egoism must ever remain indispensable to its first beginnings. For, each habitually
labouring for others, this existence develops of necessity the sympathetic affections, when it is rightly appreciated. All that is wanting, then, to these toilsome
sons of Humanity is a complete and familiar consciousness of the true nature of their life. Now this will be
the natural result of an adequate extension of Positive
education. You would even now be able to trace this
tendency, if pacific activity, still subject to no systematic discipline, were as regulated as the soldier's life,
the only life hitherto organised. But the great moral

results obtained formerly as regards this last, and of which there are still traces even in its present degradation, sufficiently indicate what the industrial life allows. Nay, we must expect from the instinct of construction sympathetic influences of greater directness and completeness than those of the instinct of destruction.

The Woman.—Guided by this last indication I begin, my father, to master the general harmony of Positivism. I already see how in it the activity, naturally subordinate to faith, can also submit to love, which at first sight it seems to reject. If so, your doctrine seems to me at length to fulfil all the essential conditions of *religion,* according to your definition of the term, since it is adapted equally to the three great divisions of our existence,—loving, thinking, acting,—which were never before so perfectly combined.

The Priest.—The more you study the Positive synthesis, the more you will feel, my daughter, how far its reality renders it more complete and efficacious than any other. The habitual predominance of altruism over egoism, in which lies the great problem for man, is in Positivism the direct result of a constant harmony between our best inclinations and all our labours, theoretical as well as practical. This life of action, represented by Catholicism as hostile to our inward growth, becomes in Positivism its most powerful guarantee. You apprehend now this contrast between two systems, the one of which admits, while the other denies, the existence in our nature of the disinterested affections. The bodily wants, which seemed destined always to keep us apart, may for the future lead to a closer union than if we were exempt from them. For acts develop love better than wishes; and besides, what wishes could you form for those who wanted nothing? We may also see that the type of real existence peculiar to Positivists necessarily surpasses, even in regard to feeling, the chimerical life promised to the disciples of theology.

The Woman.—To complete this introductory conversation, I beg you, my father, to explain shortly the general division of religion; its several main constituents you will treat later.

The Priest.—This division, my daughter, is a consequence of a just appreciation of the whole of the existence which religion has to direct. The worship, the doctrine, and the life, respectively concern our feelings, our thoughts, and our actions. Our religious initiation must begin with the worship which, by revealing to us, synthetically, Humanity, cultivates the feelings adapted to the mode of existence she prescribes. After this, in the doctrine is set forth the scientific construction which has for its object to explain the order on which all rests, and the Great Being who modifies that order. Lastly, by the life we regulate directly the conduct of each human being. In this way Positive religion embraces at once our three great continuous constructions, Poetry, Philosophy, Politics. But everything in that religion is subordinate to morals, be it the growth of our feelings, the development of our knowledge, or the course of our actions, so as to make morals our constant guide in our threefold search after the beautiful, the true, and the good.

CONVERSATION II.

THEORY OF HUMANITY.

The Woman.—Our first conversation, my father, has left me a sense of alarm at my profound incompetence as regards the " great argument " on which you are entering. Since the doctrine of the universal religion is one and the same thing as the Positive Philosophy, my mind seems too weak, or at any rate too unprepared, to grasp its explanation, however simple you may make it. I bring with me nothing beyond a full confidence, a sincere respect, and an active sympathy for the doctrine which seems calculated, after so many failures, at length to overcome our modern anarchy. But I fear that something more than these moral dispositions is needed for me to enter with any chance of success on so difficult a study.

The Priest.—Your uneasiness, my daughter, calls for some introductory remarks, which I hope will soon re-assure you. Our sole object here is to effect, for the new religion, a general exposition equivalent to that which formerly taught you Catholicism. This second operation ought to be even easier than the former, for not only is your reason now mature, but the doctrine is, by its nature, more intelligible as always demonstrable. Remember, besides, the admirable maxim which our great Molière put into the mouth of the man of taste in his last masterpiece—

> Je consens qu'une femme ait des clartés de tout ;
> —Femmes Savantes, Act i. sc. 3.

I consent that a woman should have clear ideas on all subjects—

and remark further that what was then, "I consent," would be now, "It is *fitting.*"

In strict truth, the priesthood and the public had always the same intellectual domain, allowing for the difference of cultivation, which was systematic in the one case, quite unsystematic in the other. This essential agreement, without which no religious harmony would be conceivable, in Positivism becomes at once more direct and more complete than it could ever be in theologism. The true philosophic spirit consists in reality, as simple good sense, in knowing what is, in order to foresee what shall be, with a view to bettering it where possible. One of the best Positive precepts even denounces as faulty, or at any rate premature, every systematisation not preceded and prepared by a sufficient spontaneous

development. This rule is an immediate consequence
of the dogmatic verse by which Positivism characterises
our existence as a whole—

> Act from affection, and think to act.

The first half answers to the spontaneity, the second to
the systematisation which follows it. Action, unguarded
by reflection, may occasion many inconveniences, but
nothing else can, as a general rule, supply the raw
material for effectual meditation, which will allow us
to act better.

Consider lastly, that no intellect can abstain from
forming some opinion on the order of the world, whether
external or human. You now know that religious
dogma always had the same essential object, with this
single general difference—that the knowledge of laws
henceforth takes the place of the inquiry into causes.
Now, illusory hypotheses as to causes cannot seem to
you more intelligible than real notions upon laws.

Women and proletaries, for whom this exposition is
chiefly meant, cannot and ought not to become professors,
neither do they wish it. But all need sufficient mastery
of the spirit and the method of the universal doctrine to
enforce on their spiritual chiefs an adequate scientific
and logical preparation, the necessary foundation for the
systematic exercise of the priestly office. Now, this
discipline of the intellect is, at the present day, so contrary to the habits resulting from our modern anarchy,
that it never could prevail unless enforced by the public
of both sexes on those who claim to guide its opinion.
This social condition will always give a great value to
the general spread of religious instruction, over and above
its proper object of guiding the conduct of men, whether
as individuals or as societies. But this service becomes,
at the present day, of capital importance, as the means of
finally terminating the anarchy of the West, the prominent characteristic of which is the revolt of the intellect.

Could this Catechism but convince women and proletaries that their would-be spiritual guides are radically incompetent to deal with the high questions of which the solution is in blind confidence left them, it would largely help to calm the West. Now this unanimous conviction can, at the present day, spring only from a sufficient appreciation of the final doctrine, such as to place beyond dispute the general conditions of its systematic cultivation.

As for the difficulties which now frighten you in this indispensable study, you attach too little weight, as to overcoming them, to your excellent moral dispositions. No existing school would hesitate to pronounce authoritatively that the intellect thinks at all times as if the heart were not. But women and proletaries have never lost sight of the powerful reaction of the feelings on the intellect—a reaction explained at last by Positive Philosophy. Your sex in particular, whose pleasant but unconscious task it was to hand down to us, as far as was possible, under the pressure of modern anarchy, the admirable habits of the Middle Ages, recognises daily the error of the metaphysical heresy which separates these two great attributes. Since, according to the beautiful maxim of Vauvenargues, the heart is necessary to the intellect for its most important inspirations, it must also aid in understanding their results. Its powerful assistance is peculiarly available for moral and social conceptions; for in them, more than elsewhere, the sympathetic instinct can aid the spirit of synthesis, whilst without that aid its greatest efforts could not overcome their difficulties. But it may also be of use in the lower theories, by virtue of the necessary interconnection of all our real speculations.

Of the two fundamental conditions of religion, love and faith, the first should certainly take the first place. For though faith be well adapted to strengthen love, the inverse action is stronger as more direct. Not only does

feeling preside over the spontaneous inspirations required
originally by every systematic creation, but it sanctions
and assists this creation, when it has once felt its
importance. No woman with experience is unaware
of the too frequent inadequacy of our best affections
when not aided by firm conviction. This word *convince* would suffice, if we look to its etymology, to recall
the power deep-seated beliefs have to strengthen the
within by binding it to the without.

Lastly, the intellectual deficiency which alarms you at
this point rests on the usual confusion of instruction
with intelligence. Your familiarity with, and admiration for, the unrivalled Molière have not kept you from
the common error in this respect, an error carefully kept
up by our Trissotins of all professions. And yet we
ought to blush at being in the present time behind the
Middle Ages, when all could appreciate the profound
intellectual eminence of persons who were very un-
lettered. Have you not sometimes found in such people
more real capacity than in most professors? Now more
than ever is instruction really necessary only to construct and develop science, which should always be so
framed as a whole as to be directly within the reach of
all sound intellects. Otherwise our best doctrines would
soon degenerate into dangerous mystifications : this
deviation, natural to all theoricians whatsoever, can only
be effectually checked in them by a due surveillance on
the part of the public of both sexes.

The Woman.—Encouraged by your introduction, I
ask you, my father, to begin the systematic exposition
of the Positive doctrine by a more direct and complete
explanation of its universal principle. I already understand that your conception of the true Great Being by
its very nature condenses the whole real order, not only
human but external. This is why I feel the want of a
clearer and more precise definition as regards this
fundamental unity of Positivism.

The Priest.—To reach it, you must first, my daughter,
define Humanity as *the whole* of human beings, past,
present, and future. The word *whole* points out clearly
that you must not take in all men, but those only who
are really assimilable, in virtue of a real co-operation
towards the common existence. Though all are necessarily born children of Humanity, all do not become her
servants, and many remain in the parasitic state which
was only excusable during their education. Times of
anarchy bring forth in swarms, nay, even enable to
flourish, these sad burdens on the true Great Being.
More than one of them has recalled to you the energetic
reprobation of Ariosto, borrowed from Horace, (Ep. i.
2. 27)—

> Venuto al mondo sol per far letame:
> —*Sat.* iii. 33.

Born upon the earth merely to manure it :

and, still better, the admirable condemnation of Dante—

> Che visser senza infamia e senza lodo.
> .   .   .   .   .
> Cacciarli i ciel per non esser men belli,
>   Nè lo profondo inferno li riceve,
>   Ch' alcuna gloria i rei avrebber d' elli.
> .   .   .   .   .
> Non ragioniam di lor, ma guarda e passa.
> —*Inferno*, iii. 36-51.

> .   .   .   . Who lived
> Without or praise or blame .   .   .   .
> .   .   .   .   . Heaven drove them forth,
> Not to impair its lustre, nor the depth
> Of Hell receives them, lest the accursed tribe
> Should glory thence with exultation vain.
> .   .   .   .   .
> Speak not of them, but look and pass them by.
> —CARY's *Translation.*

So you see that, in this respect as in all others, the inspiration of the poet was far in advance of the systematic view of the philosopher. Be this as it may, if these mere digesting machines are no real part of Humanity, you should, as a just compensation, associate with the new Supreme Being all its worthy animal auxiliaries. All useful habitual co-operation in forwarding the destinies of man, when given voluntarily, raises the being which gives it into a real element of this composite existence, with a degree of importance proportioned to the dignity of its species and its own service. To estimate rightly this indispensable complement of human existence, let us imagine ourselves without it. We then do not hesitate to look on many horses, dogs, oxen, etc, as more estimable than certain men.

In this primary conception of human concert, our attention is naturally directed to solidarity rather than to continuity. But though the latter is at first less felt, because it requires a deeper examination to discover it, it is an idea which must ultimately predominate. For the progress of society comes very soon to depend more on time than on space. It is not to-day only that each man, as he exerts himself to estimate aright his indebtedness to others, sees that his predecessors as a whole, in comparison with his contemporaries as a whole, have much the larger share in that indebtedness. The same superiority is manifested, in a less degree, in the most remote periods; as is indicated by the touching worship then always paid to the dead, as was beautifully remarked by Vico.

Thus the true social existence consists more in the continuity of succession than in the solidarity of the existing generation. The living are, by the necessity of the case, always and more and more, under the government of the dead: such is the fundamental law of the human order.

To grasp it more fully, we must distinguish two successive lives in each true servant of Humanity : the one, temporary but conscious, constitutes life properly so called ; the other, unconscious but permanent, does not begin till after death. The first, being always bodily, may be termed *objective;* especially in contrast with the second, which, leaving each one to exist only in the heart and mind of others, deserves the name of *subjective.* This is the noble immortality, necessarily disconnected with the body, which Positivism allows our *soul,* preserving this valuable term to designate the sum of our intellectual and moral functions, without any allusion to a corresponding entity.

According to this lofty conception, the true human race is composed of two masses, both of which are always essential, while the proportion between them is constantly varying, with a tendency to strengthen the power of the dead over the living in every actual operation. If the action and its result are most dependent on the objective element, the impulse and the rule are principally due to the subjective. Largely endowed by our predecessors, we hand on gratuitously to our successors the whole domain of man, with an addition which becomes smaller and smaller in proportion to the amount received. This necessary gratuitousness meets with a worthy reward in the subjective incorporation by which we shall be able to perpetuate our services under an altered form.

Such a theory seems at the present day to be the last effort of the human intellect under systematic guidance ; yet its germ, anterior to all such guidance, is always traceable in the most remote forms of man's evolution, and was already recognised by the most ancient poets. The smallest tribe, nay, even every family of any consideration, soon looks on itself as the essential stock of this composite and progressive existence whose only impassable limits, in space or time, are those of the normal constitution of the planet it occupies. Though the Great Being is not yet sufficiently formed, its most extensive conflicts never concealed its gradual evolution, which, rationally judged, supplies now the only possible basis of our ultimate unity. Even under the Christian egoism, which dictated to the stern St. Peter the characteristic maxim, "*As strangers and pilgrims*," we see the admirable St. Paul even then by feeling anticipating the conception of Humanity, in this touching but contradictory image, " *We are every one members one of another.*" It devolved on the Positivist principle to disclose the one ·trunk to which, by the law of their being, belong all these members which were instinctively confounded.

The Woman.—I feel compelled, my father, to admit this fundamental conception, whatever difficulties it still presents. But I am frightened at my own insignificance in presence of such an existence, the immensity of which reduces me to nothing more completely than did of old the majesty of a God with whom, though feeble, I felt myself in some definite and direct relation. Now that you have mastered me by the ever-growing preponderance of the new Supreme Being, I need to have re-awakened in me the just consciousness of my individuality.

The Priest.—This will follow, my daughter, from a more complete appreciation of the Positive doctrine. It is sufficient if we see that, whilst Humanity as a whole always constitutes the principal motor of all our operations, physical, intellectual, or moral, the Great Being can never act except through individual instruments. This is why the objective part of the race, notwithstanding its increasing subordination to the subjective, must always be indispensable for the subjective to exercise any influence. But on analysing this collective participation, we find it ultimately the result of the free concurrence of purely individual efforts. Herein we have what should raise each worthy individuality in presence of the new Supreme Being more than could be the case in respect to the old. In fact, this latter had no real need of any of our services except to give him vain praises, the childish eagerness for which tended to degrade him in our eyes. Remember this conclusive verse of the *Imitation :*—

I am necessary to thee, thou art useless to me.

> Tu mei indiges :
> Non ego tui indigeo.
> —*Imitatio Christi*, iv. 12, 38, 39 (ed. Hirsche).

Doubtless but few men are warranted in thinking themselves indispensable to Humanity : such language is only applicable to the true authors of the principal steps in our progress. Still every noble human being may and should habitually feel the utility of his personal co-operation in this immense evolution, which must cease at once should all the individual co-operators have simultaneously disappeared. The development, and even the preservation, of the Great Being must then always depend on the free services of its different children, though the inactivity of any one in particular, generally speaking, admits of an adequate compensation.

This summary exposition of the fundamental dogma of our religion enables me, my daughter, now to proceed to the explanation, first in the general, then in detail, of the Positivist worship. The study of it will make you feel, I hope, that the poetical power of Positivism is certainly on a level with its philosophical, though it has not produced as conclusive results.

First Part.

—◆◆—

EXPLANATION OF THE WORSHIP.

CONVERSATION III.

THE WORSHIP AS A WHOLE.

The Woman.—The two preceding conversations, my father, have cleared up for me the theory of religion and the conception of Humanity, the centre of the whole Positive system. I ask you now to teach me directly to love better, in order to know better, and to serve better, the incomparable Goddess whom you have revealed to me, and into whom in the end I hope to deserve incorporation. In such a subject our conferences may assume the character of real conversations. I shall only interrupt your teaching in order to throw light on, or set forth more fully, points on which you do not sufficiently dwell. I even hope to take an active part by anticipating some of your explanations, thus rendering your exposition more rapid without detracting from its completeness. For in the worship we enter the domain of feeling, where the inspiration of woman, though it keep its empirical character, can really aid the priesthood in its construction.

The Priest.—I rely greatly, my daughter, on this

spontaneous co-operation to shorten this part of our Catechism as compared with the two following. But in order to make the best use of your present disposition, this new conversation, which concerns merely the worship in general, must begin by a systematic general plan of our religion, though you are already familiar with it.

As all combinations, physical even, and still more logical, must always be binary, as is pointed out clearly by the etymology of the word, the rule is applicable necessarily to any division whatever. The fundamental division of religion obeys it naturally, by partitioning out the domain of religion between love and faith. Wherever evolution, individual or collective, follows its normal course, love first leads us to faith, so long as the growth is spontaneous. But when it becomes systematic, then the belief is constructed to regulate love. This leading division is equivalent to the true general distinction between theory and practice.

The practical domain of religion necessarily again breaks up into two, as a consequence of the natural distinction between feelings and acts. The theoretical part corresponds to the intelligence only, the sole possible basis of belief. But the practical part embraces all the rest of our existence, quite as much our feelings as even our acts. Universal custom, prior to all theory—and such custom is the best rule of language—gives a direct sanction to this view, by designating as religious *practices* the habits which relate to worship, quite as much as, if not more than, those habits which more particularly concern the regime. This apparent confusion rests on a basis of profound though empirical wisdom, through which the people, and particularly women, early learnt, as the priesthood learnt, that the perfecting of our feelings is a more important and difficult task than the immediate improvement of our actions. Our love never becoming mystic, Positive worship normally forms part of the practical domain of the true religion ; we love more in order to serve better. But on the other hand, from the true religious point of view, our acts may always have an essentially altruistic character, since the main object of religion is to dispose us and teach us to live for others. Inspired by love, our actions in return tend to develop love. Directly visible in the case of intellectual improvement, when rightly guided, this natural faculty extends even to material progress, provided it proceed on right principles. This is why the regime, under its religious aspect, appertains to the domain of love as much as does the worship.

These two principles, which make our worship practical, our regime affective, yet without ever confusing them, could not be discovered whilst religion remained theological. Then the worship and the regime were thoroughly heterogeneous, one having God for its object, the other man. The worship rose above the regime only because the second of the two beings was necessarily subordinate to the first. Both were essentially egoistic in character, in accordance with the thoroughly individual constitution of a faith which never could be reconciled with the existence in our nature of the benevolent instincts, an existence allowed by Positivism alone. Under the older faith, the division between the regime and the worship was as marked as that which separates the worship from the doctrine; so that the general plan of religion became unintelligible, as a result of our just dislike to ternary combinations.

In the final state, on the contrary, the divisions of religion are as favourable to the reason as to the feelings. In it the doctrine differs from the worship and the regime much more than these last differ from one another. It is in this way that the ordinary constitution of religion again becomes ternary, but becomes so by a division which is still binary, its main division being completed by a single subdivision, heretofore absurdly placed on a level with it. These three constituent parts together

ultimately form a regular progression, such is the natural
homogeneity of its different elements. It leads without
effort from love to faith, or the reverse ; according as we
take the subjective or the objective course, in the two
most important periods of religious initiation, respectively
under the direction of woman or the priest. To idealise
the doctrine in order to idealise the regime, such was
always the destination proper of the worship, which thus
becomes capable of representing the whole of religion.
Its study will make you sensible, I hope, that the poetic
capacity of Positivism is really on a level with its philosophic power, though not as yet able to produce such
conclusive results.

The Woman.—A very natural eagerness to enter at
once on the direct study of our worship made me, at the
outset, overleap, my father, the general preamble you
have just set before me. I now feel how much I needed
it in order to gain a clear conception of the plan of
religion, of which I had previously not sufficiently co-
ordinated the three parts. This valuable explanation,
however, seems to me now so complete, that I hope to
study immediately the whole system of the worship to
be paid to our Goddess.

The Priest.—We adore her not as the older God, to
compliment her, my daughter, but in order to serve her
better, by bettering ourselves. It is important here to
recall this normal aim of the Positive worship, in order
to anticipate or correct the tendency to degenerate into
mysticism, to which we are always liable under a too
exclusive attention to the feelings, as it disposes us to
neglect, or even to forget, the acts which they should
govern. With my greater tendency to system, I am
more prone than you to such an error, the practical evils
of which would be soon pointed out by your instinctive
wisdom, which would even remedy them in a degree by
some happy inconsistency in theory. It is of particular
importance for me to avoid this mistake in the present

conversation, for by its more abstract and general character it makes it more easy and more serious. Your
corrections, drawn from experience, would always ultimately bring me right, I doubt not, but often too late;
so as at times to lay me under the necessity of laborious
efforts to repair the error.

With this precaution constantly in view, let us look
on the whole worship as having for its object to form
a systematic connection between the doctrine and the
regime by idealising both. As for the doctrine, the worship completes it and condenses it, by rendering the
conception of Humanity at once more familiar and more
imposing, through an ideal presentation of it. But, as
type of the regime, the worship must tend directly to
ameliorate our feelings, never losing sight of the modifications they habitually undergo from the three stages
of human life—personal, domestic, and social. At first
sight, these two general modes of apprehending and
instituting the worship may seem irreconcilable, yet a
natural agreement arises from the aptitude inherent in
a worthy idealisation of the Great Being to consolidate
and develop the love which is the basis of its whole
existence. If so, the original difference in no way tends
to break up the worship into two separate domains—
one belonging exclusively to the intellect, the other to
feeling. Such a division would be ordinarily as impracticable as the distinction generally drawn between algebra
and arithmetic, which can really stand alone only in very
simple cases, and these mostly of our own making; and
yet the two, though constantly mixed, are never confused. This comparison gives a fair idea of the closeness
of the connection which naturally binds together the two
aspects, intellectual and moral, or theoretical and practical, under which we are justified in viewing either the
whole Positive worship or each of its parts. But, in
spite of the spontaneousness of their connection from the
nature of the religious system to which both relate, to

combine them wisely is really the chief difficulty to be met with in instituting our worship. For the worship is liable, as the doctrine, and even more, to degenerate into mysticism or empiricism, according as generalisation and abstraction are in excess or defect. Now these two contrary errors produce, in the moral point of view, equal evils; for the social efficacy of man's feelings is equally impaired by their becoming too refined or too coarse.

The Woman.—The better to estimate this general difficulty, I may—may I not, my father?—bring it down to the difficulty of rightly instituting the subjective life, on which of necessity rests the whole Positive worship, whether we view it intellectually or morally. Our Great Being is formed much more by the dead in the first place, then by those to be born, than by the living, most of whom even are only its servants, without the power, at present, of becoming its organs. There are but few men, and still fewer women, who admit of being satisfactorily judged in this respect before the completion of their objective career. During the greater part of his actual life each one has it in his power to balance, and even far to overbalance, the good he has done by the evil he may do. So the human population is essentially made up of two kinds of subjective elements, the one determinate, the other indefinite, between which its objective element, though more and more diminished in importance, alone forms an immediate and close connection. If so, I see that, to represent to us the true Great Being, Positive worship must largely develop in each of us the subjective life : which, by the way, it seems to me, will render it eminently poetic. At the same time such practices, in which thought works chiefly by the aid of images, become very apt for the direct cultivation of our best feelings.

The intellectual condition then appears quite compatible with the moral aim, on the principle which you have just given me. But this necessary means seems

itself to raise a new general difficulty. For I hardly
see how it will be possible to institute, still more to
secure unanimous assent to, the daily realisation in
private or in public of the subjective life, and yet its
universal practice becomes indispensable for our religion.
No doubt the entire regeneration of education will procure us, on this point, immense resources, which it is
difficult to estimate at the present time. Nevertheless,
I fear that these resources will always be too weak to
overcome the difficulty; one on which the Past seems to me
to offer, directly at least, no ground for general hope.

The Priest.—On the contrary, my daughter, I hope
soon to dispel your uneasiness, natural though it be, by a
judicious survey of this long initiation, now finally ended,
as is clearly shown by the very construction of this
Catechism. It is impossible, in fact, to mistake the
natural and universal capacity of our species for living
a subjective life, when we see such a life, under different
forms, prevail with it during forty centuries. The
emancipated now know that during this immense pro-
bation the brains of all were habitually under the sway
of beings purely imaginary, though believed to have a
real and distinct existence. But the various theologists
are almost as convinced on this point; since each belief
judges so of all the others; yet the supporters of those
others, put together, were always in a strong majority,
especially in the present dispersive state of supernatural
belief. Each one thinks illusion the rule, his own fiction
the single exception.

So prone are we to the subjective life that it is more
prevalent the nearer we ascend to the simple age of full
spontaneity, individual or collective. The greatest effort
of our reason consists, on the contrary, in so subordinating
the subjective to the objective that our mental operations may represent the external world, in the degree required by the position we occupy, whether for action or
submission, in relation to its unalterable predominance.

This normal result is obtained, in the individual as in the species, only in the period of complete maturity, and it constitutes the best sign of that maturity. Though this transformation tends radically to change the conduct of the human understanding, it will never prevent our developing the subjective life, even beyond all the needs of Positive worship. We shall always need a certain discipline to keep within due limits our natural disposition to substitute in excess the within for the without. You need feel, then, no serious uneasiness on this head; unless you judge man, as he will be, by the present tendency of scientific specialities to crush the imagination and to wither the heart; whereas this is only one of the natural symptoms of modern anarchy.

The only essential difference between the new and the old subjectivity must lie in this, that the new will be fully felt and acknowledged, no one ever confusing it with objectivity. Our religious contemplations will consciously be carried on internally; whereas our predecessors made a vain effort to see without them what had no existence but within, always on the understanding that they might fall back on the future life for the ultimate realisation of their visions. This general contrast is easily condensed by confronting boldly the two ways of conceiving the principal subdivision of the intellect. In the normal state, contemplation, even when inward, is easier and less eminent than meditation; for in it our intellect remains nearly passive. In a word, we contemplate in order to meditate, because all our important studies always are concerned with the without. To theologists, on the contrary, meditation must have always seemed less difficult and less exalted than contemplation, at that time made the highest effort of the understanding. They only meditated in order to be able to contemplate beings which were always eluding them. A familiar sign will soon mark this distinction for the greater part of the private worship. For the Positivist shuts his eyes during

E

his private prayers, the better to see the internal image ;
the believer in theology opened them to see without him
an object which was an illusion.

The Woman.—Although this conclusive explanation
dispels at once my previous uneasiness, I still continue,
my father, to look on the institution of the subjective
life as the capital difficulty in Positivist worship. Only,
the new subjectivity now appears to me always to admit
of being satisfactorily reconciled with the deep reality
which distinguishes our faith. But this agreement, it
seems to me, must require special and unceasing efforts.

The Priest.—You have duly apprehended, my daughter,
the essential condition which I must now fulfil. For the
best contrast is drawn between the worship and the
regime, if we assign them, as their respective domains,
the subjective and the objective life. Though each is at
one and the same time connected with both, the subjective evidently prevails in the worship, the objective in
the regime. Nothing is more adapted to characterise
the higher dignity of the worship as compared with the
regime ; by virtue of the necessary preponderance of
subjectivity over objectivity throughout the whole of
man's existence, even the individual, and still more the
collective existence.

The Woman.—Your systematic sanction of my unaided
conclusion induces me, my father, now to ask you in what
consists the true theory of the subjective life. Though
it is impossible here to do more than give an outline of
such a doctrine, its fundamental principle seems to me
absolutely indispensable. No Positivist can do without
a general explanation of this point; for his worship,
public or private, will require it for almost everyday use,
as a preventive against any degeneration into mysticism
or empiricism.

The Priest.—To satisfy your legitimate desire, my
daughter, conceive of the fundamental law of the subjective life as ever consisting in its due subordination to

the objective. The without never ceases essentially to regulate the within, whilst it nourishes and stimulates it; as well in regard to the life of the brain as to our bodily life. Let our conceptions be as fantastical as they may, they always bear in an appreciable degree the impress of this involuntary dominion, though it becomes less simple and even less complete, in proportion as it is more indirect. All this is a necessary consequence of the indisputable principle which I shall explain to you when expounding the doctrine, and on which I have rested our whole intellectual theory, dynamical as well as statical, thus connected with the fundamental system of biological conceptions.

The order we make never being anything but the perfecting the order we find, and that mainly by developing it, we feel here, as everywhere else, and even more than elsewhere, that our true liberty is essentially the result of a due submission. But in order properly to extend to the subjective life this general rule of the objective, we must begin by examining under this fresh aspect the natural constitution of the universal order. For all the laws which form it are far from being equally applicable to the subjective life. To make your ideas more definite, I will specify only the simplest and most common case, namely, when we employ the subjective worship to bring back as in life one whom we have loved. Without this precise determination, in which the heart aids the intellect, it would be easy to go astray in the study of such a domain. But all the ideas formed in this way in reference to our most private and most easily appreciated worship, will be easily applied, with fit modifications, to the rest of sociolatry.

The Woman.—I thank you, my father, for such consideration, which I feel to be indispensable to me. This doctrine is as new as it is difficult, for this attractive problem could not be stated even, under the reign of supernatural beliefs, which forbade us to represent to ourselves our dead otherwise than in a mysterious condition, generally left vague. Such a state allowed of no analogy on essential points between us and them. Supposing us free from all uneasiness as to their ultimate fate, we could never form for them a subjective life which made every one guilty of impiety in giving to the creature the affection due to the Creator. But if this affecting question is peculiar to Positivism, not less does the general answer appertain to it, as having alone revealed the true laws of man's intellect, of which you have already given me a glimpse. I grasp, then, at once the general method of subjective worship and its normal basis, which converts this ideal existence into a simple prolongation of the real. But would you explain to me directly the modifications which such prolongation allows?

The Priest.—They consist, my daughter, in the suppression, or at least in the neglect, of all the lower laws, so as to allow fuller predominance to the higher. During the objective life, the dominion of the outer world over the world of man is as direct as it is unbroken. But in the subjective life, the outward order becomes simply passive, and no longer prevails except indirectly, as the primary source of the images we wish to cherish. Our beloved dead are no longer governed by the rigorous laws of the inorganic order, nor even of the vital. On the contrary, the laws peculiar to the human order, especially the moral, though not excluding the social, govern, and that better than during life, the existence which each one of them retains in our brain. This existence, thus purely intellectual and affective, is composed essentially of images, which revive at once the feelings with which the being snatched from us inspires us and the thoughts which he occasioned. Our subjective worship is reduced, then, to a species of internal evocation, the gradual result of an exertion of the brain performed in accordance with its own laws. The image always remains less clear and less vivid than the object, in obedience to the fundamental law of our intellect. But since the contrary is often the case in diseases of the brain, a judicious culture may bring the normal state nearer to this necessary limit, far beyond what could be believed possible hitherto, so long as this beautiful domain remained vague and dark.

To determine more exactly this general subordination, observe that the subjective evocation of the loved object is always connected with the last objective impressions he left us. This is most evident as to age, which death withdraws from all increase. Our premature losses are thus found to invest the object of our affections with eternal youth. This law, from the original adorer, extends of necessity to his most remote adherents. No one will ever be able to represent to himself, after Dante, his sweet Beatrice otherwise than as at the age of twenty-five. We may think of her as younger, we cannot imagine her older.

The objective and the subjective life then differ fundamentally in this, that the first is under the direct control of physical laws, the second under that of moral laws ; the intellectual laws applying equally to both. The distinction becomes less marked when we see that, in both cases, the more general order always prevails over the more special. For the difference is then limited to the mode in which we estimate the generality, measured first by the phenomena, then by our conceptions, as will be explained when we are studying the doctrine.

Be this as it may, this necessary preponderance of the moral laws in the subjective life is so congruous to our nature that it was not merely involuntarily respected, but known and appreciated, at the earliest dawn of man's intelligence. You know, in fact, that the empirical outline of the great moral laws was long anterior to any full recognition of the lowest physical laws. Whilst the fictions of poetry set aside without scruple the general conditions of the inorganic order, and even of the vital, they conformed with admirable exactness to the leading

ideas of the social, and still more of the moral order.
Men found no difficulty in admitting invulnerable heroes,
and gods who took any shape at pleasure.   But the
instinct of the people, as the genius of the poet, would
at once have rejected any moral incoherence—if, for
example, a writer had ventured on attributing to a miser
or a coward, liberality or courage.

The Woman.—By the light of your explanations, I
see, my father, that in the subjective worship we may
neglect physical laws in order to cling more closely to
the moral, the real knowledge of which is to perfect so
greatly this new order of institutions.   Our imagination
easily frees itself from the most general conditions, even
of space and time, provided that the human requirements
are always respected.   But I would know how we are to
use such liberty, so as to facilitate our attainment of the
main end of subjective worship, that is to say, the
cerebral evocation of the beings dead to us.

The Priest.—So stated, my daughter, your question is
easily answered, so evident is the observation, that the
better to concentrate our strength on this holy object,
we must divert none of it on superfluous modifications of
the vital, nor even of the inorganic order.   Be careful,
then, to retain all the outer circumstances which were
habitual to the being you adore.   Use them even to reani-
mate more effectually its image.   You will find on this
point, in the *System of Positive Politics,* an important
remark :—"Our personal memories become at once
clearer and more sure, when we fix definitely the material
environment before we place in it the living image."   I
even advise you in general to break up this determination of the outward into its three essential parts, always
proceeding from without inwards, according to our hierarchical principle.   This rule of worship consists in fixing
with precision, first the place, then the seat or the attitude,
and lastly the dress, belonging to each particular case.
Though the heart may at first be impatient of the delay,

it soon acknowledges its deep efficacy, when it sees the loved image gradually acquire by these means a strength and a clearness which at first seemed impossible.

These operations, which are essentially æsthetic, are more easily understood by comparing them with the operations of science, by virtue of the necessary identity of the chief laws of both. In strict truth, science, when it tells us beforehand of a future often distant, ventures on a still bolder effort than that of art when it would call up some cherished memory. Our brilliant successes in the former case, though there the intellect derives much less aid from the heart, authorise us to hope for more satisfactory results in the other, wherein alone we have the certainty of arriving at a solution. It rests, to say the truth, entirely on our knowledge of the laws of the brain, of which our conceptions are still so confused. Our astronomical previsions, on the contrary, depend most on the simplest and best known of external laws. But whilst this distinction is sufficient to explain the inequality of our actual success in the two cases, it shows it to be simply provisional.

When the higher laws shall be sufficiently known, the Positive priesthood will draw from them results more precious, and susceptible of greater regularity, than those of the most perfect astronomy. For the previsions of astronomy become uncertain, and often unattainable, as soon as the planetary problems become very complicated, as we see almost always in the case of comets. Without justly incurring the charge of chimerical presumption, the providence of man can and ought to aspire to give more regularity to the order which is most amenable to its action, than can prevail, as regards the majority of events, in the order which obeys only a blind fatality. The greater complication of the phenomena will ultimately yield, in these high cases, to the paramount sagacity of the modifying agent, when the human order shall be sufficiently known.

The Woman.—I feel, my father, that to subordinate
the subjective to the objective is at once the constant
obligation and the chief resource of Positive ·worship.
You have made me quite understand that, far from with-
drawing ourselves from this necessary yoke, we ought
freely to accept it, even when we might neglect it. For
this full submission makes our subjective life much
easier, at the same time that it economises all our most
valuable strength. But I do not see, from this point
onwards, in what consists our own action in this inner
existence, which yet ought, it seems to me, in its own
way, to become even less passive than the outer.

The Priest.—It consists, my daughter, in idealising
almost always by subtraction, and rarely by addition, even
when in adding we observe all proper precautions. The
ideal must improve upon the real, or it is inadequate
morally; herein lies its normal compensation for its
great inferiority in clearness and liveliness. But it must
ever be subordinate to the real, otherwise the presentation would be untrue, and the worship would become
mystical; whereas by a too servile adherence to reality
it would remain empirical. Our rule avoids equally these
two contrary deviations. It is naturally indicated by
our tendency to forget the defects of the dead in order
to recall only their good qualities.

So regarded, see in it only a particular deduction from
the dogma of Humanity. For if our Divinity only incor-
porates into herself the really worthy dead, she also takes
away from each the imperfections which in all cases
dimmed their objective life. Dante had, in his own way,
a presentiment of this law, when he formed the beautiful fiction in which, to prepare for blessedness, the soul
drinks—first of the river of oblivion, then of Eunoe,
which restores only the memory of good. Add, then, to
the beings you take as types but very secondary improvements, so as never to change their true character, even
outwardly, and still more morally. But give free scope,

though always with prudence, to your natural disposition to clear them of their different faults.

The Woman.—So, my father, the true theory of the subjective life makes our worship ultimately leave the external order as it is, to concentrate with greater effect on the human order our chief efforts after inward improvement. The noble existence which perpetuates us in others becomes thus the worthy continuation of that by which we deserved this immortality; the moral progress of the individual and of the race is ever the most important aim of both lives. The dead with us are freed from the laws of matter and of life, and they leave us the memory of their subjection to these laws only that we may recall them better as we knew them. But they do not cease to love, and even to think, in us and by us. The sweet exchange of feelings and ideas that passed between us and them, during their objective life, becomes at once closer and more continuous when they are detached from bodily existence. Although under these conditions the life of each of them is deeply mingled with our own, its originality, both morally and mentally, is in no way impaired thereby, when it had a really distinct character. We may even say that the chief differences become more marked, in proportion as this close intercourse becomes more full.

This Positive conception of the future life is certainly nobler than that of any theologists, at the same time that it alone is true. When I was a Catholic, my most fervent belief never prevented my feeling deeply shocked on studying the childish conception of blessedness which we find in a father of such high moral and intellectual excellence as St. Augustine. I was almost angry when I found him hoping some day to be free from the laws of weight, and even from all wants connected with nutrition, though, by a gross contradiction, he kept the power of eating what he liked, without any fear, it would seem, of becoming inordinately fat. Such comparisons are well adapted to make us feel how greatly Positivism perfects immortality, at the same time that it places it on a firmer footing, when it changes it from objective to subjective. Still, clear as the superiority is, it does not prevent my regretting in the old worship the great institution of prayer, which does not seem to me compatible with the new faith.

The Priest.—Such an omission, my daughter, would be extremely serious, if it were real; since the regular practice of prayer, private or public, is the capital condition of any worship whatever. Far from failing therein, Positivism satisfies it better than Catholicism : for it purifies this institution at the same time that it develops it. Your mistake on this point arises from the low notion still formed of prayer, which is made to consist above all in petitions, too often for external objects, in accordance with the profoundly egoistic character of all theological worship. For us, on the contrary, prayer becomes the ideal of life. For to pray is, at one and the same time, to love, to think, and even to act, since expression is always a true action. Never can the three aspects of human life be united with so intimate a union as in these admirable effusions of gratitude and love towards our Great Goddess or her worthy representatives and organs. No interested motive any longer stains the purity of our prayers.

Still, as their daily use greatly improves our heart and even our intellect, we are warranted in keeping in sight this valuable result, without fearing that such a degree of personality will ever degrade us. Though the Positivist prays especially in order to give free expression to his best affections, he may also ask, but only for a noble progress, which he ensures almost by the asking. The fervent wish to become more tender, more reverential, more courageous even, is itself in some degree a realisation of the desired improvement; at least by the sincere confession of our actual imperfection, the first condition of the subsequent improvement. This holy influence of prayer may extend, moreover, to the intellect, were it only by urging us to new efforts to improve our thinking. On the contrary, to ask for an increase of wealth or power would, in our worship, be a practice as absurd as it is ignoble. We do not envy the theologists the unlimited command over the external order which they hope to obtain by prayer. All our subjective efforts are limited to perfect as far as possible the human order, at once nobler and more susceptible of modification. In a word, Positivist prayer takes complete possession of the highest domain formerly reserved for supernatural grace. Sanctification with us systematises more particularly the progress which previously was looked on as alien to all invariable laws, although its pre-eminence was already felt.

The Woman.—Accepting this explanation as decisive, I beg you, my father, to point out to me now the general method suited to Positivist prayer.

The Priest.—For that, my daughter, you must distinguish in it two successive parts, the one passive, and the other active, which concern respectively the past and the future, with the present for connecting link. Our worship is always the expression of a love springing from and developing through an ever-increasing gratitude. All prayer then, private or public, ought to prepare us by commemoration for effusion, this latter usually lasting half the time of the former. When a happy combination of signs and images has sufficiently rekindled our feelings towards the being we adore, we pour them forth with real fervour, which soon tends still further to strengthen them, and so to make us more ready for the concluding evocation.

The Woman. —Satisfied with these hints, I ask you, my father, to complete your general examination of our worship, by directly explaining its fundamental influences on our highest improvement. Although I feel them profoundly, I could not define them so as to secure

a fair judgment upon them. This is why I ask you, on
this point, for a systematic explanation, as a guide, first
in my own practice, and next in my legitimate efforts
to convert others.

The Priest.—Though our worship improves the heart
and the intellect simultaneously, it is important, my
daughter, to examine separately its reaction on our
moral state and its influence on our intellect.

The first is an immediate consequence of the chief law
of animal life. For worship is always a real *exercise*, and
even a more normal exercise than any other ; as is shown
by ordinary language, here, as elsewhere, the faithful
picture of human existence. Such a view of it is in the
highest degree indisputable when prayer is complete, that
is to say, when it is oral as well as mental. In fact, we
bring into play in expression, whether by sounds, or by
gestures or attitudes, the same muscles that we do in
action. So every true expression of our feelings has a
tendency to strengthen and develop them, in the same
way as when we perform the acts which they suggest.

I ought, however, on this point, to guard against a
dangerous exaggeration, by urging you never to confuse
these two great moral influences. Notwithstanding the
similarity of their most important laws, in no case can
they be looked on as equivalent. By universal experience, fully confirmed by our cerebral theory, acts will
always have more weight than expression, not merely in
the external result, but also in our inward improvement.
Still, second to the practice of good actions, nothing is
more adapted to strengthen and develop our best feelings
than their due expression, supposing it become sufficiently
habitual. Now, this general means of amelioration is
ordinarily more within our reach than even action, which
often requires materials or circumstances beyond our
reach, so as at times to confine us to barren wishes. It
is by virtue of their being thus accessible that the
practices of worship come to be, for our moral progress,

a valuable supplement to active life, which is, moreover, fully compatible with them, such is the perfect homogeneity of the Positive religion.

The Woman.—Understanding now the moral influence of our worship, I need, my father, more full explanations as to its reaction on the intellect, which is by no means so clear to me.

The Priest.—Keep distinct, my daughter, its two main cases, according as its efficacy is limited to art or passes to science.

From the first point of view, the power of the Positive worship on the mind is direct and striking, first as regards the general art, and even afterwards as regards the two special arts of sound or form. Poetry is the soul of the worship, as science is of the doctrine, and industry of the regime. Every prayer, private as well as public, becomes in Positivism a real work of art, inasmuch as it expresses our best feelings. As its spontaneous character must never be departed from, every Positivist must be, in some respects, a kind of poet—at least for his own personal worship. Though its forms should become fixed in order to secure more regularity, they will originally in all cases have been drawn up by him who uses them, or he will find that they have no great efficiency. Besides, this fixedness is never complete, since it affects only the artificial signs, which by their uniformity bring out better the spontaneous variations of our natural language, always, whether musical or mimic, more æsthetic than the other.

This poetical originality will be largely developed when the regeneration of education shall have sufficiently trained all Positivists in the conceptions, and even in the compositions, it requires, as I will point out to you in the third part of the Catechism. Then the general art will always derive fitting assistance from the special arts; since all will then be familiar with singing, the essential basis of music, and with drawing, the general source of the three arts of form—painting, sculpture, or architecture. Lastly, in the construction of his worship, each will generally introduce special ornaments, chosen with judgment from the æsthetic treasure of Humanity. Though additions of this kind seem limited to public worship, private worship may adopt them frequently and with profit, provided it borrows with discretion and moderation. True poets having at all times given expression to the leading feelings of our unchanging nature, their productions are often in sufficient consonance with our own emotions. When this agreement, without being complete, is nearly so, we may find in what we borrow from the poets more than the mere intellectual merit of a more perfect expression. We find in them, in particular, the moral charm of a personal sympathy. The older the ornaments, the better they suit us, as they sanction our affections by this spontaneous agreement, not merely with the great poet, but also with all the generations which in succession that poet has aided in the expression of their feelings. But the full efficacy of this valuable aid depends on its always remaining quite secondary, though the degree in which it is admitted must vary as the cases vary, as I will shortly point out to you.

The Woman.—Before you explain to me the influence of the Positive worship on science, would you, my father, clear up a serious difficulty naturally arising from the preceding explanation? Worship and poetry seem to me, in our religion, to melt so entirely one into the other, that their simultaneous growth would appear to require a priestly class quite distinct from that which develops and teaches the doctrine. I feel that this separation would become very dangerous by establishing an unmanageable rivalry between the two bodies, to decide which should have the ultimate direction of the regime, both being equally competent. So serious does such a conflict seem to me that you must settle it, under penalty of radically compromising the general organisation of our priesthood, thus incapacitated from presiding over private life and still more over public life.   But, on the other hand, I do not see how we can quite avoid it, as poetic culture and philosophic study seem to require wholly different treatment.

The Priest.—This mistake, which it is very important to correct, constitutes, my daughter, one of the chief results of modern anarchy, which tends throughout to disperse our strength by a lamentable specialism, as absurd as it is immoral.   In the normal state, it is only practice that really admits of specialism, as no one can do everything.   But as each must embrace the whole range of conception, scientific culture must, on the contrary, always remain indivisible.   Its division is the first sign of anarchy.   So thought the ancients under the theocracy, the only complete organisation as yet.   When in it the poet separated from the priest, its decline began.

Though the genius for philosophy and the genius for poetry cannot ever, at one and the same time, find a high destination, intellectually they are completely identical in nature.   Aristotle might have been a great poet, Dante an eminent philosopher, had the times in which they lived called for less scientific power in the one or less æsthetic power in the other.   All these scholastic distinctions were invented and upheld by pedants who, themselves without any kind of genius, could not even appreciate it in others.   Mental superiority is always similar as between the several careers of man ; the choice of each is settled by his position, especially his position in time ; for the race always rules the individual.

The only important difference that really exists in this respect arises from the services of philosophy being naturally continuous, whereas the services of poetry are necessarily intermittent.   Great poets alone are of value, even intellectually, but still more morally ; all the others do much more harm than good : whereas the humblest philosophers can be made of real use when they have

honesty, good sense, and courage. Since art has for its
main object to develop in us the sense of perfection, it
never tolerates mediocrity ; true taste always implies
lively distaste. From Homer to Walter Scott, we have
had in the West but thirteen poets really great, two
ancient, eleven modern, including even three prose
writers. Of all the rest you could not name more than
seven who could or should be read daily. As for the
rest, doubtless they will be almost completely destroyed,
as equally hurtful to the intellect and the heart, when the
regeneration of education shall have allowed us to extract
all useful documents, especially the historical. There is no
opening, then, in sociocracy less even than in theocracy,
for the foundation of a definite class exclusively devoted to
the cultivation of poetry. But the priests, whose habitual
character is the philosophical, will become for the time
poets, when our Goddess shall stand in need of fresh
effusions for general use, which may then suffice, during
several ages, both for public and private worship. Minor
compositions, naturally more frequent, will be generally
left to the spontaneous impulses of women or proletaries.
As for the two special arts, the long apprenticeship they
require, particularly the art of form, will compel us to
devote to them some select masters, whom the Positive
education will, in its natural course, point out to the
directing priesthood. They will become true members
of the priesthood, or remain merely pensioners, according
as by nature they are more or less synthetical.

The Woman.—After this elucidation you may pass
at once, my father, to your last general explanation of
the efficacy of the worship. Its æsthetic power seems to
me evident. But I do not see in what can consist its
scientific influence.

The Priest.—In a better general development, my
daughter, of the universal logic, always based on the due
co-operation of signs, images, and feelings towards assist-
ing the mind in its working. The logic of feeling is more

direct and energetic than any other; but its method is deficient in precision and pliancy. Eminently accommodating and sufficiently numerous, artificial signs make up, by these two properties, for the inferiority in logical power due to the weakness and indirectness of their connection with our thoughts. But this sum of intellectual aids must receive its complement from images, which indeed alone can satisfactorily give it, as being intermediate by their nature. Now, it is especially in reference to this normal bond of our true logic that the worship should be efficacious, though it also develops the two other constituents. In this respect, the child who prays rightly is exercising more healthily his meditative organs than the haughty algebraist who, from a deficiency of tenderness and imagination, is really only cultivating the organ of language, by the aid of a special jargon, the legitimate use of which is very limited.

This remark affords a clear glimpse of the most important scientific result of the Positive worship. It thus touches only the method properly so called, very slightly the doctrine; allowing for the moral, nay, even the intellectual notions, naturally furnished us by our religious practices. But the method will always have more value than the doctrine, as feelings have more value than acts, morals than politics. The scientific labours hitherto accumulated have for the most part hardly more than a logical value: they often teach us notions that are useless, and at times even worse than useless. Although this provisional contrast will become much weaker, when an encyclopedic discipline shall have delivered us from all the rubbish of academies, the true logic will always stand higher than science properly so called, more particularly for the public, but also for the priesthood.

The Woman.—All that remains, my father, is to ask you what is to be the special object of the two other conversations you promised me on the Positive worship.

F

However much I may feel that we have not thoroughly explored this fair domain, I do not see to what point in it we are now to direct our efforts.

The Priest.—You will see this, my daughter, if you consider that our worship, if it is not to fail utterly, must be first private, then public. These will be the respective objects of the two following conversations. But before we proceed to them, it is desirable to bring your attention generally to bear directly on this great subordination, on which depends after all the chief efficacy of the Positive religion.

The better to grasp it, look on these two worships as addressed respectively, the private to Woman, the public to Humanity. You will then feel that our Goddess can have no sincere worshippers but those who have prepared themselves for her august worship by the steady practice of private homage daily due to her best organs, her subjective organs especially, but also to her objective. In a word, the true Church has ever for its original basis the simple Family, still more in the moral order than from the purely social aspect. The heart can no more avoid this first step, retained afterwards as an habitual stimulus, than the intellect can disdain the lower steps in the encyclopedic scale in its rise to the highest, which constantly enforce on it the need of renewing its strength at the fountain-head.

It is the constant practice of private worship that more than anything else will ultimately distinguish true Positivists from the false brethren with whom we shall be burdened as soon as the true religion shall prevail. Without this mark, an easy hypocrisy would soon usurp the consideration due only to the sincere worshippers of Humanity. Between Her and the Family, we shall even have to develop the normal intermedium originating in the natural feelings, at present vague and weak, which bind us specially to the Country properly so called. The impossibility of rightly cultivating these intermediate affections otherwise than in associations of moderate extent, will ever be the best ground on which to rest the reduction of the large existing states to simple cities with their due adjuncts—a process I shall have to explain to you later.

CONVERSATION IV.

PRIVATE WORSHIP.

The Woman.—It seems to me, my father, that private worship, as private life, must be composed of two very distinct parts, the one personal, the other domestic, the separation of which seems necessary for its explanation.

The Priest.—This natural division, which I was bound not to mix up with the main division of the worship, settles, my daughter, in truth the plan of our present conversation. Two great institutions of sociolatry, the one relating to the true guardian angels, the other to the nine social sacraments, will in it characterise respectively, first our personal, then our domestic worship. The reasons for making the latter depend on the former are, in lesser degree, essentially similar to those which represent the whole private worship as the only solid basis of the public. More inward than any other, personal worship alone can sufficiently develop firmly-rooted habits of sincere adoration, without which our domestic ceremonies, and still more our public solemnities, could have no moral efficacy. Thus sociolatry institutes, for the heart of each, a natural progression, in which individual prayers duly pave the way for the collective ceremonies, through the regular intermedium of the domestic consecrations.

The Woman.—Since the private worship is thus made the primary basis of all our religious practices, I beg you, my father, to explain to me directly its real nature.

The Priest.—It consists, my daughter, in the daily
adoration of the best types which we can find to per-
sonify Humanity, taking into account the whole of our
private relations.

The whole existence of the Supreme Being resting on
love, which alone unites in a voluntary union its separ-
able elements, the affective sex is naturally its most
perfect representative, and at the same time its chief
minister. Never will art be able worthily to embody
Humanity otherwise than in the form of Woman. But
the moral providence of our Goddess is not exerted solely
through the collective action of your sex upon mine.
This fundamental source is especially the result of the
personal influence that every true woman is unceasingly
putting out in the bosom of her own family. The
domestic sanctuary is the continual source of this holy
impulse which can alone preserve us from the moral
corruption to which we are ever exposed by active or
speculative life. Without this private root the collective
action of woman on man would moreover have no permanent efficacy. It is within the family also that we
gain an adequate appreciation of the affective sex, for
each can only really know the types of it with which he
lives in close intimacy.

Thus it is that, in the normal state, each man finds
around him real *guardian angels,* at once ministers and
representatives of the Great Being. The secret adoration
of them, strengthening and developing their continuous
influence, tends directly to make us better and happier,
by ensuring the gradual predominance of altruism over
egoism, through the free play of the former and the compression of the latter. Our just gratitude for benefits
already received thus becomes the natural source of fresh
progress. The happy ambiguity of the French word
patron marks sufficiently this twofold efficacy of the
personal worship, in which each angel must be equally
invoked as a protector and as a model.

The Woman.—This first general view leaves me, my father, too uncertain as to what the personal type is ; it might apparently be taken indifferently from each of the greater family relations.

The Priest.—We must really, my daughter, duly combine three of them for the worship of angels to have its full effect. This plurality is indicated in our doctrine by the plurality of the sympathetic instincts, each of which answers specially to a leading female influence. The mother, the wife, the daughter, must in our worship, as in the existence which it idealises, develop in us respectively veneration, attachment, and benevolence. As for the sister, the influence she exercises has hardly a very distinct character, and may in succession be connected with each of the three essential types. Together they represent to us the three natural modes of human continuity, as regards the past, the present, and the future ; as also the three degrees of the solidarity which binds us to our superiors, our equals, and our inferiors. But the spontaneous harmony of the three can only be satisfactorily maintained by observing their natural subordination, which ought habitually to give the supremacy to the maternal angel, yet so that her gentle presidency never impair the influence of the other two.

For the main object of this private worship, which, as a general rule, concerns the maturity of each worshipper, one of the three feminine types has most frequently become subjective, whilst another still remains objective. This normal mixture increases the efficacy of such homage, in which the strength and clearness of the images are thus better combined with coherence and purity of the feelings.

The Woman.—Your explanation seems to me very satisfactory, yet I feel, my father, that it leaves a great void as to my own sex, whose moral wants it appears to neglect. Yet the tenderness which is our especial distinction cannot free us from the need of such habitual cultivation.

The Priest.—You have, my daughter, an easy and legitimate solution of this grave difficulty in the plurality of the angelic types, when otherwise it would be insurmountable. In fact, the principal angel alone must be common to both sexes, each borrowing from the other the two angels that complete the institution. For the mother has, for both sexes equally, a preponderance, not merely as the main source even of our physical existence, but still more as normally presiding over the whole of our education. To her, then, as the common object of adoration, your sex adds the worship of the husband and the son, on the grounds assigned above for mine as regards the wife and daughter. This difference by itself is enough to meet the respective wants which require a patronage specially adapted, to develop in the one case energy, in the other tenderness.

The Woman.—Notwithstanding the attraction this great institution even now has for me, still I find in it, my father, two general imperfections, whether as not using all our private relations, or as not having sufficiently foreseen the too frequent inadequacy of the natural types.

The Priest.—These two difficulties disappear, my daughter, if you take into account the several subordinate types which naturally connect with each of our three chief types, by virtue of conformity of feelings and the similarity of the tie. Around the mother we group naturally first the father, and sometimes the sister, then the master and the protector, besides the analogous relations which may be largely increased in number within the family, and still more without. Extend the same method to the two other types, and we form a series of adorations, less and less close to us, but more and more general, the result being an almost insensible transition from the private to the public worship. This normal development enables us also to supply, as far as possible, exceptional deficiencies, by substituting, in case of need, for one of the primary types its best subordinate. In this way we can subjectively re-create families whose composition is defective.

The Woman.—After this complementary explanation, it only remains for me, my father, to ask you for some more precise explanations as to the general system of prayers adapted to this fundamental worship.

The Priest.—It requires, my daughter, three daily prayers : on getting up, before going to sleep, and in the midst of our daily occupations whatever they be. The first, longer and more efficacious than the other two, ·begins each day by the due invocation of the guardian angels, which alone can dispose us to the habitual right use of all our powers. In the last, we express the gratitude owing to this daily protection, so as to secure its continuance during sleep. The mid-day prayer should for a time disengage us from the impulses of thought and action, in order to penetrate both more fully with that influence of affection from which they always tend to withdraw us.

This object at once indicates the respective times of the three Positivist prayers, and even the mode of their performance. The first, prior to all work, will be said at the domestic altar arranged in agreement with our best memories, and in the attitude of veneration. But the last should be said when in bed, and as far as possible be continued until we fall asleep, the better to ensure a calm brain when we are least protected from evil tendencies. The hour for the intermediate prayer cannot be so accurately stated, as it must vary with individual convenience; yet it is important that each one, in his own way, should fix it very strictly, thereby attaining more easily the frame of mind it requires.

The respective length of our three daily prayers is also pointed out by their proper object. It is fitting, in general, that the morning prayer be twice as long as the evening, the mid-day half as long. When the private worship is completely organised, the chief prayer natu-

rally occupies the whole first hour of each day. It does
so especially from the division of its opening portion into
two, each as long as the concluding; the commemoration
common to all the days of the week being made to precede that which is proper to each separately. The result
is the division in practice of the morning prayer into
three equal parts, in which precedence is given respectively, first to images, then to signs, and last to feelings.
The two other prayers do not admit of the same proportion between commemoration and effusion. Whilst in the
morning, effusion in all lasts only half as long as commemoration, the ratio is inverted in the evening, and
equality marks the mid-day prayer. You will find no
difficulties in these minor differences. But I ask you to
observe that, as follows from these indications when combined, the total length of our daily worship only reaches
two hours, even for those who are led to repeat during
the night the prayer of mid-day.

Every Positivist, then, will devote to his daily personal
improvement less time than is now absorbed by bad
reading and by useless or pernicious amusements. There
alone takes place the decisive growth of the subjective
life by our identifying ourselves more and more with the
Being we adore, whose image, gradually purified, becomes
more clear and vivid with every new year of worship.
By these secret practices each prepares himself to feel
aright the awakening of sympathy, which will be a result
of the publicity which belongs to our other sacred rites.
Such a combination of moral faculties will, I hope, enable
the rules of sociolatry to overcome, in the best of both
sexes, the present coarseness of Western manners. Ordinary and uncultivated minds still regard as lost all time
not occupied by work in the common sense. In the
cultivated classes, there is already a recognition of the
value inherent in purely intellectual exertion. But since
the close of the Middle Ages, there has been a universal
forgetfulness of the direct higher value of moral cultiva-

tion properly so called. Men would almost blush to devote to it as much time as the great Alfred allotted to it daily, without in any way impairing his admirable activity.

To complete this special theory of the daily prayers, I must point out to you the unequal share assigned in them to the ornaments, always mere adjuncts, borrowed with discretion from the æsthetic treasures of Humanity. By their nature they are more adapted to aid effusion than commemoration. As such their aid is more available in the evening than in the morning. But its special purpose is to relieve us from original effort which we usually find impracticable in regard to the intermediate prayer, in which the effusion at its close may consist almost entirely in a judicious choice of passages from the poets. When singing and drawing shall have become as familiar to all as speaking and writing, this help from without will more fully satisfy our internal wants, in the too frequent languor of our best emotions.

The Woman.—Now that I understand our private worship, I am endeavouring, my father, to anticipate you as to the constitution of the domestic worship properly so called. But I cannot, of myself, as yet form a satisfactory idea of it. I quite see that the domestic, like the private worship, can institute a constant adoration of the types common to the whole family. So also it can reproduce for this elementary society the collective invocations which the public worship addresses directly to Humanity. These two kinds of religious practices, under the natural priesthood of the head of the family, are susceptible no doubt of a high moral influence. Still something is wanting to stamp on our domestic worship a character quite its own, so that it be kept distinct from either of those between which it is to be the intermediary.

The Priest.—The institution of the social sacraments fulfils, my daughter, this necessary condition. It is

through it that the domestic worship is strongly marked
off from the two others, at the same time that it affords
them a natural transition.   It consists in consecrating
all the successive phases of private life by connecting each
with public life.   Hence our nine social sacraments :—
*Presentation, initiation, admission, destination, marriage,
maturity, retirement, transformation*, and lastly, *incorporation.*   Their unchanging succession forms a series of
preparations by which, during the whole of his objective
life, the worthy servant of Humanity proceeds, in a
gradual course, to the subjective eternity which is ultimately to constitute him a true organ of the Goddess.

The Woman.—Though the normal limits of this Catechism preclude you, my father, from a really complete
explanation of all our sacraments, I hope you will be
able in it to give a sufficient idea of each.

The Priest.—By the first, my daughter, the final religion gives systematic consecration to every birth, as all
the preliminary religions instinctively did.   The mother
and the father of the new scion of Humanity come to
present it to the priesthood, which receives from them a
solemn engagement to prepare the child properly for the
service of the Goddess.   This natural guarantee is completed by two additional institutions, which Positivism
thinks it an honour to borrow in germ from Catholicism,
developing it in a social spirit.   An artificial couple, to
be chosen by the parents, but with the approbation of
the priesthood, freely offers the new servant of the
Great Being a fresh protection, mainly spiritual, but
at need temporal, all the special witnesses concurring.
He also receives from his two families two special patrons,
the one a theorician, the other a practician, whom he
will complete at the time of his emancipation, by taking
a third name, derived, as the other two, from the consecrated representatives of Humanity.

In the ancient civilisation, this first sacrament was
often refused, especially to those who were judged incom-

petent for the destructive activity which then prevailed.
But as modern social life more and more finds a use for
natures of every order, the *presentation* will almost invariably be accepted by the priesthood, allowing for cases
too exceptional to need prevision.

The second sacrament is termed *initiation*, as marking
the first dawn of public life, when the child passes at
fourteen from its unsystematic training under the direction of its mother, to the systematic education given by
the priesthood. Till then the advice of the priest was
given to the parents only, whether natural or artificial,
to remind them of their essential duties during the first
period of childhood. But now the new being receives
directly the counsels of religion, destined specially to
forearm his heart against the injurious influences too
often attendant on the intellectual training which he is
to undergo. This second sacrament may be put off, and
sometimes, though very seldom, refused, if the home
education has not succeeded to the extent required.

Seven years later, the young disciple, first presented,
then initiated, receives, as the consequence of his whole
preparation, the sacrament of *admission*, which authorises
him freely to serve Humanity, from whom hitherto he
received everything, giving nothing in return. All civil
codes have recognised that it is necessary to put off,
and even to refuse, this emancipation in the case of those
whom an extremely defective organisation, uncorrected
by education, condemns to perpetual infancy. A more
accurate judgment will lead the priesthood to measures
of equal severity, the direct consequences of which will
never extend beyond the spiritual domain.

This third sacrament makes the child into the servant
without being able as yet to mark out his special career,
often different from what was supposed during the
practical apprenticeship which coincided naturally with
his scientific education. He alone can properly decide on this point, as the result of trials freely made and

prolonged for a sufficient time. Hence the institution of
a fourth social sacrament, which at twenty-eight, allowing
for a delay, either at his own request or enjoined, conse-
crates the *destination* thus chosen. The old worship
offered us the rudiment of this institution only in the
case of the highest functions, in the ordination of priests
and the coronation of kings. But Positive religion must
always give a social institution to all the useful professions, with no distinction of public and private. The
humblest servants of the Great Being will come to receive
in her temple from her priests the solemn consecration of
their entrance on their co-operation, whatever form it take.
This is the only sacrament that admits of a true repeti-
tion, which, however, must always be an exception.

The Woman.—I understand, my father, this series of
consecrations prior to *marriage*, itself to be followed by
our four other sacraments. As for this chief sacrament,
which alone gives completeness to the whole series of
man's preparations, I already know the main points of
the Positivist doctrine. Above all, I sympathise most
deeply with the great institution of eternal widowhood,
long looked for by the hearts of all true women. Besides
its importance for the family and even for the state, it
alone can sufficiently develop the subjective life for our
souls to rise to the familiar representation of Humanity,
by means of an adequate personification. All these
precious notions had I made almost my own before I
became your catechumen. I know also that you will
return to this subject, from another point of view, when
explaining the regime. We may then enter on the last
series of our consecrations.

The Priest.—First, however, my daughter, we must
settle the normal age for the chief social sacrament. As
marriage is to follow, and not precede, the particular
destination, men cannot be admitted to it as a religious
ordinance till they have accomplished their twenty-eighth
year. The priesthood will even advise the government

to extend the legal veto of the head of the family to the age of thirty, the better to guard against any precipitation in the most important of all our private actions. For women, the sacrament of destination necessarily coincides with that of admission, their vocation being always known and happily uniform. They are therefore ready for marriage at the age of twenty-one, an age, moreover, which gives better security for harmony in marriage. These lower limits of age must not be lowered for either sex, save on very exceptional grounds, which the priesthood must thoroughly weigh, on its moral responsibility. But in general no higher limits should be fixed, though women should almost always marry before twenty-eight, men before thirty-five, when married life shall have taken its right constitution.

The Woman.—The first of the sacraments after marriage seems to me, my father, sufficiently explained by its mere definition. You had already made me observe the general coincidence of the full development of the human organism with the completion of man's social preparation, about the age of forty-two. I am here thinking only of your sex, as it alone is concerned with the sacrament of *maturity.* The vocation of woman is at once too uniform and too fixed to admit either of the two consecrations that precede and follow marriage.

The Priest.—Though you have, my daughter, grasped without help from me the true nature of our sixth sacrament, you would hardly be able, if you stopped at this point, to appreciate duly its peculiar importance. During the twenty-one years which separate it from the seventh, the man is living his second objective life, on which alone depends his subjective immortality. Till then our life, mainly preparatory, had naturally given rise to mistakes at times of a serious character, but never beyond reparation. Henceforth, on the contrary, the faults we commit we can hardly ever fully repair, whether in reference to others or to ourselves. It is important, then, to impose solemnly on the servant of Humanity the stern responsibility on which he is entering, with special reference to his peculiar function, now clearly determined.

The Woman.—For the next sacrament I see, my father, no other purpose but to mark the normal termination of the great period of complete and direct action of which the sixth consecration marked the beginning.

The Priest.—On the contrary, my daughter, the sacrament of *retirement* is one of the most august and best determined of our sacraments, when we consider the last fundamental service which is then rendered by each true servant of Humanity. In the Positive arrangements, every functionary, especially every temporal functionary, always names his successor, subject to the sanction of his superior, and allowing for exceptional cases of moral or mental unworthiness, as I shall shortly explain to you. You see at once that it is the only means of satisfactorily regulating human continuity. When the citizen at sixty-three, of his own free will, withdraws from an activity which he has exhausted, in order to have scope in future for his legitimate influence as an adviser, he solemnly exercises this last act of high authority, and by so doing places it under the control of the priesthood and the people, which may lead him to modify it in a noble spirit. With the rich, this transfer of office is completed by the transmission, in accordance with the same rules, of that portion of the capital of the race which forms the working-stock of the functionary, after he has made provision for his own personal wants.

The Woman.—Now, my father, I see the full social bearing of our seventh sacrament, in which I saw at first only a kind of family festival.

As for the eighth, I am now familiar enough with the true religion to understand of myself in what it consists. It is to replace the horrible ceremony in which Catholicism, freed from all check on its anti-social character, openly tore the dying person from all human affections, to place him alone before the judgment-seat of God. In our *transformation*, the priesthood, mingling the regrets of society with the tears of the family, estimates justly as a whole the life that is ending. First securing, where possible, the reparation of evil, it generally holds out the hope of subjective incorporation, but without ever committing itself to a premature judgment.

The Priest.—As your appreciation of the last objective sacrament is adequate, my daughter, I have now to explain to you the final consecration.

Seven years after death, when all disturbing passions are sufficiently quieted, the best special documents remaining yet accessible, a solemn judgment, the germ of which sociocracy borrows from theocracy, finally decides the lot of each. If the priesthood pronounces for *incorporation*, it presides over the transfer, with due pomp, of the sanctified remains which, previously deposited in the burial-place of the city, now take their place for ever in the sacred wood that surrounds the temple of Humanity. Every tomb in it is ornamented with a simple inscription, a bust, or a statue, according to the degree of honour awarded.

As to the exceptional cases of marked unworthiness, the disgrace consists in transporting in the proper way the ill-omened burden to the waste place allotted to the reprobate, amongst those who have died by the hand of justice, by their own hand, or in duel.

The Woman.—These clear indications as to the nine social sacraments leave me, my father, a general regret as regards my sex, which does not seem to me sufficiently considered. Still, I in no way object to our natural exclusion from three of these consecrations, since it rests on grounds which are in the highest degree honourable to women, whose quieter life requires less religious attention. But I cannot conceive that the subjective paradise should not admit those whom our religion proclaims most apt to deserve it. I do not, however, see

how, in the general, we should share in personal incorporation, which seems to me only to be possible as a
result of public life, and public life is rightly forbidden
our sex, except in very rare cases.

The Priest.—You will supply, my daughter, this
serious omission by considering that the incorporation
of man is to include all the worthy auxiliaries of every
true servant of Humanity, not even excepting our animal associates.

The chief function of woman being to form and perfect
man, it would be as absurd as unjust to honour a good
citizen, and neglect to honour the mother, the wife, etc.,
to whom his success was mainly due. Around and at
times within each consecrated tomb, the priesthood will
consequently be bound to collect in the name of Humanity, all the individuals who took a worthy part in the
services such tomb rewards. Although your sex, by
its superior organisation, tastes more keenly the pure enjoyment that results from the mere formation and exercise of good feelings, it should never renounce its claim
to just praise, much less to the subjective immortality
which it so thoroughly appreciates.

The Woman.—After this complementary explanation
it only remains for me, my father, to ask you wherein
lies the obligation for each to receive our different
sacraments.

The Priest.—They must always, my daughter, be
purely optional, so far as any legal obligation is concerned, without ever imposing more than a simple moral
duty, a duty demonstrated in our education and sanctioned by opinion.

The better to preserve this purely spiritual character,
the chief condition of their efficacy, our sacraments must
have side by side with them parallel institutions, established and maintained by the temporal power, as alone to
be required in each case. Its judgment, less discrimi-
nating and less strict, will dispense with the religious

rites for those whom they might alarm, and who can yet
render society services which it would be a pity to lose
or impair.

For instance, we must not consider as anarchical,
though of revolutionary origin, the institution of civil
marriage, as a necessary preliminary to the religious,
from which it may legally dispense. The contrary custom
arose from an usurpation on the part of Catholicism
which Positivism will never imitate. Those who revolt
from the law of widowhood, which yet is essential to the
performance of a Positivist marriage, need to contract a
civil union to preserve them from vice and secure the
legal status of their children. The same holds good, in
lesser degree, for most of the other social sacraments,
especially admission and destination. The priesthood
ought, in case of need, to urge the government to institute legal rules with the object of moderating the just
strictness of our religious prescriptions, the persistently
free observance of which will never have any other reward than that of conscience and opinion.

CONVERSATION V.

PUBLIC WORSHIP.

The Woman.—When entering on the direct study of
our public worship, I should submit to you, my father,
the answer which I have already given of myself to
superficial but honest criticisms, directed against this
solemn adoration as a whole. It is urged that each
Positivist is glorifying himself when paying honour to
a being which is of necessity composed of its own worshippers. Our private worship is in no way open to
this reproach : it applies solely to the direct worship of
Humanity, especially where the homage is collective.
But we can easily repel it by the true idea of the Great

Being which is predominantly subjective in its composition. They who testify their gratitude to her are in no way assured, in general, of their final incorporation. They have only the hope of this reward, because they count on deserving it by a worthy life, the judgment on which always rests with their successors.

The Priest.—Your correction is fully in agreement, my daughter, with the true spirit of our public worship, in which the present glorifies the past the better to prepare the future, naturally putting itself out of sight before these two immensities. Far from stimulating our pride, these solemn prayers tend unceasingly to inspire us with a sincere humility. For they make us profoundly conscious to what a degree, despite our best collective efforts, we are incapable of ever rendering to Humanity more than a very small part of what we have received from her.

The Woman.—Before you explain to me the general outline of this public worship, would you, my father, give me some sufficient idea of the temples in which it is to be performed? As for the ministering priesthood, I feel that its essential constitution will be adequately stated in your exposition of the regime.

The Priest.—Our temples, my daughter, cannot at present be adequately conceived. For, as architecture is the most technical and the least æsthetic of all the fine arts, each new synthesis reaches it more slowly than any other art. Not till our religion be not only thoroughly worked out, but also widely spread, can the public wants indicate the true nature of the edifices which suit it. Provisionally then, we shall have to use the old churches, in proportion as they fall into disuse ; though this inevitable preliminary ought to last a less time in our case than in the case of Catholicism, which, for several centuries, was confined to polytheistic edifices.

The only general indication that can at present be given on this point relates to site and direction, even now determined by the nature of the Positive worship. Since Humanity is essentially composed of the dead who deserve to live after death, her temples must be placed amid the tombs of the elect. On the other hand, the chief attribute of Positive religion is its necessary universality. In all parts of the earth, then, the temples of Humanity must turn towards the general metropolis, which for a long time, as the result of the whole past, must be Paris. Thus Positivism turns to account the happy if rudimentary conception of Islam in respect of a valuable institution, wherein the common attitude of all true believers brings out more fully the touching solidarity of their free homage.

This is all I have to tell you as to our sacred buildings. As for the arrangement of their interior, all we need at present observe is the need of reserving the chief sanctuary for women duly chosen; so that the priests of Humanity may always find themselves in the midst of her best representatives.

The Woman.—This last remark leads me, my father, to complete my former question, by asking you what will be the symbols of our Goddess. As the decision regards painting and sculpture, it should even now be more attainable than that of our temples, the two first arts of form being more rapid in their motion than the third.

The Priest.—In truth, my daughter, the nature of the Great Being leaves now no room for hesitation as to its plastic representation. In painting or sculpture, the symbol of our Goddess will always be a woman of thirty with her son in her arms. The pre-eminence, religiously, of the affective sex ought to be the prominent feature in this emblem, in which the active sex should remain placed under its holy guardianship. Though groups with more figures might render the presentment more complete, it would not be synthetic enough to come into really common use.

. Of the two modes adapted for the expression of this

normal symbol, sculpture is suitable for the image fixed
in each temple, in the midst of the nobler women, and
behind the sacred desk.   But painting is preferable for
the movable banners which are to head our solemn pro-
cessions.   Whilst their white side will present the holy
image, the sacred formula of Positivism will occupy the
green, turned towards the procession.

The Woman.—As the last of my introductory questions, I ask you, my father, to explain the sign which
in ordinary use may suffice to represent this characteristic formula.

The Priest.—We get it, my daughter, from our
cerebral theory, as I shall carefully explain when we
study the doctrine.   We may repeat our fundamental
formula whilst placing the hand in succession on the
three chief organs of love, of order, and of progress.   The
first two adjoin one another, the last is only separated
from them by the organ of veneration, the natural
cement of the whole they form ; so that the gesture
may become continuous.   When the habit is sufficiently
formed, we soon suppress the words—the expression by
gesture is enough.   In fine, as the rank of the cerebral
organs indicates fully their functions, the sign, at need,
is reducible to the mere succession of the corresponding
numbers in the cerebral table (*see Conversation* viii.)
Thus it is that, without any arbitrary institution, Positivism is already in possession of signs for common use
more expressive than any of those adopted by Catholicism
and Islam.

The Woman.—Now, my father, I ought not any
longer to delay your direct exposition of the system of
public worship.

The Priest.—You will find it, my daughter, fully expressed in the table I here offer you (*Table A*).   This
part of our worship, as the two preceding portions, has
two objects : to make us better understand and better
live the life which it represents.   We must then, idealise

first the fundamental ties which constitute that existence, then the indispensable preparations which it requires, lastly the normal functions which go to make it
up. Such will be respectively the objects of the three
systems of monthly festivals which are to fill the Positivist year, divided consequently into thirteen months of
four weeks, with one complementary day consecrated to
the dead in the aggregate.

You already know the four fundamental classes—
affective, speculative, patrician, and plebeian—which are
essential to society in its normal form. As for the preparatory stages, we cannot, without confusion, condense
them more, so profound are the intellectual and social
differences, which must always distinguish fetichism,
polytheism, and monotheism, even in the spontaneous
initiation of every Positivist. With regard to the
primary ties, we must certainly begin by celebrating the
most universal, and then honour each of the private
affections which alone can ensure it a real consistency.
Now these elementary relations are really five in number:
marriage, the parental, filial, fraternal, and domestic
relation ; ranking them, in obedience to our hierarchical
principle, by the increase in generality and decrease in
intimacy.

The number of the Positivist months, though at first
sight paradoxical, becomes then sacred when we enter
into its religious grounds. Repeated experience has
moreover shown that it can easily prevail when the
faith on which it rests prevails. Again it is for the
universal religion alone to establish the regularity in
point of time attained by our exact division of each
month into four weekly periods. However great the
practical advantages of such an arrangement, they would
not secure its adoption, were it not that the needs
of our worship dispelled the hesitation always attendant
on mere business reasons.

The Woman.—At the first general view of the

sociolatric table, I see, my father, no serious difficulty
in it except as regards the domestic relation, the importance of which seems to me exaggerated, when it is placed
among the fundamental ties.

The Priest.—Such an objection reminds me, my
daughter, that by birth you are a northern, although
happily preserved from Protestantism. For the southern
nations of the West retain, in this respect, more perfectly
the true human feelings, so nobly developed in the
Middle Ages.

So far from domesticity being destined to pass away,
it will become more and more important, clearing itself
more completely of all the original servitude. When
completely voluntary, it furnishes many families with the
best means of rendering worthy service to the Great
Being, by affording her true servants, philosophical or
practical, an aid which is indispensable. This share in
promoting the public good, though indirect, is more
complete and less uncertain than that of most whose
co-operation is direct. It may also better cultivate
our best feelings. We form too restricted an idea of it
when we confine it to certain classes. In all ranks of
society, above all in the proletariate, every citizen passed
through this condition so long as his practical education
lasted. We must then idealise domesticity as the complement of the family ties and the starting-point of the
civic relations.

The Woman.—My heart wanted, my father, nothing
but this rational correction to rise above the anarchical
prejudices which prevented me from fraternising as I
ought with the noble types, especially among women,
which this position, so little understood, often presented.
Your wholesome explanation leaves me only the wish
for one last general one, in respect to the other extreme
in our scheme of sociolatry. The respective positions of
the patriciate and proletariate seem to me there reversed.
Political considerations may rank them so, according to

the order of material power; but religion, which classes by moral worth, ought, it seems to me, to arrange them differently.

The Priest.—You forget, my daughter, that in the Positive religion there must always be an exact correspondence between the worship and the regime. But I easily excuse your mistake from the nobleness of its motive. I have myself at times thought as you do, from allowing too much weight to the extreme imperfection of the actual patriciate, so often unworthy of its high social destination. Real superiority of the brain, whether intellectual or still more moral, is at the present day more common in proportion among the classes which have been preserved from an education and power which degrade. Still, though we must carefully take into account this undeniable exception when organising the transition of the West, we must be able systematically to put it aside when constructing the abstract worship of Humanity, destined mainly for the normal state. If we looked too much to the present and not enough to the future, we should certainly be led to place even · the priesthood below the proletariate; for its actual imperfection greatly exceeds that of the patriciate, whether one judges it as it exists among the ruins of theology or in its rudimentary state in metaphysics and science.

In the Positive worship, as in the normal existence which it idealises, the worthy patrician stands higher as a general rule than the true plebeian, as much in true nobleness as in real power. When we rank the classes of men by their capacity to represent the Great Being, the importance and difficulty of the peculiar services of the patriciate, as the education they require and the responsibility they involve, always place it above the proletariate. It is in the very name of such classification that the wisdom of the priesthood, duly aided by the sanction of women and the support of the people, must remind the patricians, singly or collectively, of their eternal social duties, when they come to neglect them seriously. But these extraordinary remonstrances would miss their main object if the normal worship did not pay sufficient honour to the necessary ministers of our material providence. By placing the proletariate at the lower extremity of the social scale, the worship will remind us that its characteristic aptitude to control and correct all the powers of society is derived especially from a situation which is essentially passive, and which displays no marked tendency. Our sacred synopsis, as the regime it embodies, must then insert the two great powers, the spiritual and the temporal, between the two masses, women and proletaries, which react uninterruptedly on their sentiments and conduct. Were the patriciate lowered, the Positive harmony would be infringed quite as much in sociolatry as in sociocracy.

The Woman.—I am sufficiently familiar already with the public worship as a whole for you to explain to me, my father, your division by weeks of the thirteen monthly commemorations. This final development, which will leave no one of our weeks without its general festival, must strongly support the moral aim of the great worship, thus recurring under widely varied yet always convergent aspects.

The Priest.—Before I enter on this explanation, I should, my daughter, say that Positivism retains unchanged the established names for the days of the week. I had thought of substituting others, but I have abandoned the project, which will leave no other trace but a successful essay, some touching domestic prayers, adapted to connect the public with the private worship, and composed by M. Joseph Lonchampt, for each day of our week. The old names have the advantage of recalling the whole of the past in its three stages, fetichist, polytheist, and monotheist.*

To make our worship completely regular, it was

---

* See *Pos. Pol.* vol. iv. pp. 135, 404 (120, 351, *E. Tr.*)

necessary that each day of any week whatever should always hold the same place in the year. This invariability is obtained by affixing no weekly name, first to the complementary day with which every Positivist year ends, then to the additional day which follows it if it is leap year, according to the rule adopted in the West. Each of these two exceptional days is really sufficiently marked by its festival. With this precaution, our calendar holds good for all years—a point as important for the regime as for the worship.

The Woman.—I grasp, my father, the full moral efficacy of such invariability, by which any day whatever of our year might receive, as the last day does, a purely religious name ; a result which Catholicism never attained but by exception.

The Priest.—This preliminary settled, I may, my daughter, begin to state directly in their order the ceremonies appointed for the seventh day in all our weeks. The sociolatrical table shows you how each monthly commemoration is subdivided into four weekly festivals. All I have to do, then, is to give reasons for this division and to make it clear by some summary explanations.

Our first month, dedicated to Humanity, needs little in this respect. After opening the Positivist year by the most august of all our solemn rites, this direct festival of the Great Being has its completion in the four weekly festivals, in which we respectively appreciate the several essential degrees of the social union. They are ranked according to the decrease of extension and the increase of intimacy in the collective relations. The first festival glorifies the bond of religion, the only one that can be universal ; the second, the connection due to old political relations which have disappeared, but not without leaving a considerable community of language and poetry. In the third, we celebrate directly the effective union springing from the free acceptance of one common government. The fourth honours the least extended, but the most complete of civic relations, in which the constant proximity of habitation brings us nearest to the intimacy of the family.

To give its full value to the month of marriage, its first solemnity glorifies the conjugal union in all its fulness, at once exclusive and indissoluble, even by death. In it the priesthood brings home, both to heart and intellect, the general advance of this admirable institution, the primary basis of all human order, by delineating each of its essential phases, from the primal polygamy down to the Positivist marriage.

In the following festival is honoured the voluntary and perpetual chastity which weighty moral or physical reasons may enjoin on a noble couple. The capital object of marriage, the mutual improvement of both sexes, comes out more clearly in such an exceptional union ; without its obliging them, however, to renounce the affections that concern the future, always within their reach by a judicious adoption. There will also be brought into suitable relief its tendency to control at length human procreation, while inherited disease is not allowed to preclude the benefits of marriage.

The third week of this month ends with honouring the exceptional unions in which a disparity, often not without excuse, does not exclude the main benefit of marriage, especially when the habits of the final state shall limit the difference to age. Lastly, the fourth festival honours the posthumous union which will often be a result of the normal constitution of human marriage, the deepest pleasures of which are strengthened and developed by the purification and constancy attendant on subjective love.

One explanation will suffice for our three following months, their weekly subdivisions being naturally the same. For the most important, its first half is devoted to the paternal relation in its complete form, first involun-

tary, then adoptive; its second half to the incomplete
paternal relation which, in every regular society, results
from spiritual authority or temporal patronage. Hence
spring, in a descending order, the four normal degrees
of paternal affection, respectively honoured in the four
weekly festivals of the third Positivist month. Now
the same distinctions and gradations necessarily recur
in the case of the filial and fraternal relations, thus dis-
pensing with any fresh explanation for the fourth and
fifth months.

As for the sixth, it honours, first, permanent domesticity, which will always mark off a very numerous but
a special class, then the analogous position in which every
man as a rule finds himself during his practical training.
The first case clearly requires an important subdivision,
the practical distinction being the residence; according
as the domestic relation is complete, as in the case of
the servant proper, or incomplete, as in that of the
clerk, who has simply to perform a certain office. When
the manners of the normal state shall have made domestic
service, especially that of women, consistent with the full
development of the family affections, Positive worship
will make the moral superiority of the first position
deeply felt, for in it the devotion is purer and more
living. The same distinction is applicable, though in a
less marked degree, to temporary domesticity, and is
there again determined by the dwelling. Hence the
last two festivals of the sixth month, respectively devoted
to pages and to apprentices, according as the masters are
rich or poor.

The Woman.—All these details as to the different
fundamental ties offer me, my father, no difficulty.
But I fear lest my weakness in history prevents my fully
understanding the second series of social festivals. For
the preparation of man as a whole is as yet only very
imperfectly known to me.

The Priest.—That is enough, my daughter, to enable

you even now to understand in outline the succession of the three preliminary states mentioned in our synopsis of sociolatry. But as for the weekly division of each of them, you will, it is true, hardly be able to enter into it till after the two historical conversations with which this Catechism will end. I limit myself, therefore, to the co-ordination of the chief divisions, recommending you to complete it for yourself when you shall have gained the requisite knowledge.

The fictitious synthesis, in all cases based on the search after causes, may take two different forms, according as the wills to which events are attributed inhere in the bodies themselves or in external beings, habitually beyond the reach of our senses. Now the direct form, which is more spontaneous than any other, constitutes the initial fetichism ; whereas the indirect distinguishes the theologism which follows it. But this last state, more alloyed and less lasting than the first, offers in succession two distinct constitutions, according as the gods are many or are condensed into one. Theologism, which after all but forms an immense spontaneous transition from fetichism to Positivism, takes its rise from the one as polytheism and leads to the other by monotheism. Complete this mental advance by the corresponding social progress, and the whole initiation of man finds adequate expression, as you will soon feel.

You will then be able to see how well adapted is our second series of social festivals to pay due honour to all the essential phases of this long preparation, from the first upward movement of the smallest tribes down to the twofold development of the modern transition. This full celebration of the past of man in twelve weekly festivals is a consequence of the historical condensation which the abstract worship by its nature allows.

The Woman.—We can then, my father, now enter on the last sociolatrical series. The month dedicated to the moral providence offers me no difficulty, so clearly marked is the distinction between the types of woman assigned to its four weekly festivals. But I am at a loss as yet as to the subdivision of the sacerdotal month.

The Priest.—Take for your guide, my daughter, the different forms or degrees of the Positive priesthood, ranked according to their increasing completeness. This great ministry calls for a rare union of the moral qualities, active no less than affective, with intellectual capacities, both for art and science. If, then, these last alone are remarkable, their possessors, after proper cultivation, must remain, perhaps for ever, mere pensioners of the spiritual power, without ever aspiring to be incorporated into it. In these cases which are fortunately exceptional, the finest genius for poetry or philosophy cannot supply the place of tenderness and energy in a functionary who must habitually be animated by deep sympathies and who has often to engage in difficult struggles. This incomplete priesthood allows for the due cultivation of all true talent without detriment to any social function.

As for the complete priesthood, it requires, first, a preparatory stage, beyond which the candidate will not proceed if, in spite of the announcement of his vocation, he does not successfully pass through the proper noviciate. After this decisive trial, at thirty-five he obtains the true and definitive priesthood, but exercises it for seven years in the subordinate position, which marks the vicar or substitute. When he has worthily gone through all the phases of our encyclopedic teaching, and even entered upon the other priestly functions, he reaches at forty-two the chief degree, becoming irrevocably a priest in the fullest sense. Such are the four classes of theoricians which are honoured respectively by the weekly festivals of the eleventh month.

The Woman.—The next, my father, requires no particular explanation. Though not familiar with active life, its definite character enables me to understand fairly the normal division of the patrician body into four essential classes, in accordance with the decreasing generality of functions and the increasing number of functionaries. Perhaps even, in our anarchical time, women are more apt than the proletaries, and still more than their teachers, to appreciate rightly this natural hierarchy, as they are more thoroughly preserved from disturbing passions and from sophistical views. I am glad, then, that the four weekly festivals of our twelfth month yearly honour. and by honouring moralise, these several necessary forms of the material power, on which rests the whole economy of society. But I am not so clear as to the subdivision of the last month.

The Priest.—It depends, my daughter, on the generality which attaches naturally to the proletariate, in which all the great attributes of Humanity require a distinct ideal expression. This immense social mass—the necessary stock of all the special classes—is mainly devoted to active life, the direct subject of the first weekly festival of the plebeian month. After this active proletariate, we must pay a separate tribute to the affective proletariate which necessarily accompanies it. This special tribute to the proletary women can alone give due completeness to the general celebration of the types of women, considered in the tenth month from a point of view which embraced all classes, but viewed here in their popular manifestation.

The third festival of our thirteenth month should picture worthily the contemplative proletary, especially the artistic, or even the scientific, who, not able to gain admission into a priesthood of necessarily limited numbers, yet feels himself more the theorician than the practician. We shall have at times to compassionate these exceptional types, and in all cases to respect them, in order to turn them to good account by wisely guiding their instinctive tendencies. From them principally must come the general control of the proletariate over the special powers, whereas the general impulse it ought to give requires more active natures.

Finally, the last festival of our popular month has reference mainly to mendicity, temporary, or even permanent. The best social order will never entirely preclude this extreme consequence of the imperfections inherent in practical life. So the idealisation of our social state would be incomplete unless the priesthood closed it with a just appreciation of this exceptional existence. Where there is adequate justification and worthy conduct, such an existence may often deserve the sympathy, at times even the praise, of all honourable minds. More fluctuating than any other, this complementary class naturally connects with all ranks of society, which must in turn draw from it and feed it. It thus becomes well qualified to develop the general influence of the proletariate on all the powers of society. There would then be as great improvidence as injustice in not giving mendicants a separate idealisation.

The Woman.—As for the complementary day, I understand, my father, why Positivism transfers to the end of our year the collective commemoration of the dead, happily introduced by Catholicism. This touching commemoration, the insertion of which would have disturbed the normal economy of our public worship, is its proper completion as a whole and a natural preparation for its annual recurrence. It was fit that the festival proper of the Great Being should be preceded by the glorification of all its organs without exception.

The additional day in leap-year is equally easy. My sex having it scarcely ever in its power to deserve an individual and public apotheosis, the abstract worship, without degenerating into a concrete worship, was bound to pay this honour collectively to the women worthy of an individual celebration. The ideal expression of human existence is thus completed by glorifying the right use of the various exceptional powers which woman's nature admits, when its distinctive character is not impaired thereby.

The Priest.—As you have of yourself, my daughter, satisfactorily finished the explanation of our public worship, the first part of this Catechism is quite complete. We must now proceed to the study of the doctrine, which, as the worship itself, is a direct preparation for the regime—the ultimate end of the whole Positive initiation.

Second Part.

—⬩—

EXPLANATION OF THE DOCTRINE.

CONVERSATION VI.

THE DOCTRINE AS A WHOLE.

The Woman.—In our second conversation, my father, you made me know Humanity. In the three following conversations, you have taught me the worship we owe Her. I ask you now to set before me the systematic co-ordination of the whole system of Positive doctrine around such an unity.

The Priest.—You should, to that end, renounce first of all, my daughter, all aspirations after an absolute, external, in one word, an objective unity; which will be easier for you than for our professors. Such a wish, compatible with the inquiry into causes, is in contradiction with the study of laws, meaning by laws constant relations traced in the midst of immense variety. These admit only a purely relative, human, in one word, a subjective unity. In fact, laws are of necessity plural, by virtue of the impossibility that notoriously exists of ever reducing under the other either of the two general elements of all our real conceptions, the world and man. Even if we succeeded in condensing each of these two great studies around one single law of nature, as the two must remain separate, scientific unity would still be unattainable. Though the knowledge of the world presupposes man, the world could exist without man, as is perhaps the case with many stars that are not habitable. So again, man is dependent on the world, but he is not a consequence of it. All the efforts of materialists to do away with spontaneous vital action by exaggerating the preponderating influence of the inorganic environment on organised beings have ended in nothing but discrediting the inquiry, as useless as it is idle, henceforth abandoned to the unscientific mind.

But further, it is far from being the case that objective unity can ever be established within the limits of each general element of the above dualism. The various essential branches of the study of the world or of man reveal to us an increasing number of different laws, which will never be susceptible of being reduced the one under the other, despite the frivolous hopes inspired at first by our planetary gravitation. Though for the most part still unknown, and many ever to remain so, we have made out enough of them to guarantee against all attacks the fundamental principle of the Positive doctrine, namely, the subjection of all phenomena whatsoever to invariable relations. The all-pervading order which is the outcome of the sum of natural laws bears the general name of *fate* or of *chance*, according as the laws are known to us or unknown. This distinction will always remain of great practical importance; since the ignorance of these laws is, for our action, equivalent to their non-existence, as it precludes all rational prevision, and so all regular interference. Still we may hope to discover for each of the more important cases empirical rules which, insufficient from the theoretic point of view, yet suffice to keep us from disorderly action.

In the midst of this growing diversity, the dogma of Humanity gives to the whole of our real conceptions the only unity they admit, and the only bond that we need.

To apprehend its nature and formation, we must first
distinguish three kinds of laws, physical, intellectual,
and moral. The first by their nature belong to the
active, the last to the affective sex, whilst the intermediate order forms the proper province of the priesthood, which, having to reduce to system the joint action
of the two sexes, shares in unequal degree the life of
both. This is why the two extreme studies were
cultivated empirically at all times to meet the corresponding wants, but with very different success. In
fact, physical laws being, at bottom, independent of
moral laws, men could, in regard to them, establish convictions which, though incoherent, were firm. On the
contrary, as moral laws are necessarily dependent on
physical laws, women could, in this department, construct
no impregnable system, and their efforts were only
valuable for their influence on the affections. It was,
then, from the physical order that sound scientific culture
must originate, on the basis of a sufficient detachment
from the details of action. As, however, the moral order
is the ultimate goal of all our real meditations, logical
and scientific unity was unattainable unless by some
adequate connection of these two extreme domains.
Now the intermediate domain can alone unite them, for
it naturally connects with each. Thus it is that the
construction of a true theoretic unity depends in the
last resort on a sufficient elaboration of the special laws
of the understanding.

The Woman.—Your conclusion seems a difficult one
to get at, yet I feel no difficulty, my father, in at once
admitting it. My meditations on moral subjects have
often made me feel to what an extent a knowledge of
the laws of the intellect would be indispensable to their
practical coherence; since the rules proper to the function that judges always mingle with those of each func
tion judged. Men, however, are naturally less sensible
of this connection in the case of the physical laws which

engross the attention of their sex. You may pass on, then, without further preamble, to the direct exposition of these laws of the mind, on which all systematic unity depends.

The Priest.—I must at the outset, my daughter, divide them, here as elsewhere, into *statical* and *dynamical*, according as they concern the invariable arrangements of the object under consideration, or its inevitable variations. These two correlative terms are become indispensable to any serious exposition of Positivism, and through it they will soon become popular. Not that they can ever have for your sex the moral attraction which you will shortly find in the terms *objective* and *subjective*, the ultimate and chief destination of which is to express with pleasantest shading our best emotions. But their purely intellectual application must not strip them of the respect due to their scientific utility. For the rest, these two pairs of philosophical expressions are the only ones that I am obliged to require you to accept.

The preceding definition renders it easy for you to see that, in any department whatever, the statical study necessarily precedes the dynamical, which could never be entered on without such a preparation. It is necessary, in fact, to have determined the fundamental conditions of any existence before considering its different successive states. The ancients, who saw everywhere stationariness, were completely alien to any dynamical conceptions, even in mathematics. Whereas the incomparable Aristotle, the eternal prince of true philosophers, even then laid down all the essential bases of the highest statical studies, of life, of the intelligence, and of society. But, following this necessary course, the dynamical complement comes to be everywhere indispensable. Without it, the statical appreciation can never be anything but provisional, so as to be defective as a guide to practice, where it would, if isolated, lead to serious errors, especially in the more important cases.

The statical law of our understanding becomes, in Positivism, a simple application of the fundamental principle which in all cases subordinates man to the world. In fact, it consists in the constant subordination of our subjective constructions to our objective materials. The genius of Aristotle gave its rudimentary general conception in this admirable statement :—*There is nothing in the understanding that did not originally spring from sensation.* But as modern writers often pressed this axiom too far to the point of representing our intelligence as purely passive, the great Leibnitz was obliged to add an essential restriction, with the aim of formulating the spontaneous character of our mental dispositions. This explanation, which was limited in reality to the clearer development of Aristotle's maxim, was completed by Kant, by introducing the distinction never to be forgotten between the objective and the subjective reality of all human conceptions. Still, this principle was not really systematised till Positivism connected it in due form with the general law which, in all vital phenomena, places every organism in constant dependence on its environment. For our highest spiritual functions, equally as for our most corporeal acts, the external world serves us at once for nourishment, stimulus, and control. Whilst in this way the subordination of the subjective to the objective no longer stood isolated, Positive Philosophy also supplied its necessary complement, without which the statical study of the intellect could not have been sufficiently connected with the dynamical. It consists in recognising the fact that, in the normal state, the subjective images are always less vivid and less clear than the objective impressions from which they are drawn. Were it otherwise, the without could never regulate the within.

By virtue of these two statical principles, all our conceptions necessarily have their origin in an uninterrupted interchange between the world which supplies their

materials and man who shapes them. They are profoundly relative, both to the subject and to the object,
and as these vary respectively, so necessarily are the
conceptions modified. Our great merit, in the scientific
point of view, consists in so perfecting this natural
subordination of man to the world that our brain may
become the faithful mirror of the external order, the
future results of which then admit of prevision by virtue
of our internal operations. But this representation cannot be, and is not required to be, absolutely exact. The
degree of approximation is determined by our practical
wants, which give us the standard of precision desirable
for our theoretical previsions. Within this necessary
limit there is generally left for our intellect a certain
liberty in speculation, which it should use to secure fuller
satisfaction for its own inclinations, whether in the
direction of science or even of the fine arts, by giving
to our conceptions greater regularity, greater beauty
even, but not less truth. Such, under its mental aspect,
is Positivism, which, always occupied with the study
of law, holds on its way between two paths of equal
danger—mysticism which seeks to penetrate to causes,
and empiricism which confines itself to facts.

The Woman.—There seems to me, my father, one
serious omission in this statical theory of man's intellect,
in that it appears solely to have reference to the state
of reason properly so called, without being able to embrace
madness, which yet it ought to explain not less than the
other. Actual life offers daily so many intermediate
shades between these two states of mind that all these
cases must obey the same great laws, with differences
only of degree, as in the case of our bodily functions.]

The Priest.—It will be enough, my daughter, to consider more attentively the preceding doctrine to see that
it does really contain the true theory of madness and of
idiocy. These two opposite states are the two extremes
of the normal proportion which the state of reason

requires between objective impressions and subjective suggestions. Idiocy consists in the excess of objectivity, when our brain becomes too passive; and madness, in the strict sense, in the excess of subjectivity, from undue activity of that organ. But the mean state, which is reason, itself varies with the regular variations to which all human existence is subject, the social no less than the individual. The judgment of madness thus becomes the more delicate in that we must take into account in it times and places, in short, circumstances generally, as is so well impressed on us by the admirable composition of the great Cervantes. It is the case in which we most clearly realise to what an extent the statical study of the intelligence remains inadequate without its dynamical complement.

The Woman.—After this striking reflection, I would, my father, if you think proper, at once enter on this complementary study, which alone can allow my own meditations to grasp at length this great spectacle as a whole. Whatever the changes in the opinions of men, they can never in any case become purely arbitrary, though I cannot in any way unravel their general course.

The Priest.—It consists, my daughter, in the passage of every theoretical conception necessarily through three successive states : the first, theological, or fictitious; the second, metaphysical, or abstract; the third, positive, or real. The first is always provisional, the second simply transitional, the third alone definitive. This last differs from the two former, especially in its characteristic substitution of the relative for the absolute, when at length the study of laws replaces the inquiry into causes. There is, at bottom, no other difference between the two others, in point of theory, than the reduction of the primitive deities to mere entities. But as this transformation takes from the fictions of supernaturalism any firm consistence, socially above all, but also mentally, metaphysics always remain a mere solvent of theology, without power

ever to organise their own domain. Hence this doctrine
of revolt and modification has no other utility, in our
original evolution, whether individual or collective, but
to allow the transition from theology to Positivism to
be gradual. It is the better suited for this transitional
office from the circumstance that its equivocal conceptions can alternately become, either abstract representatives of supernatural agents, or general expressions for
the phenomena in question, according as we are nearer
the fictions or the real state.

The Woman.—This dynamical law finds already sufficient confirmation in my own experience ; yet I desire,
my father, to get as firm hold as possible of the intellectual principle of this evolution.

The Priest.—It is, my daughter, a consequence of the
statical law, which compels us to draw upon ourselves
for the subjective connections of our objective impressions, which otherwise would always be incoherent. The
true relations of things always requiring for their per-
ception a difficult and gradual analysis, which I shall
explain to you, our first hypotheses were purely instinctive, and as such fictitious. But this general tendency,
which would now be an excess of subjectivity, was at first
quite in conformity with our mental state, in which the
evolution could only originate in such an initial step.
A long experience, even yet inadequate for the more
backward minds, could alone unveil to us the absolute
futility of the inquiry into causes. Now, this useless
problem long had for us an invincible attraction, both
in speculation and in action, as promising us the power
of always proceeding by deduction without requiring any
special induction, and of modifying the world at our
pleasure. Thus, the two motives which impelled the
primeval thinker coincide essentially with that which
will always guide our intellectual efforts. It is the same,
at bottom, as regards the logical principle of this primitive regime. For the whole of sound logic is reducible

to this one rule : always form the simplest hypothesis compatible with the whole of the information possessed. Now, the thinkers of the theological period, and even of the fetichist, applied this rule better than the greater part of our modern doctors. Their object being to arrive at causes, they limited themselves to explaining the world by man—the only possible source of theoretic unity—by attributing all phenomena to superhuman wills, it matters not whether in the phenomena or external to them. Such a problem admits, by its nature, no other solution— one far superior to the misty fictions of our atheists or pantheists, whose mental state is nearer madness than the *naïve* simplicity of the true fetichists. This superiority is made most evident by the respective results. Whilst German ontology is at the present day retrograding to its Greek source, without inspiring any real and durable thought, the primitive theology opened to the human mind the only path which was practicable in our primitive state. Though it never could lead us to the determination of causes, its provisional colligation of facts led, by a natural sequence, to the discovery of laws.

This last study, at first looked on as quite secondary, soon tended to become the chief, under the impulse of practice which showed it to be more adapted for the previsions required for our activity. In strictness, the better minds never sought the cause except when they could not find the law ; and no blame can attach to the course they adopted, as more fitted than any torpor of the intellect to pave the way for this ultimate attainment. Our intelligence has even such a preference for Positive conceptions, especially on the ground of their superior practical value, that it often exerted itself to substitute them for the fictions of theology, long before the preparation required had been duly made. The end of our mental evolution is consequently still less uncertain than its opening phase.

The Woman.—This explanation of your *Law of the three*

states leaves me, my father, much in a mist, as regards the numerous cases in which the human mind seems to me at one and the same time, theological, metaphysical, and positive, according to the questions on which it is engaged. If unexplained, this co-existence would compromise directly your dynamical law, which, however, appears to me indisputable. Free me, I beg, from this perplexity.

The Priest.—It will disappear, my daughter, if you will observe the unvarying order which directs the simultaneous advance of our different theoretical conceptions according to the decreasing generality and increasing complication of the phenomena with which they deal. Hence results a complementary law, without which the dynamical study of the human understanding would continue obscure, and even almost inapplicable. It is easy for you to understand that, more general phenomena being necessarily more simple, the speculations which concern them must be easier and their progress therefore more rapid. This gradation, which is verified even in the different phases of theologism, is especially true in the Positive state, owing to the laborious preparations it requires. Thus it is that certain theories remain metaphysical, whilst others of a simpler nature have already become Positive, though more complicated ones still remain theological. But never do you meet with the reverse—a full and sufficient answer to the objections arising from their disparity at any one time.

The natural order which I have just indicated as existing between our different conceptions, and from which I shall deduce the true encyclopedic scale, alone allows a thorough understanding of their general advance. It founds the Positive logic, by revealing to us the connection in which our different theoretical studies must follow one another if they are to issue into any permanent construction. Though each class of phenomena has always its proper laws, which presuppose special

inductions, these last could hardly ever be of real value
were it not for the deductions supplied by the previous
knowledge of simpler laws. This subjective subordination
is a result of the objective dependence of less general
phenomena on all those which are more general. So the
unbroken order of our studies, rising ever from the world
to man, is not only justified by the logical training for
which simpler speculations are more adapted ; it rests
also on the dependence scientifically of the higher theories
on the lower, a consequence of the subordination of their
respective phenomena.

The Woman.—You have now, my father, made clear
to me the laws of the intellect, dynamical as well as
statical ; but I do not as yet see springing from them
the construction I looked for in respect to the whole
system of Positive doctrine. I want, then, to see directly
how Humanity, as an all-pervading principle, can at
length establish, by virtue of these laws, a real speculative unity, by connecting the moral with the physical
laws.

The Priest.—Your legitimate wish, my daughter, will
be satisfied by considering from a new general point of
view the complementary law of the intellectual movement which I have just stated. So conceived, it is
chiefly subjective, as must be the law which it supports.
But you are aware also that this classification admits by
its own force of an objective application, in determining
the general interdependence of the several phenomena.
Under this new light its destination becomes statical in
the main, and serves to characterise, not the co-existence
of our several intellectual advances, but the fundamental
order which governs all events whatsoever. Then the
law of classification is found to be entirely distinct from
that of filiation, though the simultaneous discovery of
the two is sufficiently explained by their close connection.

Before I set out to you this great theoretical hierarchy, I must limit with sufficient accuracy its general

sphere. This follows, in reality, from the true philosophical distinction between speculation and action.
Whilst action of necessity remains special, true theory is
always general. But it never acquires its characteristic
generality except by the aid of a previous abstraction,
which more or less impairs the reality of its conceptions.
Whatever be the dangers in practice of this impairment,
we must resign ourselves to it to attain the coherence
which can only be secured by the absolute universality
of theoretic laws. It is a true maxim of common sense
that every rule has its exceptions. Still, our intellect
throughout needs to find ultimately rules which never
fail, in order to avoid indefinite vacillation.

The only way of attaining this is to break up, as far
as possible, the study of beings, generally the only direct
study, into the study of the several general events
which compose the existence of each. Thus we obtain
abstract laws, the different combinations of which then
explain each concrete existence. Though very numerous
in themselves, these irreducible laws, on which rests all
our speculative wisdom, are much less numerous than
the special rules which depend on them. These last,
putting aside their number, will, from their natural
complication, always defy all our best efforts either
inductive or deductive. But on the other hand, to know
them would be practically useless, except in the rare cases
in which they really influence our destiny. For these
exceptional cases, practical genius, become the only competent authority, can always find empirical rules sufficient for our guidance, by availing itself wisely of the
general indications furnished by the speculative genius.
For the regularity of the compound events, if not so
easy to see as the regularity of their constituent general
elements, is a necessary consequence of it, so that observation will detect it if directed on the point for a
sufficient length of time.

For instance, we shall never know the general laws of

the variations peculiar to the normal constitution of the
atmosphere.   Yet the sailor and the agriculturist know
how, from. their observations of the locality or the
weather, to draw special rules, which, though empirical,
supersede in the main the so-called science of meteorology.
It is the same with all the other concrete studies, geo-
logical, zoological, and even sociological.   Whatever lies
beyond the grasp of practical genius will always remain
an idle question.   True science, then, is necessarily
abstract.   Its general laws, relating to the few categories
under which all observable phenomena may be brought,
are sufficient always to demonstrate the existence of concrete laws, though most of these last neither can nor
ought to be ever known, except for practical purposes.

The Woman.—I catch a glimpse, my father, of the
great simplification introduced into your philosophical
construction by this fundamental analysis which brings
the study of beings under that of events.   But I am
frightened at the constant abstraction required by such a
scientific regime, though, fortunately, I am exempt from
it.   Its institution seems to me even beyond the power
of our intellect, if all orders of phenomena are to be
directly studied in the Great Being which alone presents
them to us in their entirety.

The Priest.—For your comfort, my daughter, all that
is required is to consider under a new aspect the general
principle of the abstract hierarchy.   Though directly it
establishes only the subordination of events, indirectly it
should also lead to that of beings.   For phenomena are
only more general in so far as they belong to more numerous existences.   The simplest of all, though existing
everywhere, must then be found in beings which offer
us no other, and where, therefore, the study of them in
themselves becomes more accessible.   In strict truth, the
second step in science will never be separated from the
first ; this it is, more even than the nature of the phenomena, which constitutes the increase in complication.

But whatever be these successive accumulations, each fresh category of events may be studied in beings independent of the succeeding categories, though dependent on the preceding, the previous knowledge of which will allow us to concentrate attention on the new class. Even supposing the beings not always distinct, the Positive method will keep its main efficacy if they are seen in different states, and this condition cannot fail, by the nature of such a classification. Thus, the scientific hierarchy that I am going to set before you, though its original purpose was to furnish a scale of phenomena, necessarily constitutes the true scale of beings, or, at any rate, of existences. It becomes by turns abstract or concrete, according as its purpose is subjective or objective. This is why the encyclopedic subordination of the arts essentially coincides with that of the sciences.

The Woman.—Before you proceed, my father, to the exposition of this hierarchy, of which I begin to see the general principle, I beg you to explain to me the course we are to follow. To cement the fundamental union between the world and man, it would seem that it might start equally from either whilst making for the other. Its habitual use seems even to require that it should be apt, as every other scale, to become indifferently an ascending or descending one. But I do not know whether these two paths are suited to its construction.

The Priest.—The regular concurrence of these two methods, the one objective, the other subjective, is as necessary, my daughter, for the formation as for the application of the hierarchy of science. Its spontaneous elaboration depended on the first; but its systematic institution required the second. The initiation of each individual must in this, as in every other important point, essentially reproduce the evolution of the race, only for the future we shall do consciously what was formerly done blindly. The combination of these two methods alone allows us to secure the advantages of both and

neutralise their dangers. To ascend from the world to
man, without having first descended from man to the
world, exposes us to the excessive cultivation of the lower
studies, whilst losing sight of their true scientific destination, so as to waste our scientific efforts on academic
trifling, as adverse to the intellect as to the heart. Connection and dignity are then sacrificed to reality and
clearness. Still this was the course necessarily adopted
by abstract Positivism, during the long scientific introduction which extends from Thales and Pythagoras to
Bichat and Gall, in order to elaborate in succession the
materials of the ultimate systematisation. The higher
wants of our intellect then received their satisfaction,
and that an imperfect one, only from the heterogeneous
guardianship still vested in the theologico-metaphysical
spirit. But at the present day, when the universal
principle of the definitive synthesis is irreversibly established as a result of this immense preparatory movement,
the subjective method, become at last as Positive as the
objective, must take the direct initiative in forming the
encyclopedia. It alone can properly originate the construction which the other will then be able worthily to
work out. This rule is as applicable to each great
scientific inquiry as to the whole system of the sciences.

The Woman.—You see me then ready, my father, to
adopt fully the religious sanction given by the dogma of
Humanity to all the essential portions of abstract science
in succession, strengthening the highest and ennobling
the lowest through the connection of all with it.

The Priest.—The better to define such a synthesis, you
should, my daughter, recall at the outset the persistent
aim of human life, the preservation and perfecting of the
Great Being whom we must at once love, know, and
serve. Each of his own spontaneous action discharges
these three offices, which religion systematises by the
worship, the doctrine, and the life. Though the philosophical construction is then necessarily prior to the

two others, it is, at bottom, only destined to consolidate them and to develop them. In itself, the direct study of Humanity may degenerate as much as the lower sciences, if we forget that we are to know her only to love her more and serve her better. When attention to the means makes us mistake or neglect the end, the philosophical advance has really less to recommend it than the natural development of ordinary men.

Thus you see why, at the top of the encyclopedic scale, I place MORALS, or the science of the individual man. Since the Great Being never operates but through organs which are in the last instance individual, these organs must first be studied with special care, in order that their service may be properly rendered during the period of their objective existence, on which will depend their subjective influence. It is thus that Positivism definitely ratifies the primary precept of the initial theocracy : *know thyself, to better thyself*. In it the intellectual principle and the social motive act in concert. As a fact, the most useful of all the sciences is also the most complete, or rather the only one which is complete ; since its phenomena subjectively embrace all the other, though, by that very fact, they are objectively subordinate to them. The fundamental principle of the scientific hierarchy gives then a direct predominance to the moral point of view as the most complicated and the most special.

But at this point the philosophical conformity of Positivism with theologism necessarily ceases. The latter, always occupied with causes, placed the study of morals under the immediate control of the supernatural principles by which it explained everything. Thus evoking purely internal observation, it gave a sanction to the personality of an existence which, bringing each into direct connection with an infinite power, isolated him entirely from Humanity. Positivism, on the contrary, only seeking the law in order the better to guide the activity, always in its essence social, bases moral science far more on the observation of others than of oneself, in order to establish conceptions at once real and useful. Then we feel how impossible it is properly to enter on such a study without a previous study of society. In all respects, each of us depends entirely on Humanity, especially with regard to our noblest functions, always dependent on the time and place in which we live ; as you are reminded by these fine verses in Zaïre—

> J'eusse été, près du Gange, esclave des faux dieux,
> Chrétienne dans Paris, Musulmane en ces lieux.
> —*Act* i. *sc.* I.

> I had been, by the Ganges, the slave of false gods,
> Christian in Paris, Musulman where I am.

Thus it is that morals, regarded as our chief science, begins by instituting SOCIOLOGY, the phenomena of which are both simpler and more general, in accordance with the spirit of the whole Positive hierarchy.

The Woman.—Allow me, my father, to detain you a moment on this first step, to resolve the contradiction it seems to offer between these two conditions of your classification. For here the complication seems to grow, exceptionally, with the generality. I have always thought the moral point of view simpler than the social one.

The Priest.—That is solely, my daughter, because you have hitherto proceeded on feeling rather than on reason ; morals being justly for your sex an art rather than a science. If we had to compare the number of cases, you would see that the number of individuals is greater than that of nations, which absorbs your attention. But limiting ourselves to its native complication, you forget that moral science, besides all the influences taken into account by social science, must also appreciate impulses which social science may set aside as almost inappreciable. I mean the strong mutual influences which are in constant action, in obedience to laws as yet

I

too little known, between the physical and moral nature of man. Though very powerful for the individual, sociology pays no particular attention to them, because their conflicting results in different individuals cancel one another in regard to nations. On the contrary, any moral judgment which should neglect them would expose us to the most serious mistakes, from attributing to the soul what proceeds from the body, or the reverse, as you see every day.

The Woman.—I now understand, my father, what made me stop you at the outset of your hierarchical series, which I now beg you to follow out to the end, fearing no fresh interruption, which would prevent my mastering the general filiation.

The Priest.—Your objection, my daughter, is in itself a very natural one, and it answers the purpose here of bringing into greater prominence our first step in the encyclopedia, the indispensable type of all the others, which will be more easily taken in consequence, as in the case of any scale whatever. I hope that you will descend without effort from one science to the next, under the same impulsion as that which has just led you from morals to sociology, looking always to the natural subordination of the respective phenomena.

This fundamental principle makes you feel at once that the systematic study of society requires a previous knowledge of the general laws of life. Indeed, as nations are beings gifted in an eminent degree with life, the vital order necessarily governs the social, the statical condition of which and its dynamical progress would be deeply changed were the constitution of our brain, or even of our body, to change in a notable degree. In this case, the simultaneous increase of generality and simplicity admits of no doubt. Thus it is that sociology, first constituted by morals, constitutes in its turn BIOLOGY, which has, moreover, its direct relations with the master science. Biology having to study life only in what it presents in common in all the beings which enjoy it, animals and plants form its proper province, though it is ultimately destined for man, whose true study, however, it can only sketch in rude outline. Thus regarded, biology examines judiciously the bodily functions by the light derived from the study of those existences in which they are naturally clear of all higher complication. When this logical direction of biology exposes it to academic degeneracy by laying too much stress on insignificant beings or acts, the discipline of philosophy must recall it to its true vocation, without ever fettering the method indispensable to its inquiries.

These first three sciences are so closely connected that I make the name of the middle one stand for the whole in the encyclopedic table which I have arranged (*Table B.*) to render easier for you a general estimate of the Positive hierarchy. For sociology may be easily regarded as absorbing biology by way of introduction, and morals as conclusion. When the word *Anthropology* shall be in more common and sounder use, it will become preferable as the collective term, since its literal meaning is the *Study of man.* But for a long time it will be desirable to use here the term *Sociology*, in order to mark more clearly the principal superiority of the new intellectual regime, which consists most particularly in the introduction into our encyclopedia of the social point of view, alien in the main to the earlier synthesis.

Living beings are of necessity bodies, which, despite their greater complication, always obey the more general laws of matter, the invariable predominance of which presides over all their peculiar phenomena, always, however, leaving them their spontaneity. A third step in our encyclopedia, in full analogy with the preceding ones, places, then, biology, and consequently sociology and morals, in dependence on the great inorganic science which I have called COSMOLOGY. Its true domain is the general study of man's planet, the necessary environment of all the higher functions, vital, social, and moral. A better name would then be *Geology*, for this conveys the required meaning directly. But academical anarchy has so spoilt this term that Positivism must renounce its use, until we eliminate, as we soon shall, the would-be science which has been decorated with it. Then we shall be able better to conform to the laws of language, and apply to the whole of the inorganic sciences a more exact denomination, the concrete nature of which is even more calculated to remind us that we need to study each existence in its least complicated form.

This would be the limit of my encyclopedic operation, without any decomposition of cosmology, had I only in view the final state of man's reason, which will be bound to contract the inferior sciences and expand the higher. But at present I must also provide for the special wants of the initiation of the West, the essential equivalent of which will always recur in the evolution of each individual. These two reasons compel me to divide cosmology into two equally fundamental sciences, one of which, under the general name of PHYSICS, studies directly the whole material order. The other, simpler and more general, justly termed MATHEMATICS, is the necessary basis of physics, and as such of the whole scientific edifice, as treating of the most universal form of existence, reduced to the only phenomena which recur everywhere. Without this division, we could not understand the spontaneous advance of the Positive philosophy, which could only begin by such a study, the more rapid completion of which caused it at first to be considered as the only science. Although its name reminds us too strongly of this original privilege, which has long disappeared, it should be kept till such time as the natural superiority of this type of scientific and logical study has duly controlled the general progress of the encyclopedic laws. Then a less vague and better constructed name may demarcate the true domain of the science, acting as a systematic check on the blind scientific ambition of its too exclusive professors.

Be this as it may, you should feel the necessity of descending as far as mathematics to find a natural basis for the encyclopedic scale—a basis able to make the whole system only the gradual development of the good sense of mankind. In fact, physics themselves, far simpler than the other sciences, are yet not simple enough. Their special inductions cannot be reduced to system without the aid of more general deductions, as in every other case; only in physics this logical and scientific want forces itself less on the attention. It is only in mathematics that you can use induction without previous deduction, such is the extreme simplicity of its domain, where induction often escapes notice; so much so, that our academic geometricians only see in it deductions, which are consequently unintelligible, as resting on nothing. There can exist nowhere convictions really proof against attacks except those that are based ultimately on this eternal foundation of all Positive philosophy. Such will always be the necessary termination of the subjective connection, guided by which every man of intellectual ability and honest heart will at any time be able, as I have just done, to form the fundamental series of the five principal encyclopedic steps.

The Woman.—It is to this reaction of feeling upon the intellect that I attribute, my father, the ease I find in following such a construction, so dreaded by me at the outset. With its attention constantly riveted on morals, the only solid basis of its legitimate influence, my sex will always set a high value on securing it at length systematic foundations, capable of resisting the sophisms of bad passions. At present more than ever, we are alarmed as we contemplate the moral ravages already caused by the intellectual anarchy, which threatens at no distant period to dissolve all the bonds which bind men together, unless irresistible convictions at length prevent its unchecked ascendency. True philosophers may therefore count on the secret co-operation and heart-felt gratitude of all women worthy of the name, when they reconstruct morals on Positive foundations, as a final substitute for its supernatural bases, too evidently worn out. Women who shall feel, as I do now, the necessity of descending with this object to the most abstract sciences, will know how to appreciate duly this un-expected help that reason at length steps forward to give to love. I thus understand why the encyclopedic table which I am going to study proceeds in an inverse direction to that of the exposition which it summarises. For we must become most familiar with this ascending order, according to which the several Positive conceptions will always develop. By instituting it as you have just done, you have obviated the chief repugnance women naturally feel for too abstract a course, which hitherto they have seen lead so often to dryness and pride. Now that I can always keep in sight and recall the moral aim of the whole scientific elaboration, and the conditions peculiar to each of its essential phases, I shall have as much satisfaction in ascending as in descending your encyclopedic scale.

The Priest.—This alternation will become easier to you, my daughter, if you remark that, in both direc-tions, the method may rest on the same principle, in all cases following the decrease of generality. All that this requires is to refer the fundamental series at one time to the phenomena themselves, at another to our own concep-tions, according as it is to be used objectively or subject-ively. In truth, moral notions necessarily comprehend all the others, which we draw from them by successive abstractions. It is in this above all that consists their greater complication. The science of morals, then, has more subjective generality than all the lower sciences. Inversely, the phenomena of mathematics are the most general solely as being the most simple. Their study,

then, offers more objective but less subjective generality
than any other. Alone applicable to every form of
existence within our ken, it is also the science which
gives us least knowledge of the beings with which
it deals, for it can only reveal their commonest laws.
All the intermediate sciences present, in less degree, this
twofold contrast which exists between mathematics and
morals.

But whether you ascend or descend, the encyclopedic
course always represents morals as the supreme science,
since it is at once the most useful and the most complete.
It is there that theory, having lost by degrees the abstraction of its beginnings, forms a systematic union
with practice, after completing all that was indispensable
as preparation. And therefore the wisdom of mankind,
systematised by Positivism, will always insist on respect-
ing the admirable equivocal designation, so regretted by
our pedants, which, in morals alone, fuses the art and
the science in one appellation.

In this apparent confusion moral science happily finds
an equivalent for the discipline which, in all the others,
anticipates or corrects the scientific aberrations attendant
on our upward course of intellectual culture. In fact,
the general rule is to restrict each phase of the encyclopedic scale to the degree in which it is necessary as a
preparation for the next above it; reserving, be it remembered, for practical genius the more detailed studies
which it may judge suitable in any particular case.
Despite the declamations of academicians, we now know
that such a discipline sanctions all theories of real interest, excluding only scientific puerilities, of which, at
the present day, the combined needs of the intellect and
the heart demand the suppression. Now, this rule, so
valuable everywhere else, fails of necessity for the science
which stands at the top of the encyclopedic scale.

Were moral theories as much cultivated as the rest,
their greater complication, in this special absence of dis-

cipline, would expose them to more frequent and more
dangerous aberrations. But the heart then offers a better
guidance to the intellect, by recalling more forcibly the
universal subordination of theory to practice, by virtue of
a happy ambiguity of designation. Philosophers ought,
in fact, to bring the same dispositions as women to the
study of morals, in order to draw from them the rules
of our conduct. Only, their deductive science gives a
generality and consistence to the inductions of women
which they could not get otherwise, and which yet are
almost always indispensable to secure the social, or even
private, efficacy of the precepts of morality.

The Woman.—The true regime of the intellect being
thus constituted, I ask you, my father, to close this long
and difficult conversation by delineating generally the
properties of your encyclopedic series, viewed for the
future as an ascending series, with which I shall soon be
familiar. I see without your aid the intellectual and
moral dangers inherent in this objective culture, so long
as it remained unprovided with the subjective discipline
just explained. Then the unavoidable succession of the
several encyclopedic phases compelled the scientific intellect provisionally to adopt a system of dispersive
specialism, directly counter to the full generality which
should characterise theoretical views. Hence naturally
followed, more especially in the learned, and as a consequence even in the public, an increasing tendency on
the one hand to materialism and atheism, on the other to
the slighting of the softer affections and the neglect of the
fine arts. I have long been aware how greatly, under all
these aspects, true Positivism, far from offering any real
solidarity with its scientific preamble, is on the contrary
its best corrective. But I cannot by myself alone apprehend the essential attributes which I am now to appreciate in the whole system of your theoretical hierarchy.

The Priest.—Reduce them, my daughter, to two chief
ones, which correspond to its two general objects, equally

subjective and objective, or here rather, logical and scientific, according as the attention is directed mainly to the method or the doctrine.

Under the first aspect, the encyclopedic series points out at once the necessary course of scientific education and the gradual development of true reasoning. Mainly deductive in its cradle in mathematics, where the requisite inductions are almost always spontaneous, the Positive method becomes more and more inductive in proportion as it enters on speculations of a higher order. In this long elaboration, we must distinguish four capital divisions, in which the growing complication of the phenomena makes us successively develop observation, experiment, comparison, and historical filiation. Each of these five logical phases, including the mathematical starting-point, spontaneously absorbs all its predecessors, as a consequence of the natural subordination of their respective phenomena. Sound logic thus becomes complete, and as such systematic, as soon as the definitive foundation of sociology gives rise to the historical method, as biology had previously introduced the art of comparison, after that physics had sufficiently developed observation and experiment.

Fortunately for your sex, its ignorance relieves it at present from the philosophical demonstrations by which Positivism labours to convince men that to learn reasoning the only way is to reason, with certainty and precision, on clear and definite cases. Those who are most aware that every art should be learnt by practice alone, still listen to the sophists who teach them to reason, or even to speak, by only reasoning or speaking on reasoning or speech. But although you were taught grammar and perhaps rhetoric, at least you were spared logic, the most pretentious of the three scholastic studies. By being spared it, your own reason, judiciously trained under your cherished Molière, soon did justice to the two other classical absurdities. Strengthened now by systematic convictions, you will not hesitate to treat with just ridicule the Trissotins who would teach you the art of deduction, without having themselves ever made the least use of it in mathematics. Each essential branch of the Positive method must always be studied especially, in the department of science which first gave it birth.

The Woman.—This first judgment having, fortunately, no difficulty for me, as I see in it simple good sense, I beg you, my father, to pass at once to the second general property of your encyclopedic series.

The Priest.—It consists, my daughter, in the systematic conception of the universal order, as is indicated by the second title of our conspectus. From the material to the moral order, each order is superposed on its predecessor, in obedience to this fundamental law, the necessary consequence of the true principle of any hierarchy : *The noblest phenomena are, in all cases, subordinate to the lowest.* This is the only rule of really universal application discoverable by the objective study of the world and man. As it cannot in any way supersede the necessity of less general laws, it cannot by itself ever constitute the barren external unity vainly sought by all philosophers, from Thales to Descartes.

But, whilst renouncing this futile stimulus, which finds a more valuable substitute in the moral destination of all our scientific efforts, we are glad to trace, between all our abstract doctrines, an objective connection inseparable from their subjective co-ordination. Social action above all must turn to account such a view of the sum of real fatalities. Our dependence and our dignity becoming thus inter-connected, we shall be better disposed to feel the value of voluntary submission, on which depends mainly our moral, and even our intellectual improvement.

Observe, in fact, to give completeness to this great law, that, from the practical point of view, it represents the order of nature as increasingly susceptible of modification in proportion as it governs more complicated phenomena. Improvement always implies imperfection, which everywhere increases with complication. But you see also that man's providence then becomes more efficient, as having more varied agents at its command. Such compensation is still, doubtless, inadequate; so that the simplest order generally remains the most perfect, though under a blind government. Still, this general law of modifiability makes morals the chief art in two ways, first for its superior importance, next because it offers a larger field for our wise action. Practice and theory then combine to justify more and more the predominance which Positivism systematically allows to morals.

The Woman.—Since you have now explained to me sufficiently the Positive doctrine as a whole, I would wish, my father, before leaving you to-day, to know beforehand the proper object of the two other conversations you promised me on this second part of your Catechism. I do not see, in fact, what is left for me to know as regards this systematic basis of the Universal Religion, in order to fit me to pass to the direct and special study of the life, which is finally to engage my attention.

The Priest.—The foregoing conceptions, my daughter, are too abstract and too general to leave a sufficient impression if not completed by some less general explanations of a more definite character, of which too I shall make frequent use. Without detaining you at each particular phase of the encyclopedia, as will be the case in the new Western education, I simply ask you to appreciate separately the two unequal parts which historically make up the whole Positive philosophy.

This natural division consists in dividing the universal order into external and human. The first, answering to cosmology and biology, formed, under the name of *natural philosophy*—a term ordinarily adopted in England—the sole scientific domain of antiquity, and even this it could only treat statically and in outline. Besides that the true scientific spirit did not admit then of a more complete upward growth, the state of society was naturally adverse to a premature extension, which could for long end only in compromising the existing order without really aiding ulterior progress.   Only, the exceptional genius of Aristotle, after reducing to a system, as far as was possible, natural philosophy, prepared the way for a sound moral philosophy, by an adequate, if inchoate, treatment of the two essential parts of human statics—first collective, then individual.   And therefore he was not really appreciated till the Middle Ages, when the provisional separation of the two powers led to the direct advance of our most important speculations.   But this precious social impulsion could not relieve the true philosophic spirit from the long scientific preamble which still separated it from its highest domain.   Hence this provisional division lasted on to our own day.   It must therefore preside over the last transition of the Western reason, directed by Positivism.

CONVERSATION VII.

THE EXTERNAL ORDER, FIRST INORGANIC, THEN VITAL.

The Woman.—By studying the table which summarizes our fundamental conversation, I understand, my father, the necessity for the two others on the Positive doctrine which you promised me at its close.   My heart must first make me feel the need of each encyclopedic phase for the moral systematisation which is the grand object of this immense scientific construction.   It is necessary now that my intellect should see how the separate stages of this abstract edifice succeed one another, from the base to the summit, without, however, penetrating into their interior.   This systematic ascent becomes the indispensable complement of the descent which serves as its foundation and which I made under your guidance.

If the mind of man can really mount, by an almost insensible progression, from the lowest mathematical notions to the sublimest moral conceptions, it will be for me the most admirable of all sights. Though my sex never can follow such a filiation in its details, it should at the present day grasp its feasibility in the general, in order to be sure that systematic morals can thus be rested on really safe foundations. Then the opinion of women will brand, as you wish, the anarchical sophists who, though theological belief is absolutely decayed, oppose the advent of the Positive faith, in order to prolong indefinitely a religious interregnum which favours their unworthiness and their incapacity. Fear not then to fix my attention first on the mathematical step, where is found, according to you, the only solid base for the body of scientific theories. The marked aversion this study arouses in all our metaphysical make-mischiefs predisposes me to feel the organic power you attribute to it.

The Priest.—To get a clear conception of this logical and scientific base of the whole abstract edifice, it is enough for you, my daughter, to estimate aright the general domain assigned it in our encyclopedic table. Mathematics study directly universal existence, reduced to its simplest, and consequently lowest phenomena, on which necessarily rest all other real attributes. These fundamental properties of any being whatever are number, extension, and movement. Whatever cannot be considered under these three points of view can have no existence except in our understanding. But nature shows us many beings of whom we can know nothing beyond these elementary attributes. Such are in especial the stars, which, being from their distance only accessible to investigation by the sight, admit only of this mathematical study, quite sufficient, it must be allowed, to regulate duly our true relations towards them. So astronomy will always furnish us the most direct and complete application of mathematical science. Still, if the general laws of number, extension, and motion, could have been studied nowhere but in these heavenly bodies, they would for ever have escaped us, despite their extreme simplicity. But, as they recur everywhere, they were open to discovery in more accessible cases, after putting aside, by unconscious abstractions, the other material attributes which then complicated their examination.

Observe even here how our hierarchical principle presides over the true internal distribution of each great science, as naturally as over the general co-ordination of the sciences. For, these three ultimate elements of mathematics, the calculus, geometry, and mechanics, form, from the historical no less than the dogmatic point of view, a progression essentially analogous to that which is seen more palpably in the whole of the abstract system. The ideas of number are certainly more universal and simpler than those even of extension, and these, on the same ground, in their turn, precede those of motion.

In the case of most of the stars, our real knowledge is limited ultimately to accurate enumeration, without our being able even to say what their shape or size is, nor are we much concerned with them. Numbers are as applicable to phenomena as to beings. This point of view, which draws no distinctions, is, at bottom, the only one universally applicable, as alone extending to all our thoughts whatsoever. Its native roughness does not preclude a noble use, that of perfecting in all directions harmony and stability, the best types of which it originates for us. So you see children of themselves begin their initiation in abstract thought by purely numerical speculations, long before they come to think on geometrical properties.

As for motion, you easily see the increase of complication and the decrease of generality which place its study highest in the domain of mathematics. This is why the Greeks, forward as they were in geometry, could only attain a rudimentary grasp of mechanics in some cases of equilibrium, never having a glimpse of the elementary laws of motion.

Comparing these three essential parts of mathematics, we see that the calculus, of which algebra rather than arithmetic is the principal development, subserves mainly a logical purpose, over and above its peculiar and direct utility. Its essential province is to enlarge to the utmost our powers of deduction. The study of extension and that of motion acquire through it a generality and coherence which they could not have unless all their problems were transformed into mere questions of number. But, from the scientific point of view, geometry and mechanics are the main constituents of mathematics ; for they alone establish directly the theory of universal existence, passive first, then active.

Mechanics thus take a very important encyclopedic position, as the necessary transition between mathematics and physics, the characteristics of which severally are in close combination in mechanics. In them the whole logical ordering does not seem purely deductive, as it is supposed to be in geometry, owing to the extreme facility of the required inductions. In mechanics we begin to feel distinctly the need of an inductive basis, already become difficult to trace amongst our concrete observations, in order to allow the free growth of the abstract conceptions which are to connect with it the general problem of the composition and communication of motion. It was mainly owing to the want of such external foundation that the science of mechanics could not be developed till the seventeenth century.

Up to that time the mathematical spirit had only brought out subjective laws, alone perceptible in geometry and the calculus, in thinkers who did not as yet comprehend their necessary connection with objective laws.

But these last became distinct objects of cognizance from the great difficulty they presented to the founders of mechanics. The three fundamental laws of motion are so important and so universal that I must state them to you here, as the best types of true laws of nature—simple general facts allowing of no explanation, but, on the contrary, serving as a basis for all rational explanations. Though the metaphysical regime greatly hindered their discovery, it was most delayed by its own inherent difficulty. For it was the first capital effort of the genius of induction, discerning at length, in the midst of the commonest events, general relations which had hitherto escaped all the efforts of man's intellectual activity.

The first law, discovered by Kepler, consists in this, that motion is naturally rectilinear and uniform. Hence curvilinear or any motion which is not uniform can only result from a continuous composition of successive impulsions—impulsions again either active or passive. The second law, due to Galileo, proclaims the independence of the inter-connected movements of a plurality of bodies as regards any common movement of the system they form. But this community of movement must be complete, in velocity no less than in direction. Only on this condition do the particular bodies remain in the same relative state of rest or motion as if the system were motionless. So this second law is not applicable to rotatory movements, from which in fact came the untenable objections which met its discovery. Lastly, the third law of motion, that of Newton, consists in the constant equality between reaction and action, in every mechanical collision; provided that, in measuring each change, proper regard be paid to the mass as well as to the velocity. This law is the proper basis of all notions relating to the communication of motion, as that of Galileo governs all those that concern its composition, that of Kepler having throughout determined, to begin with, the nature of each movement. These three laws together suffice for the general problem of mechanics to be approached deductively, by bringing gradually the more complicated cases under the more simple, by mathematical artifices often difficult to invent in particular cases.

These general laws will be of direct use to you in explaining numbers of phenomena of daily occurrence, in the midst of which you live without understanding, or even perceiving them. They are eminently fitted to make you feel what it is that constitutes the true scientific genius. Finally, you should observe how each of them naturally comes under a law common to all phenomena whatever, social and moral quite as much as simply material phenomena. The first connects with the law of persistence which reigns everywhere; the second with the law which recognises the independence of the action of the part as regards the conditions common to the whole, whence, in social questions, is derived the reconcilement of progress with order. As for the third, it at once admits of an universal application, which never varies save so far as concerns the measure of the several influences. This philosophical comparison completes our estimate of the importance, from the encyclopedic point of view, attaching to the extreme limit of the domain of mathematics.

The Woman.—Though these considerations by their abstractness and novelty are naturally, my father, beyond my grasp to-day, I feel that, on sufficient reflection, I shall be able to master them. I beg you then to pass at once to the direct study of the material order.

The Priest.—To place it on its proper philosophical footing I am compelled, my daughter, to require of you one last encyclopedic effort, that of decomposing the second cosmological science, which in its collective form I called Physics, into three great and really distinct sciences. They are, in the ascending order, now becoming familiar to you, first, Astronomy, next, Physics properly so called which keeps the common name, lastly, Chemistry,

K

as you may find from the secondary division in our table. So, the hierarchy of science has finally to offer you seven encyclopedic degrees, in place of the five you have hitherto recognised. We pass from one form to the other by simply drawing out more fully the second of the five original degrees, as you lengthen a pocket telescope by drawing out its tube. It is only when you come to apply them that you will see which arrangement you should prefer in each case.

In fact, this fundamental series allows of several different arangements, according as you contract it or expand it, the better to satisfy our different intellectual wants, never inverting the order of succession. Its most condensed form is as clearly indicated in our table as the most expanded. When further advanced, you will often reduce the whole encyclopedic bundle to the simple dualism, cosmology and sociology; to do which at the outset would expose you to vagueness. But you will never contract it more, so evidently impossible is it to reduce objectively one under the other two primary groups, which can only be united by the subjective conception of them, when we place ourselves directly at the true religious point of view.

After having, by the help of very familiar language, pointed out to you this expansion of the encyclopedia, I am especially bound to give reasons for it, by explaining its nature.

The Woman.—From the slight knowledge I have, from hearsay, of the three sciences you have just introduced, I guess, my father, why you intercalate them here. For their introduction anticipates a wish I was on the point of laying before you, as to the continuity of the encyclopedic series. When comparing, in this respect, the lower and higher sciences, our primitive scale of five degrees offered me a serious disparity. I understand without effort, by the simple connection of the phenomena, how we rise insensibly from biology to sociology, and from sociology to morals, though I need on this point your special explanations, to give greater precision to my ideas.   On the other hand, I could not at first understand to my satisfaction the transition from mathematics to the direct study of the inorganic order, and still less that from cosmology to biology.   That might doubtless arise from my more complete ignorance of the lower conceptions.   But I felt also that this want of harmony must be connected with the very constitution of our first scale, though I could in no way see the remedy, nor even know that there was one.   I shall easily, then, accustom myself to the seven encyclopedic steps, if by this slight complication I feel my sense of order satisfied. Still I allow, that had you begun with seven at first, I should have felt too great a difficulty in conceiving your abstract hierarchy as a whole.

The Priest.—Since you have guessed the ultimate motive of this final modification, it only remains for me, my daughter, to complete your own unaided effort, by pointing out in a systematic way the nature and object of the three sciences introduced.

Positive religion defines astronomy as the study of the earth as a heavenly body ; that is to say, the knowledge of our geometrical and mechanical relations to the stars which can affect our destinies by influencing the state of the earth.   It is then around our globe that subjectively we condense all astronomical theories, absolutely rejecting all such as, disconnected with it, become at once mere idle questions, even granting them to be within our reach. Hence finally we eliminate, not merely the so-called sidereal astronomy, but also the planetary studies which concern stars invisible to the naked eye, and as such necessarily without any real influence on the earth.   The true domain of astronomy for us will then, as originally, be limited to the five planets always known, together with the sun, the centre of our movements as of theirs, and the moon, our only satellite in the heavens.

The whole difference between our doctrine and that of the ancients, here as elsewhere, consists essentially in substituting at length the relative for the absolute, a centre which was long objective being made purely subjective. This is why the discovery, or rather the proof, of the double movement of the earth constitutes the most important revolution in science belonging to the preliminary state of human reason. One of the most eminent precursors of Positivism, the sagacious Fontenelle, explained admirably to your sex its philosophical bearing, so far as was then desirable, in a charming little work, the apparently trifling character of which did not deprive it of the immortality it deserves.

In fact, it is by virtue of the earth's motion that Positive doctrine has come to be directly incompatible with all theological doctrine, by its making our largest speculations profoundly relative, whereas previously they were able to retain an absolute character. The discovery of our planetary gravitation was at no long interval its scientific consequence and its philosophical complement. Though academical routine has greatly hampered the influence of these two theories in an encyclopedic point of view, Positivism finally establishes them as the primary general basis for the direct study of the inorganic order, thus brought into immediate connection with the mathematical basis of the whole doctrine.

In this initial step, this order is, in fact, regarded simply under its geometrico-mechanical aspect, to the exclusion of all inquiries, as absurd as they are idle, as to the temperature of the stars or their internal constitution. But, on passing from astronomy to physics proper, a passage made almost imperceptibly through planetary mechanics, we penetrate more deeply into the study of inert nature. In order, however, to give a truer idea of this new science, we must first gain a conception of the highest cosmological science, the more decided character of which will enable us subsequently to more easily grasp pure physics, somewhat indefinite in themselves. This course allows you to observe one of the most important logical precepts of Positivism, which bids us, in all cases, look first to the two extremes if we wish to form a right conception of the intermediary by which they are connected. Chemistry was actually introduced, as a distinct science, in the East as in the West, several centuries before physics, which Galileo created on his own impulse in order to establish a sound transition from astronomy to chemistry, in place of their previous chimerical connection.

To shorten and simplify the explanation of the two, consider chemistry and physics as in the main subject to the same general influences, which only differ, at bottom, in the greater or less intensity of the modifications which the constitution of matter receives from them. But this sole difference never leaves any ambiguity as to the true nature of each case, despite the confusion due to academic teaching. In their full intensity, states of heat, of electricity, even of light, modify the constitution of matter sufficiently to change the internal composition of substances. In this case the event belongs to chemistry ; that is, to the study of the general laws of composition and decomposition. These processes can and ought to be looked on always as purely binary. They rarely allow more than three successive combinations, the union becoming more difficult and less stable in proportion as it becomes more complicated. At lower degrees, the same influences modify at farthest the condition of bodies without ever altering their substance. In this case matter is only studied under the strictly physical aspect. Though both these sciences are equally universal, the decrease of generality is as sensible as the increase of complication when we pass from the one to the other. For physics, as they study the whole of the properties which make up every material existence, consider equally all bodies, with mere differences of degree. Its several branches must then correspond to the different senses which unveil to us the external world. Chemistry, on the contrary, considers all substances as in their nature distinct; and chiefly addresses itself to the problem of determining these radical differences. Though the phenomena it studies are always possible in any body whatever, they are practically never found in it except under special conditions, the rare and difficult concurrence of which often demands the intervention of man.

Of these two neighbour sciences, physics are logically the most important, chemistry scientifically, on a comparison of their encyclopedic value, when we have once allowed the indispensable necessity of each of them, both for theory and practice. It is from physics most of all that the genius of induction takes a vigorous spring, by the development of observation, too spontaneous in astronomy; and then of experiment, which nowhere else leads to such unequivocal results. But chemistry carries the day as to the encyclopedic importance of the notions we derive from it. Its extreme imperfection as a science, which can only cease under the discipline of Positivism, has not prevented its exercising a luminous influence on the whole reason of the West. This valuable power is derived especially from the general analysis of our earthly environment, gaseous, liquid, and solid, completed by the equally indispensable analysis of vegetal and animal substances. We may thus at length apprehend the fundamental economy of nature, previously unintelligible, because we had not recognised, in all real beings, lifeless as well as living, material elements essentially identical in character.

You understand, then, how chemistry properly so called alone forms a normal transition between cosmology and biology, in accordance with your legitimate wish for unbroken continuity. You would set a still higher value on this great encyclopedic condition, as favourable ultimately to the heart as to the intellect, were I to point out the true internal arrangement of astronomy, physics, and chemistry, as I did at the outset in the case of mathematics. But we must keep such developments for more special conversations, which are not immediately indispensable from the religious point of view. This initial type must suffice here to make you feel the general possibility of a really gradual ascent from mathematics to morals, by the application, with increasing exactness and detail, of the unchangeable principle of our hierarchy.

If we complete this subjective or logical appreciation by an equivalent objective or scientific appreciation, the general succession of these three abstract studies begins to disclose to you a real concrete scale, if not of beings, at least of existences. In astronomy you observe only simple mathematical existence, which, previously almost a mere idea, becomes there a reality in the case of bodies which we cannot examine under any other point of view, and which become therefore its best type. But in physics, we rise to phenomena of a higher and nearer kind, which tend to approach man. Lastly, chemistry offers you the noblest and deepest form of material existence, always subordinated to the antecedent forms, according to our universal law. Though the great objective conception emanating from this progression can only find its adequate development in biology, it is important to notice its germ in cosmology, in order thoroughly to master the true principle of classification for beings of whatever order.

The Woman.—This admirable continuity enables me, my father, better to judge the noisy disputes which at times arise between the different departments of science. The natural predilection of my sex for moral explanations disposed me to look on these scientific discussions as in the main attributable to the passions of men. I now see a more justifiable origin for them in the profound uncertainty which, from want of encyclopedic principles, the different classes of savants must often have felt as to their legitimate sphere, in consequence of this almost imperceptible succession of their respective domains.

The Priest.—This continuity, my daughter, is the most important philosophical result of the sum of the efforts made by modern reason. For the true scientific genius is shown above all in connecting, as closely as possible, all phenomena and all beings. Practical genius completes later this general result ; since our artificial improvements always end in strengthening and developing the natural connections. Thus you should begin to feel that the modern spirit is not exclusively critical, as it is accused of being, and that it substitutes durable constructions for the decrepit remnants of the old doctrine. At the same time, you may already see at this point the necessary incompatibility of the theological and Positive regimes, by virtue of the irreconcilable opposition between laws of nature and supernatural wills. What would become of this admirable order, which, by a graduated series, connects our noblest moral attributes with the humblest natural phenomena, if we were obliged to introduce into it an infinite power whose capricious action, allowing of no prevision, would threaten it at any moment with an entire subversion?

The Woman.—Before grasping directly this general continuity, there remains for me, my father, a great gap to fill as regards the vital order, the systematic conception of which you must now explain to me. In our encyclopedic descent I already saw its natural connection with the human order. But I cannot get to see as yet how it connects in itself with the inorganic order : for an impassable abyss seems to me to separate the domain of life from that of death.

The Priest.—Your difficulty, my daughter, is in full conformity with the historical progress of the initiation of the race. It is scarcely two generations since true thinkers were able to begin to form a clear conception of this fundamental connection, which is the capital problem of all natural philosophy. It was incumbent, in the first place, on cosmologists, through the advent of chemistry, to push the study of the material order on to its noblest and most complicated phenomena. But it was after that incumbent on biologists to descend duly to the lowest and simplest functions of life, the only ones that could connect directly with this inorganic basis. Such was the chief result of the admirable conception due to the true founder of the philosophy of biology, the incomparable Bichat. As the result of a profound analysis, the most noble vital functions were represented by it as always resting, even in man, on the lowest, in obedience to the general law of the order of nature. Animality is throughout subordinate to vegetality, or the life of relation to that of nutrition.

This luminous principle leads us to see that the only phenomena really common to all living beings consist in the decomposition and recomposition which their substance is constantly undergoing from the action of their milieu. The whole system of vital functions thus rests on acts which have a strong analogy with chemical effects, from which they only differ essentially by the instability of the combinations, which are, moreover, more complicated. This simple and fundamental life is found only in plants, where it reaches its highest development, since there it directly transmutes inorganic materials into organic substances, which is never done by higher beings. The general definition of animality consists, in fact, in the living nature of the substances which nourish it : whence follow, as necessary conditions, the capacity of discerning these substances and the power of seizing them ; consequently sensibility and contractility.

To consolidate his fundamental analysis of life, the great Bichat had shortly to construct an anatomical conception which might be at once its complement and its condensation. The cellular tissue, alone universal, is the proper seat of vegetative like ; whilst animal life resides in the nervous and muscular tissues. Then the general idea of biology is complete, so as to render possible in all cases a sufficient agreement between the statical and dynamical point of view, to enable us to pass properly from the function to the organ or the reverse.

In obedience to the precept of logic which bids us study all phenomena especially in the beings where they are at once most strongly marked and most free from any complication with higher phenomena, the theory of plants becomes the normal basis of biology. It establishes directly the general laws of nutrition by a consideration of the simplest case and the one where they are seen in most intensity. This is the only part of biology which could be absolutely separated from sociology, were not the subjective arrangement always paramount over the objective cultivation. It is there that is directly effected the natural transition from inorganic to vital existence.

The Woman.—I see by this, my father, that the encyclopedic continuity can be established in reference to the lower portion of the scientific hierarchy. But in starting from a vitality so low as this simple vegetality, I do not see how we can rise to the true human type, although I recognise our own subjection to the laws of nutrition, as much as to those of weight.

The Priest.—The difficulty which you experience, my daughter, corresponds in fact to the most important artifice of biology, gradually constructed, by biologists from Aristotle to Blainville, in order to form an immense scale, at once objective and subjective, destined to connect man with the plant. If these two extremes alone existed, a supposition which in no way involves a contradiction, our scientific unity would become impossible or at any rate very imperfect, in consequence of the sudden break thus introduced into encyclopedic continuity. But the immense variety of animal organisms enables us to establish between the lowest form of life and the highest a transition as gradual as our intelligence should require .

Still, this concrete series is necessarily discontinuous, by virtue of the fundamental law which upholds the essential permanence of each species in the midst of its secondary variations. The old intellectual system was a great obstacle to the upward growth of this great construction, by its vain endeavour to find therein the absolute result of the objective relations. But the predominance in our encyclopedia of the subjective method puts a final end to these sterile and endless debates, by always subordinating the formation of the animal series to its true object, which is logical rather than scientific. As we ought to study the animals only to gain a sounder knowledge of man by connecting him with the plant, we are fully authorised to exclude from such a hierarchy all the species which would disturb it. An analogous motive enables us, or rather commands us, to introduce under proper restrictions some purely imaginary races, specially created to facilitate the leading transitions, without any shock to the statical and dynamical laws of animality. The fuller study of certain animals really belongs to the domain of practice, in the case of the few species with which the human race finds itself, on various grounds, more or less connected. All other specialties in zoology would be but the result of an intellectual degeneracy, in a science which by its complication and vast extent is more exposed to academic absurdities, so numerous even in mathematics.

But the whole constituted by the animals adapted to form a true series will always have for us a profound abstract interest, as serving to throw light on the general study of all our lower functions, as we trace each of them in its gradual simplification and complication. Humanity being, at bottom, but the highest degree of animality, the highest notions of sociology, and even of morals, have necessarily their first germs in biology, for the really philosophical minds which can detect them there. Our sublimest theoretic conception thus becomes more within

our ken, when we look on each animal species as a Great
Being more or less abortive, from the inferiority of its
own organisation and the development of the predominance of man. For collective existence always constitutes
the necessary tendency of the life of relation which is the
characteristic of animality. But this general result cannot, on 'one and the same planet, be fully attainable by
more than one of the sociable species.

The Woman.—From these explanations as a whole, I
see, my father, how biology, when cultivated philosophically, can finally fill up all the serious gaps in the encyclopedia, by forming a gradual transition between the
external order and the human. This immense progression, at once of beings and phenomena, in constant conformity with the hierarchical principle of Positivism,
connects, at its lower end, with the regular succession of
the three essential modes of material existence. I thus
see attainable the full realisation of the admirable continuity which at first seemed to me impossible. But
before quitting the vital order properly so called, I should
be glad to know more clearly and precisely the two
essential parts of its domain, vegetal and animal life.

The Priest.—This legitimate wish, my daughter, will
be duly gratified by mastering the three great laws which
govern each of them. You must see in them so many
general facts, subordinate to one another but completely
distinct, and which taken together always explain, both
the continuous functions of the life of nutrition, and the
intermittent functions of the life of relation.

The first law of vegetality, the necessary basis of all
vital studies, without excepting the case of man, consists
in the renewal of its substance to which every living
being is constantly subject. On this fundamental law
follows that of growth and decay, ending in death,
which, not in itself the necessary consequent of life, is
everywhere found to be its constant result. Lastly, this
first biological system is completed by the law of repro-

duction, by which the preservation of the species compensates the loss of the individual.

The chief property of all living beings is the capacity each has to reproduce its like, as itself sprang from its like. Not merely does no organic existence ever emanate from inorganic nature. But, further, no species whatever can spring from another, either inferior or superior, allowing for the variations within very narrow limits, as yet but little known, which each species admits. There is then a really impassable gulf between the worlds of life and of inert matter, and even, though less broad, between the different modes of vitality. Whilst it strengthens the position that any simply objective synthesis is impossible, this view in no way impairs the true subjective synthesis, which throughout results from a very gradual ascent towards the human type.

As for the three laws of animality, the first consists in the alternate need of exercise and rest inherent in the whole life of relation, with no exception for our noblest attributes. This characteristic intermittence of the animal functions naturally connects with the beautiful observation of Bichat on the constant symmetry of their organs, either half of which can be in action whilst the other half remains passive. The second law, which, as in all other cases, presupposes the preceding without being its consequent, proclaims the tendency of every intermittent function to become habitual; that is to say, to reproduce itself spontaneously when the original stimulus has ceased. This law of habit finds its natural complement in that of imitation, nor are the two really distinct. According to the profound reflection of Cabanis, the aptitude to imitate others is, in fact, a result of the aptitude to imitate oneself; at least in every species endowed with sympathy. Lastly, the third law of animal life, subordinated to that of habit, consists in the perfectibility, both statical and dynamical, inherent in all the phenomena of relation. For each of them, exercise tends to strengthen the functions and organs, prolonged disuse to weaken them. This last law, which rests on the two others whilst remaining distinct, condenses the whole theory of animality, as you at first saw was the case with the last law of vegetality.

Combining these two great laws, we form a seventh law of life, that of hereditary transmission, which deserves a distinct scientific appreciation, although logically it is only a necessary consequence of the preceding laws. As every animal function or structure is perfectible up to a certain point, the capacity of every living being to reproduce its like will have power by this law to fix in the species the modifications which have taken place in the individual when they are sufficiently deep. There follows from this the improvement, limited but continuous, dynamical in the main but also statical, of every race whatever, by a succession of regenerations. This high faculty, which condenses spontaneously the two systems of biological laws, is the more developed in proportion as the race is higher and as such more modifiable as well as more active, by virtue of its greater complexity.

Although the general laws of hereditary transmission are as yet too little known, the above consideration indicates its high efficacy as regards the direct amelioration of our own physical, intellectual, and above all moral nature. It is indisputable, in fact, that vital heredity is as applicable, nay, even more applicable, to our noblest attributes as to our lowest. For phenomena become more modifiable, and consequently more perfectible, in proportion as they are by nature higher and more special. The valuable results obtained in the principal races of domestic animals can convey but a faint idea of the improvements reserved for the most eminent species, when it shall be systematically guided, under its own providence.

The Woman.—This general conclusion of the study of vitality makes me, my father, fully see its theoretical and practical importance. I feel thus prepared for the direct study of the human order, for which you reserve our last conversation on the Positive doctrine.

The Priest.—You may, my daughter, find it useful to sum up, under its most important philosophical aspect, this conversation as a whole, guided by the simple contrast which you must have observed, in our encyclopedic synopsis, between the two divisions of Positive Philosophy, the historical and doctrinal divisions. The first, which is adapted to every scientific initiation, individual or collective, brings biology nearer to cosmology; the other, which represents our ultimate state, combines it, on the contrary, with sociology. This contrast brings out clearly the principal characteristic of the vital order, as the natural link between the external and the human order.

CONVERSATION VIII.

THE HUMAN ORDER, FIRST SOCIAL, THEN MORAL.

The Woman.—Before we enter on the highest province of science, I should, my father, submit to you a general difficulty, the outcome of the metaphysical objections I have often heard urged against this capital extension of the Positive doctrine. Any subjection of social and moral phenomena to invariable laws, similar to those of life and matter, is now represented, by certain reasoners, as incompatible with the liberty of man. Though these objections have always seemed to me purely sophistical, I never knew how to break their force with the minds, still too numerous, which let them thus act as a check on their instinctive tendency towards Positivism.

The Priest.—It is easy, my daughter, to overcome this preliminary difficulty, by a direct definition of true liberty.

Far from being in any way incompatible with the order of things, it consists throughout in obeying without hindrance the laws applicable to the case under consideration. When a body falls, it shows its liberty by moving, according to its nature, towards the centre of the earth, with a velocity proportionate to the time, unless the interference of a fluid modify its natural action. So, in the vital order, every vegetative or animal function is said to be free, if it is performed according to the laws applicable to it, without any hindrance from within or from without. Our intellectual and moral existence always admits of a similar judgment which, evidently indisputable as regards action, becomes therefore necessary for affection as its motor and for reason as its guide.

If human liberty consisted in obeying no law, it would be even more immoral than absurd, as making all regulation impossible, for the individual or for the society. Our intelligence most fully evidences its liberty when it becomes, in accordance with its normal vocation, a faithful mirror of the world without, in spite of the physical or moral influences which might tend to disturb it. No mind can refuse its assent to demonstrations which it understands. Nay, more, no one can reject the opinions which are generally received by those among whom he lives, even when he knows not their true grounds, unless he be preoccupied by a counter-belief. For instance, we may challenge the proudest metaphysicians to deny the earth's motion, or still more recent doctrines, though they have no knowledge whatever of their scientific proofs. It is the same in the moral order, which would become one mass of contradictions were it possible for every one, at pleasure, to hate when he ought to love, or the converse. The will admits of a liberty similar to that of the intellect, when our good instincts acquire such ascendency as to bring the impulse of affection into harmony with its true purpose, overcoming the antagonist motors.

Thus, throughout, true liberty is inherent in and sub-

ordinate to order, human as well as external order.
But in proportion as the phenomena become more complicated, they become more exposed to disturbance, and
their normal state presupposes more effort, for which,
however, there is scope owing to their being more open
to systematic modifications. Our best liberty, then, consists in making, as far as possible, our good inclinations
prevail over our bad ; and here, too, it is that our power
is most extensive, provided that our intervention always
conform to the fundamental laws of the universal order.

The metaphysical doctrine on the so-called moral liberty
must be considered historically as a passing result of
modern anarchy. For its direct aim is to sanction complete individualism, to which has tended more and more
the insurrection of the West which naturally succeeded
the Middle Ages. But this sophistical protest against
all sound discipline, whether private or public, can in
no way hamper Positivism, though successful as against
Catholicism. It will never be possible to represent as
hostile to the liberty and dignity of man the doctrine
which places on the surest basis, and gives freest scope
to, his activity, intelligence, and feeling.

The Woman.—This preliminary explanation will enable
me, my father, henceforth to meet sophisms which have
yet too great weight with minds deficient in cultivation.
Would you then explain at once the capital extension of
the Positive doctrine to the social world ?

The Priest.—At the outset, my daughter, you must
look on this great science as made up of two essential
parts : the one statical, which constructs the theory of
order ; the other dynamical, which sets forth the theory
of progress. Religious instruction looks most to the
former, for there the fundamental nature of the true
Great Being is the direct object of study. But the
second must complete this conception, by explaining the
successive destinies of Humanity, in order to give a
right direction to our social action. These two halves of

sociology are closely bound one to another by virtue of a general principle which Positivism establishes in order to connect throughout the study of movement with that of existence : *Progress is the development of order.* Such a law, applicable even in mathematics, finds a larger application in proportion as the phenomena become more complicated. For the distinction then becomes more marked between the statical and the dynamical state; whilst the simplification produced by this connection of our studies also acquires greater value. Sociology then would naturally offer the best application of this great principle, and the true source of its systematisation. In this science it is as applicable in its inverse as in its direct sense. For the successive states of Humanity must in this way throw more and more light on its fundamental constitution, all the essential germs of which are necessarily contained in its rudimentary beginnings. But the theoretical and practical efficacy of dynamic sociology will be specially delineated in the two conversations which will conclude this Catechism. For the present, then, I should confine myself to explaining to you the principal notions of social statics.

The Woman.—Such a limitation, I may add, my father, suits my inadequate knowledge of history. Though the conceptions of social statics must be more abstract than those of social dynamics, I shall find it easier to grasp them, if I give the attention which their importance and difficulty call for. There, at any rate, I shall feel supported against my ignorance by the certainty of finding in myself the confirmation of a doctrine emanating directly from our nature.

The Priest.—It is in fact enough for you, my daughter, attentively to examine yourself to see at once the necessary constitution of the social order. For, in order to represent the general existence of Humanity, it must present unmistakably a combination of all our essential attributes. Though your own existence shows you them indistinctly, it makes you sufficiently alive to them for you to be able better to grasp their fundamental harmony, when collective organs enable each of them to have the expansion which shall fully express them.

Conceive of the Great Being then as being, as you are, only in a more marked degree, directed by feeling, enlightened by intelligence, and supported by action. At once you have the three essential elements of society, the sex in which affection prevails, the contemplative class, that is, the priesthood, and the strength of the active class. They are thus ranked according to their decrease in dignity, but also according to their increase in independence. The last then is the necessary basis of the whole economy of the Great Being, by the fundamental law, now familiar to you, that the noblest attributes are in all cases subordinate to the lowest.

In reality, the unintermitting wants arising from our bodily constitution enforce on Humanity a material activity which governs the whole of her existence. Only able to develop itself by an increasing co-operation, this activity, the most powerful stimulant of our intelligence, supplies in especial the strongest excitement to our sociability. In it our activity more and more subordinates solidarity to continuity, which is the seat of the most characteristic as well as the noblest attribute of the Great Being. For the material results of human co-operation depend more on the combined action of the successive generations than on that of the contemporaneous families. Far from being radically unfavourable to intellectual and moral advance, this continuous preponderance of active life ought then to furnish the best security for our unity, by providing the intellect and the heart with a definite direction and a progressive aim. Without this all-pervading impulse, our best mental, and even our best moral dispositions, would soon degenerate into vague and incoherent tendencies, which would end in no progress either for the individual or the community.

Still, the necessarily personal origin of this activity will at first stamp it with a profoundly egoistical character, only to become altruistic under the gradual transformation due to the collective advance. This is why, in order fully to understand the general constitution of social order, we must break up the active class into two constituents always distinct and often in opposition. They have as their special object to develop, one the practical impulse, with the personality implied in its chief energy, the other the reaction of society which more and more ennobles it.

For this indispensable decomposition, it is enough to take the active power under the heads of concentrated and dispersed, according as it is the result of wealth or of number.

Though the first can only tell indirectly, it is generally the stronger, and is so more and more even, as representing continuity, whilst the second answers to solidarity. For the material treasures which Humanity entrusts to the rich are mainly formed by a long antecedent accumulation, in spite of the permanent need for the partial replacement which their necessary consumption involves. All strong practical impulsions then must come from the patriciate in which are vested these powerful nutritive reservoirs, the chief social efficiency of which depends on their concentration in individuals. Thus it is that material property receives a direct sanction from the Positive religion, as the essential condition of our continuous activity, and so indirectly the basis of our noblest progress.

The second practical element, without which the first would be worth nothing, is the proletariate, which forms the necessary basis of every nation. Unable to gain social influence except by union, it has a direct tendency to bring into play our best instincts. Its conditions draw unceasingly its main attention towards the moral regulation of an economy the disturbances of which fall especially on it. Naturally relieved from the serious responsibility and the mental absorption which all authority habitually brings, be it theoretical or practical, the proletariate is well fitted to remind by its own action both the priest-hood and the patriciate of their social function.

The Woman.—I believe, my father, that this con-tinuous influence of the active class is not less indispen-sable to control or to compensate the exaggeration of feeling by women. Not mixing in active life, my sex is often disposed not to see or not to allow for the rough conditions it imposes. But the feeling which sways it can always make it accept them nobly, in order to attain the good which is its natural aspiration ; when this necessary stimulus leads us to a right estimate of those conditions.

The Priest.—You have thus, my daughter, reached by yourself the complete understanding of the great social function which marks the proletariate. For if even the affective sex can forget its true mission, from being too exclusively occupied with its own wants, the speculative and the active powers are naturally far more exposed to this danger, as their attention is habitually engrossed by special efforts. The moral providence of women, the in-tellectual providence of the priesthood, and the material providence of the patriciate, require then to be completed by the general providence derived from the proletariate, so to form the admirable system of human providence in its entirety. All our powers, each according to its nature, may thus always conduce to the preservation and per-fecting of the Great Being.

This general conception of our social constitution suffices to characterise its three essential elements. Ranked by their decreasing aptness to represent natu-rally Humanity, they follow the same order in the pre-dominant influence they successively exercise in every complete education. The providence of woman, which should always preside over our moral growth, first leads us to feel continuity and solidarity, by directing the un-systematic education which is given in the bosom of the family. Next the providence of the priesthood teaches us the systematic conception of the nature and destiny of the Great Being, by disclosing to us step by step the whole order of the world. Lastly, we come directly and permanently under the power of the material providence, which initiates us into practical life, the influences of which on affection and thought complete our preparation.

So a natural coincidence between our full individual development, as well of the brain as of the body, and the completion, as a general rule, of our initiation as members of society, constitutes our real maturity. Then begins our second life, a life essentially of action, following the whole series of preparations which fit us for the right service of Humanity. This fresh stage of objective existence, though usually shorter than the first, is alone decisive in gaining for each head of a family the subjective existence which shall incorporate him in due form into Humanity.

The better to understand the social constitution, we must consider separately its two most special elements, the only classes properly so called, the priesthood which counsels, the patriciate which commands. With them respectively are preserved and increased the spiritual and material treasures of Humanity, to be properly distributed, in accordance with their natural laws, amongst all her servants.

From the theoretical class in the first place comes systematic education, in the next a consultative influence upon the whole of life, in order to accord therein each particular activity with the general harmony, which active life leads us to neglect. The admirable institution of human language, though always the result of the co-operation of all, becomes the special patrimony of the priesthood, as the natural depository of religion, and the chief instrument in its exercise. By its nature imperishable, spiritual wealth may be useful to all simultaneously without ever being exhausted ; so that its conservation needs no distribution, and is but a simple adjunct of the priestly

office. Eminently synthetical and social, language consolidates and develops the natural subordination of the
human order to the external. It also increases our mutual
union, most of all by establishing a close connection between systematic wisdom and common reason.

Material products, as destined for individual consumption and as perishable by nature, have to obey quite other
laws in their preservation and use. Over and above the
collective attention of the patriciate, aided by the general
watchfulness, they require to be appropriated to individuals, as otherwise the concentration which is normal for
them would become illusory, or rather impossible. This
personal appropriation, the primary basis of the material
providence, must rest on the land, or it will not attain
the requisite stability, the land being the natural seat
and necessary source of all material production. Thus
by a natural process are formed, through the ages, the
nutritive reservoirs of Humanity, which have everywhere
to renew incessantly man's material existence, whilst
their managers direct the labours required for their
continuous replacement.

This chief office of the patriciate consists in restoring, to
each organ of society, the materials which he is constantly
consuming, as provisions for his subsistence or as the
instruments of his function. Wages have never any other
legitimate function, whatever the class that receives them.
In fact, the labour of man, that is to say, the useful
effort of man to react against his destiny, cannot be other
than gratuitous, because it does not admit of nor require
any payment in the strict sense. A true equivalence can
only exist as between the materials of labour, and not
between its essential attributes. Always recognised in
the case of the affective sex and the contemplative class,
nay, even for the practical power which pays the wages of
the rest, this inherent gratuitousness of all human services is left in doubt only as regards the proletariate, that
is to say, for those who receive the least. Such a contra-

diction clearly indicates the source historically of this anomaly, essentially due, not to the inferiority of the labour in question, but to the long servitude of those who give it. Positive religion alone can on this point overcome modern anarchy, by awakening in all the sense that no individual service ever admits of other reward than the satisfaction of rendering it and the gratitude it excites.

The Woman.—Vulgar minds may at the present day tax this view with sentimental exaggeration, but I venture to promise you, my father, that it will soon meet with a cordial reception amongst women. I have often been shocked at the prevailing egoism, which, on the strength of a very small salary, acquits us of all gratitude for important and difficult services, services which endanger the health, and sometimes the life, on each occasion, of those who perform them. This Positivist principle gives systematic consistence to feelings universally felt, which only require a formal statement and co-ordination to secure their gradual prevalence. It completes the process by which I have been brought to see that it is possible at length to stamp on our whole existence, even our material existence, a really altruistic character. All that this holy transformation in fact requires is that each, without being in a state of habitual enthusiasm, should feel deeply his real participation and that of all others in the common work. Now, such a conviction can certainly be produced by a wise education imparted to all, in which the heart will dispose the intellect ever to grasp truth as a whole.

The Priest.—To complete the fundamental view of social order, it remains for me, my daughter, to explain the three forms or degrees proper to it.

Every collective organism necessarily offers to view the several essential elements which I have just explained to you. But they have a more or less marked character, and consequently are more or less distinct, according to the nature and extent of the society under consideration.

Their respective predominance leads us to recognise three different associations, to be ranked by the decreasing closeness of the union and their increasing extent. The intermediate one rests on its predecessor and serves as base for the one that follows. The only one of which the natural foundation is love, the *Family*, is the closest and most limited society, the necessary element of the two others. Man's activity then forms the *City*, where the bond results mainly from an habitual co-operation, the sense of which would be too weak if this political association were to unite too large a number of families. Lastly comes the *Church*, where the essential tie is faith, and which alone admits of a real universality, which the Positive religion will inevitably attain. These three human societies have as their respective centres, woman, the patriciate, and the priesthood.

The family from which each comes is always part of some city or other, and even of some church or other. But this last tie, as the weaker, is susceptible of greater variations, though always within fixed limits. When it attains sufficient consistence, it alone gives us the means of reducing to its proper size the city, around which usually centres each existence, by virtue of the natural preponderance of action over intellect and even over feeling. For the social state can only be really permanent in so far as it succeeds in reconciling independence with concert, two conditions equally inherent in the true idea of Humanity. Now, this necessary agreement prescribes for political societies limits much narrower than those usual at the present day.

In the Middle Ages, the inchoate separation between the religious and the civil society made it possible even then to substitute the free incorporation of the nations of the West for the compulsory incorporation originally given them by the dominion of Rome. Thus the West presented, during several centuries, the admirable spectacle of a persistently voluntary union, founded solely on a common faith, and maintained by a common priesthood, between nations whose different governments had all the independence that was requisite.   But this great political result could not survive the premature emancipation of a power which the Positive religion alone will organise aright and definitely enfranchise.   The necessary decline of Catholicism led to a fresh concentration of the temporal power, indispensable at the time to prevent the entire political disseveration to which society was being driven by the increasing disruption of all religious bonds. Hence it was that, notwithstanding the feelings and habits of the Middle Ages the traces of which are yet visible, the nations of the West acquiesced in the formation everywhere of States on far too large a scale.

The political reasons for this exorbitant extension having in great measure ceased, even in France men begin to feel the deep-seated danger of this anomaly, and also the approach of its end.   But the Positive religion will soon reduce these monster associations to the normal size which will supersede any need of force to maintain temporal union between nations between whom spiritual union alone is admissible.   Thus shall we shortly apply the statical principle which considers the Great Being as politically the organ of the simple city, with its complement of the less condensed populations in free connection with it.   The feeling of patriotism, now so vague and weak in consequence of its excessive diffusion, will in the new order be able to develop fully all the energy attendant on this concentration of the city.   But the habitual union of the great cities will become more real and more efficacious by assuming its normal character of a voluntary concert.   The Positive faith will inspire a due sense of the solidarity, and even of the continuity, which ought finally to prevail between all the regions of the earth without exception.

The Woman.—Guided by the whole of your remarks

on the theory of society, I feel now, my father, well prepared to take my seat at last at the highest point of the encyclopedic edifice, each successive stage of which you have brought within my ken. Though moral science must be the hardest of all, its empirical cultivation is too familiar to my sex for it to feel as much alarm at it as at the others. I am therefore glad to reach in due time the systematic study of the individual man.

The Priest.—In truth, my daughter, this necessary terminus of the whole encyclopedic preparation is alone able to satisfy the intellect and the heart. Moral science is more synthetical than any other, and its direct connection with practice gives strength to this natural attribute. In it alone do all the abstract points of view meet spontaneously to build up a general guidance for concrete reason. From Thales to Pascal, every genuine thinker cultivated simultaneously geometry and morals, from a secret presentiment of the great hierarchy which was finally to combine them. The name *microcosm* or *little world* given by the ancients to man even then indicated how entirely the study of man appeared apt to condense all the others. Morals are naturally the only science susceptible of real completeness, without putting aside any essential aspect, as must be the case in each of the sciences which serve as their basis. For when we look on these latter as determining the laws which in each science concern man, they only attain this end by purposely neglecting all the properties higher than their respective provinces, into which they incorporate only the inferior attributes. By this course of decreasing abstraction, the scientific intellect is sufficiently prepared to approach finally the only study which no longer compels it to abstract anything essential from the common object of our various real speculations. Thus only is the meditation of man irrevocably united with the contemplation of woman, to constitute the final condition of human reason.

First cosmology establishes the laws of mere matter.

Then, on this basis biology constructs the theory of life. Lastly, sociology subordinates to the twofold foundation the proper study of the collective existence. But, though this last preliminary science is necessarily more complete than its predecessors, it does not yet embrace all that goes to form human nature. For our most important attributes find in it but inadequate appreciation. Sociology considers in man mainly intelligence and activity, in combination with all our lower properties, but not in direct subordination to the feelings which govern them. This collective development especially brings into relief our theoretical and practical progress. Our feelings only figure in sociology, even in statical sociology, for the stimulation they give to the common life or the modifications they receive from it. Their own laws, to be properly studied, must be studied in moral science, where they acquire the preponderance due to their higher rank in the system of human nature. This it is which often leads minds of an unsystematic order to misconceive the fulness of synthetical character which distinguishes this final science, by them limited too closely to this its chief sphere, around which as a centre all the rest must ultimately be grouped.

The Woman.—The theoretical connection between sociology and morals is still somewhat obscure to me, so I beg you, my father, to disperse these mists before you directly expound the Positive conception of human nature. I have not forgotten the indisputable reasons, which, in our fundamental conversation on the doctrine, made me recognise the objective subordination of morals to sociology; since man is always under the sway of Humanity. But on the other hand, it seems to me that the social science stands in continual need of the more important notions which we should derive from morals as to our true nature.

The Priest. — This very reasonable difficulty, my daughter, will disappear, if you take into account the unsystematic knowledge which in all cases precedes and prepares the way for systematic study. Science is always simply an extension of the common wisdom. Never does it really create any essential doctrine. Its theories are limited to the generalisation and co-ordination of the empirical insight of the reason of mankind, with a view of giving it a consistence and development otherwise unattainable. This relation between the two more especially holds good in moral studies, which, though they could not, owing to their greater complexity, be systematised till the last, always supplied, such is their paramount importance, the main food for the common meditations, especially with women. From this empirical culture there soon emerged notions of great value, in spite of their incoherence, which have been hitherto despised by the systematic intellect only because it could find no place for them in its theological or metaphysical theories. It is for the Positive spirit, alone capable of taking in the social point of view, that it was reserved to generalise them and co-ordinate them, after it had founded the last preliminary science. But its ability to systematise them allowing it to appreciate them at their value in defiance of philosophical prejudices, it was able at once to turn them to account so far as at length to construct sociology. If you examine the way in which we habitually use in sociology the knowledge of human nature, you will soon see that all that we really use is this spontaneous study, far more real than all the moral speculations of earlier philosophers. This empirical sketch may, in fact, suffice for the conceptions which concern the collective existence, before it has been reduced to the systematic shape which the final science alone can give it.

The Woman.—This explanation, my father, entirely removes the confusion in theory which the two essential aspects of the human order presented to me as a secondary question. My ignorance having preserved me from the classical theories of human nature, I could better appreciate the reality of the moral ideas which sociology employs, and see that they coincide with the results obtained by the spontaneous action of the common reason.

The Priest.—To found directly the final science, it is enough, my daughter, if we put in proper systematic form the division which this common reason early recognised in the whole of man's existence, when it distinguished therein feeling, intelligence, and activity. Traceable in the oldest poets, under different forms, this basic analysis finds in them its empirical completion by the general division of our inclinations into personal and social. Though the theories of theology, and still more of metaphysics, were for special reasons unable to embody this last idea, its self-evidence always overcame the sophisms of philosophy in the uncultivated mind. Such is the natural domain, to systematise and develop which is the essential object of moral science. The other true sciences also have always as their highest object the determining the general laws of the commonest phenomena ; as for instance chemistry, with reference to combustion and fermentation.

Although moral science could not be adequately handled by any theology, observe with due honour the original attempt of the true founder of Catholicism to meet the philosophic needs created by the new religious teaching. The great St. Paul, in constructing his general doctrine of the permanent conflict between nature and grace, really sketched, in his own way, the whole moral problem, not merely the practical, but also the theoretic problem. For, this valuable conception was provisionally a compensation for the radical incompatibility of monotheism with the innate existence of the benevolent instincts, which impel all creatures to mutual union instead of devoting themselves separately to their Creator. In spite of all the flaws inherent in such a theory, its development in the Middle Ages is really the only great advance possible for morals between its

rudimentary state in the early theocracy and its recent
formation into a Positive science. The essential results
of the common wisdom found therein, at any rate, a far
better presentment than in the lamentable ontology
which presided over the gradual dissolution of Catholicism. And so the mystics of the fifteenth century, and
above all, the admirable author of the *Imitation*, are the
last thinkers in whose writings, before Positivism, one
can really grasp human nature as a whole, so defectively
appreciated in all the metaphysical systems.

When I remind you of a moral doctrine which was
justly dear to you in your youth, it is not merely that
I wish to honour an attempt now too generally miscon-
ceived. Besides being a provisional substitute for the
Positive theory of human nature, the objective introduction to which still required a long period, it spontaneously prepared that theory by a formal demarcation of
its systematic domain. It was under this influence
that, even prior to the foundation of sociology, the true
scientific genius undertook, on this point, a decisive,
though an inadequate attempt, immediately after the
rise of the philosophy of biology.

The first step was to establish, in this highest province
of science, a general harmony between the statical and
dynamical points of view, by determining the seat of our
chief functions. Despite the metaphysical confusion
which would make the intellect all in all, assigning to it
the whole brain, the common reason had broken through
the mists of philosophical speculation, at least as to our
instincts, especially the personal instincts, on a consideration of their spontaneous energy. The older thinkers
sanctioned their distinct existence, by placing them,
though vaguely, in the several viscera of the life of
nutrition. Still, no organ was allotted to the instincts
of sympathy, and science, agreeing with theology,
always spoke of the passions as if there were only bad
ones. Moreover, the intellect remained undivided, and

its subordination to feeling could find no scientific expression.

Without this historical introduction, you could not duly appreciate the admirable effort of genius by which Gall founded the Positive theory of human nature, though unable to construct it so far as to give it real efficacy; this presupposed sociology. Under this powerful impulsion two general principles were laid down, one dynamical, the other statical, the natural inter-connection of which will always serve as a base for the true study of the soul and the brain. Gall established at once the plurality of our higher functions, mental and moral, and their common seat in the brain, the different regions of which ought to correspond to the real distinctions between them. Notwithstanding the important errors, especially in regard to the intelligence, due to a superficial analysis and an empirical localisation, he succeeded in giving an adequate idea of the general division of our existence, and even in finally sanctioning the benevolent instincts. The imaginary conflict between nature and grace was thenceforward replaced by the real opposition between the posterior mass of the brain, the seat of the personal instincts, and its interior region, where there are distinct organs for the sympathetic impulses and the intellectual faculties. Such is the indestructible basis on which the founder of Positive religion constructed subsequently the systematic theory of the brain and soul, when he had instituted sociology, from which alone could come the requisite inspiration.

The Woman.—I have a glimpse, my father, of the vast philosophical importance of the two principles laid down by the immediate precursor of Positivism. The continuous inter-action of our feelings and our thoughts, as the natural relations of our several instincts, could not be adequately accounted for with such an excessive interval between their positions as was formerly assigned them. The cerebral theory at length enabled us to apprehend these important relations, so as to perfect our real knowledge of them. Still, when we take from the nutritive organs this moral function, alien as it was to their physical, we expose ourselves, it seems to me, to a grave general omission as regards their undisputed connections with our higher functions. The reciprocal influence of the physical and moral nature, exaggerated in the ancient hypothesis, seems to me then neglected in the new view.

The Priest.—The reproach is only applicable, my daughter, to the cerebral theory in its rudimentary state. It does not apply to its definitive state, where these great relations are fully systematised. Retaining of the old opinion the true notions which so long accredited it, we must first limit these vegetative influences to the propensities properly so called, without giving them any direct bearing on the intellectual functions, or even on the active motors. The speculative and active regions of the brain have nervous communications only with the senses and the muscles, in order to perceive the outer world and to modify it. On the contrary, the affective region, which forms its largest mass, has no direct communication with the outer world, with which it is indirectly connected through its special relations with the intelligence and the activity. But, beside these cerebral connections, special nerves bind it closely to the chief organs of the life of nutrition, in consequence of the necessary subordination of all the personal instincts to the vegetative existence. If this general correspondence can be sufficiently specified in detail, as there is reason to hope it may be, it will furnish powerful means for the reciprocal improvement of man's moral and physical nature.

The Woman.—This positive conception of human nature seems to me, my father, quite in agreement with the experience of mankind, especially in that it bases our unity directly on the constant subordination of the intellect to the heart. You had already explained to me that, of the two modes admissible for this preponderance

M

of feeling, the altruistic regime alone can secure for man, even as an individual, a complete and lasting unity, one, however, more difficult to form than the egoistic unity. But this theory of human harmony presents still a serious difficulty, as to how to reconcile it with the first law of animality, which asserts the intermittence of the whole life of relation, with no power to except the functions of the brain. For the true unity cannot be discontinuous. The intellect and the activity can and ought to rest periodically, as the senses and the muscles which correspond to them. On the contrary, affection admits of no suspension. Could we ever cease to love within ourselves and without?

The Priest.—The direct connection between the affective and the nutritive life should lead you, my daughter, to regard the first as equally continuous with the second. To reconcile this necessary continuity with the intermittence common to the whole life of relation, it is enough if we consider the double structure of the brain. All the organs of the brain are, as the senses and muscles, composed of two symmetrical halves, separate or contiguous, each of which can function whilst the other rests. Such an alternation exempts feeling from all interruption notwithstanding the intermittence of the brain. Sometimes the intelligence functions in this way during sleep, if not by the organs of contemplation, in direct connection with the senses, at any rate by those of meditation, where the dependence on the senses is not immediate. This is the origin of dreams, states of temporary mental alienation, in which, as in madness, subjective impulses, without our will, get the upper hand. This occasional persistence of the intellectual functions during sleep enables us to understand, by analogy, the normal persistence of the affective functions. Nay more, it furnishes us indirect evidence of such persistence. For dreams always bear the stamp of the dominant instincts. Since the heart directs the intellect in the waking state despite external impressions, it must assert a greater power over it when these impressions are in abeyance. We may hope, then, that the cerebral theory will ultimately lead to a right interpretation of dreams, and even to their modification, in accordance with the premature aspiration of all antiquity.

The Woman.—I could not, my father, satisfactorily grasp the Positive theory of human nature, unless, after explaining the general relations to one another of the heart, the intellect, and the character, you showed me the systematic division of each of the three into really elementary functions.

The Priest.—It follows, my daughter, from the cerebral table which you see. (*Table C.*) It should become as familiar to you as our encyclopedic table. But though longer, you will find it less difficult. Any person of sufficient age, especially a woman, would soon feel the reality of such an analysis, which, by its nature, can only rest on observations within the reach of all. If special and difficult contemplations were indispensable for its verification, that would be enough to prove it defective. The great efforts it took to construct this synopsis can in no way affect its use, especially for minds preserved from our classical education. For these difficulties depended less on the nature of the problem than on the false theories which prevailed on the subject. Though the earliest sphere of our intellect, it is the last to be included in the gradually attained harmony between the theoretical and practical reason. But this fundamental agreement is at length thus introduced into it; so as to produce in it, better than elsewhere, the progress to which this agreement always gives rise.

This classification of the organs of the brain offers you throughout a fresh application of the universal principle of decreasing generality, on which you have already seen to rest the encyclopedic hierarchy. You observe it especially in the case of the instincts, which are both more numerous and more marked in character. Their decrease in generality in proportion as they become nobler and less energetic is fully verified in the whole of the animal series. In the lowest stages we find only the fundamental instinct of individual preservation, up to the complete separation of the sexes. Then in succession all the other instincts are added, first the personal, then the social, in the order indicated by the conspectus of the brain, in proportion as we rise towards man. This zoological comparison would suffice then to prove the truth of such an analysis, of which it even frequently facilitated the elaboration, always, however, under the guiding inspiration of sociology. The highest portion of the animal series, comprising the mammalia and birds, certainly offers a complete union of all our higher functions, with mere differences of degree. See how the greatest of poets had a presentiment of this fundamental resemblance, when he placed in the midst of the sublime conceptions of his Paradise, this admirable picture of the moral existence of a bird—

> Come l augello intra l'amate fronde
> Posato al nido de' suoi dolci nati,
> La notte che le cose ci nasconde,
>   Che per veder gli aspetti desiati,
> E per trovar lo cibo onde li pasca,
> In che i gravi labor gli son aggrati,
>   Previene 'l tempo in su l'aperta frasca,
> E con ardente affetto il sole aspetta
> Fiso guardando pur che l'alba nasca.
> —DANTE, *Parad.*, xxiii. 1–9.

E'en as the bird, who midst the leafy bower,
Has in her nest sat darkling through the night,
With her sweet brood, impatient to descry
Their wished looks, and to bring home their food,
In the fond quest unconscious of her toil ;
She, of the time prevenient, on the spray
That overhangs their couch, with wakeful gaze
Expects the sun, nor ever, till the dawn,
Removeth from the east her eager ken.
—CARY'S *Translation.*

In this charming description, an animal very far removed from man offers us the same normal co-operation of feeling, intelligence, and activity as exists among us. Such a brotherhood is still more precious for the heart than for the intellect, as extending our sympathies beyond our species, so as to temper our too frequent conflicts with the subordinate races.

The Woman.—Although I am very fond, my father, of watching animals, with the view of tracing in them all our leading impulses, I suppose that the synopsis of the brain may do without this verification, which is not suited to all minds.

The Priest.—Observations limited to our own species are indeed sufficient, my daughter, to dispel all uncertainty as to each part of this Positive theory of the soul and brain. Even the analysis of the intellect, more delicate than the two others as less marked in character, may be verified by facts of daily experience. It is enough to compare in this way the two sexes to see the principal distinction between the organs of contemplation and those of meditation; since the first function is more developed in woman, and the second in man. Similarly we distinguish the two organs of meditation, by remarking that your sex is more adapted for comparing facts, and mine for co-ordinating them. Were our professors as sagacious as most women, and as clear of erroneous views, the strongly marked comparisons supplied by the zoological series would not be needed to convince them on this point.

The Woman.—Before studying the cerebral table, I should like, my father, to clear up some doubts suggested by a first inspection. The instincts, as a whole, seem placed in their right light, except the maternal instinct, which I expected to find under altruism, not under egoism.

The Priest.—You confound it, my daughter, with the sympathetic influences it may have, but which are not inherent in it, since they are often wanting. The observation of animals leaves us no doubt as to this distinction, for it shows us the maternal relation in animals at too low a point in the scale to have the higher sentiments which are associated with it amongst us. But you can dispel all uncertainty without going beyond our own species. However invaluable the improvement in this instinct effected by civilisation, particularly modern civilisation, through the increasing influence of society on the family, it is still possible daily to detect its true nature in women of weak sympathies, where it is easier to isolate it. Then we see that the child, for the mother no less than for the father, is regarded directly as a mere personal possession, an object of tyranny, and often of avarice, more than of a disinterested affection. Only, as the relations which spring from maternity can give a strong stimulus to the instinct of benevolence, they spontaneously aid in the development of these latter in all kindly natures, but they never create the sympathies such a reaction presupposes. On comparing the different states of society, coexisting or successive, we see the true character of an instinct which, previous to its cultivation by the providence of man, often leads to the sale, or even the murder, of children on purely selfish grounds. Besides, look around you and see the principles on which professions are habitually chosen or marriages made ; and ask yourself whether it is not the egoism of the parents that oftenest prevails therein, now that the anarchy of modern times has weakened the influence of society on the family.

The sexual instinct was at times honoured with a similar mistake, not by your sex, which, in general, is not blind to its selfish character, but by men who equally confused it with the sympathies of which, when rightly guided, it may stimulate the growth. All the personal propensities, not excepting the destructive, are open to similar influences, which do not give rise to similar misconceptions, because they are less direct and less marked. This general relation makes it much easier to solve the great human problem, the subordination of egoism to altruism. In truth, the greater energy of the personal instincts may thus serve to compensate the natural weakness of the sympathetic instincts, by originating an impulse which these latter would not find in themselves. Once called out, the benevolent affection persists and grows by virtue of its supreme charm, though this coarser stimulant has ceased to act. The moral superiority of your sex often relieves it from the need of such a preparation, by disposing it to love as soon as it finds objects to love, without seeking in love any selfish gratification. But the coarseness of man can hardly ever dispense with this indirect beginning, which has become especially necessary to public life, to ennoble in it pride or vanity.

The Woman.—For the intellectual functions, I am surprised, my father, to find excluded from the cerebral table the classical faculties—memory, judgment, imagination, etc.

The Priest.—Look on them, my daughter, as results of the mental organisation as a whole, results long regarded as special functions. The comparison of individuals and of the sexes, completed, if necessary, by that of species, proves directly the groundlessness of the old analysis of the intellect and the soundness of the new. For such observation shows us marked and permanent differences as regards contemplation or meditation, but never leads to clear and sure results as to the faculties acknowledged by the schools. The most unimportant judgment requires an habitual concurrence of the five intellectual functions, if it is to establish, between the within and the without, that lasting and unanimous coincidence which is the characteristic of truth. So it is, even more strongly, with each effort of memory or imagination, which often calls for inductions or deductions absolutely analogous to the operations of science. As for the will, it becomes the direct result of every affective impulse sanctioned by the intellect as fit to direct our conduct.

The Woman.—Contrariwise to my last remark, I am
surprised, my father, to see language holding a distinct
place in the cerebral table, instead of being treated as a
product of the whole of our intellectual functions.

The Priest.—Your mistake depends, my daughter, on
your confusing the special aptitude to create artificial
signs with the results that follow on its due subordination to the other mental powers. The intellectual
analysis of Gall was generally inadequate, but he did
not hesitate to assign to language a separate organ, as to
the existence of which the observation of animals, of
men, and of nations, could leave him no doubt.

When left to itself, without any control from the brain,
as is often seen in illness, and at times in health, its
direct activity produces nothing but mere verbiage, which
reason alone transforms into true discourse. In other
cases, on the contrary, the exceptional atony of this organ
hinders the transmission of the most carefully elaborated
thoughts. For the rest, we must not confound, in the
animals, the proper function of language with its vocal
instruments, which do not always correspond to it. Each
higher species has its natural language, understood by the
whole race, and even by the races pretty near it in the
series : but the physical means of communication often
remain very imperfect. As for the actual language of
civilised nations, it is in reality a very complex result
of the whole of man's development. Still its primary
source equally lies in the organ of the brain which leads
us to create, by some means or other, artificial signs,
without any direct thought of the mental and moral
communications to be effected by them.

The Woman.—To complete this important appreciation, pray, my father, point out to me the general use
I ought to make of the cerebral table when I have
sufficiently studied it.

The Priest.—It can, my daughter, become your own
only by a constant application. Women practise them-

selves habitually in discerning, in our actions and language, the feelings and thoughts which really inspire them. Consider the synopsis of the brain as a general instrument for perfecting greatly this function of women. You will often acknowledge that the human soul is not impenetrable. The brain may thus become a book exempt from change, which you will read despite all the artifices of dissimulation. Complete this observation of individuals by the comparison of nations in sufficiently distinct states, and even of the animals which are easily understood, and you will have finished your initiation in the Positive theory of human nature.

But, to avoid or correct mistakes which are but too easy, you must always remember that most of the results observed, intellectual as well as moral, spring from the concurrent action of several functions of the brain. Each of these can seldom be observed alone. So your inquiry will most frequently require an analysis, the elements of which you will always find in our table, and you will combine them till your synthesis adequately represents the case under notice. For instance, envy is the result of a combination between the instinct of destruction and some one of the other six egoistic instincts; under a secret feeling of personal inferiority, mental as well as moral. There are then six kinds of envy, according as its second element is avarice or luxury, etc.

The cerebral table summarises all that is at present really demonstrated in the Positive theory of human nature. This is why the number and position of the intellectual and moral organs are alone indicated by it, without any precise statement as to their form or size. An objective study, not as yet properly organised, can alone complete this subjective theory of the brain, by determining the peculiar constitution of each organ. But we must not set too high a value on this complement, as without it the cerebral theory is sufficient for its chief object, as is shown by this Catechism.

The position of the organs is really the most important point to determine as it is also the most difficult. It at once points out the mutual influences which, without any intervention of nerves, depend on simple contiguity. It is thus easy to explain the relations, otherwise unintelligible, and yet indisputable, between the sexual and the destructive instinct. The order of the organs, especially the affective organs, gives the measure of their respective energy, by the law which you see written in the table. For instance, between two consecutive instincts, we thus see that the destructive is naturally stronger than the constructive instinct. We cannot doubt it, when we see the preference everywhere given it, with no exception for man, when a being thinks it has free choice of its means.

But the noblest use of the cerebral table consists in stating better the human problem, the ascendency of sociability over personality, as you have already so keenly felt before this direct explanation. The three practical qualities are, in themselves, indifferent to good and evil : their sole direct aim is action. As for the five intellectual functions, their true destination evidently consists in serving the three social instincts rather than the seven personal affections : it is the only method, if their own proper growth is to be large and durable. Still, their intrinsic weakness often hinders them from resisting the natural energy of the selfish impulses ; and hence arises the chief difficulty. If the intellect is not false to its holy mission, personality, in itself incoherent, easily submits to a sociability which never refuses it due satisfaction. Harmony thus established between the feeling and the intellect, the activity instinctively follows an impulsion which affords it an inexhaustible field. Ultimately then all depends on a thorough combination of the two contiguous organs which respectively preside over the chief sympathetic instinct and the properly synthetical part of the intellect. By taking the predominant organ as the representative of each of the three regions of the brain, the sacred formula of Positivism is naturally graven on every brain, since it enjoins the habitual harmony of three adjacent organs.

The Woman.—By the whole of this and the preceding conversation I see, my father, that the Positive doctrine is now adequate to the spiritual government of Humanity, as our two first conversations had led me to anticipate. Its profoundly relative character excludes the stagnation inherent in the absolute character of theological doctrine. But this immutability which it claimed really issues in death ; whereas the gradual modifications of Positivism are certain symptoms of a life as lasting as that of the race.   Without waiting for its inexhaustible improvements, I feel that it is already elaborated to the point at which it can direct the actual reorganisation of the West.

The Priest.—This definitive conviction allows me, my daughter, to proceed now to the exposition, first in the general, then in detail, of the Positivist life.   After appreciating Positivism as the true religion, first of love, then of order, we must, in the last place, recognise in it the sole religion fully adapted to human progress in its entirety, and most particularly to moral progress.

Third Part.

—◆—

EXPLANATION OF THE REGIME, OR SYSTEM OF LIFE.

CONVERSATION IX.

THE REGIME AS A WHOLE.

The Woman.—In this final study, I am aware, my father, that I have to be nearly as passive as I was toward the doctrine, though I expect to find in it fewer difficulties. The regime does not offer me an essentially affective domain, as was that of the worship, where at times I could by my own effort anticipate your explanations. Here the heart is no longer competent to inspire me with views which frequently imply the maturest experience and the deepest reflection, both naturally forbidden the sex whose contemplations can hardly pass with good result beyond the limits of private life. For it is now necessary to construct directly the general rules which should preside over human acts, the habitual most of all, but also the exceptional. Now, to determine these rules demands an accurate conception of our whole existence, collective no less than individual, in order to judge the real results attendant on each system of conduct. The aberrations of feeling must in such conception be the more shunned, in that their influence would here be more noxious, from bearing immediately on our practical and social life.

The Priest.—It must not be, my daughter, that this becoming reserve conceal from you the fundamental office assigned to your sex by the whole human regime. The Positive worship has for its main object the development of the feelings required by the disposition to live for others. All our study of the Positive doctrine leads to the conclusion that our true unity consists above all in this living for others. Resting on this double basis, the regime must now secure the direct predominance, in practical life, of this unique principle of the universal harmony. Now, such an aim necessarily implies the close and continuous union of the two sexes, for it depends as much on the heart as on the intellect. In thus passing from theoretical to practical morals, it is the intellect alone that can decide what habits should prevail, and even by what means they gain a footing. But this twofold study would almost always end in nothing if feeling did not impel us constantly to overcome its arduous difficulties. Hence the respective parts of the priesthood and the affective sex in our moral regime. Whilst the priest acts on the heart through the intellect by his judgment of the conduct of each, women should act on the intellect through the heart by securing the spontaneous ascendency of the nobler dispositions. This necessary co-operation is equally applicable in the age of preparation and in real life.

The Woman.—Encouraged by this introduction, I have to ask you, my father, what is the true field of this third part of our religion. Though the regime always concerns the life of action, as the worship has reference to the life of affection, and the doctrine to that of thought, I should find a difficulty in conceiving of its religious precepts as embracing all action indifferently. Yet I do not see on what would rest any distinction.

The Priest.—The practical domain of religion is limited,

my daughter, to the dispositions which are really common
to all, without entering into the particular discharge of
each function. It must, however, accurately appreciate
the different social functions, but only to lay down in regard to them the rules adapted to maintain and develop
the general harmony. All that concerns the detail of
execution appertains to the various modes or degrees of
government properly so called, whether private or public,
and never to the priesthood.

To give more precision to this fundamental distinction, we must now extend to progress the general division
with which your study of the doctrine has familiarised
you as regards order. As we at first divided the universal order into the external and human order, we should
treat in the same way the improvements of which it is
susceptible. We thus distinguish two species of progress,
the one external, the other human. Though both ultimately have reference to ourselves, the last alone concerns
our own nature, and the first is limited to our external
circumstances, which it improves by reacting on all the
existences which have power to influence ours. Hence
we habitually designate as material this external progress,
notwithstanding that it embraces the vital order properly
so called, but only as concerns the species which are useful to us as food or as instruments. The point of view
of progress being necessarily more subjective than that
of order, the uniformity of the language we use cannot
always correspond to the identity of conceptions.

This distinction is a sufficient and apt introduction to
the fundamental division between the practical spheres
of the government and the priesthood. Whilst all the
social forces are, in our view, equally devoted to the perfecting of the whole, we must by this division distinguish
them according as they improve the outward order or
the human. Such is the truest elementary source of the
normal separation of temporal from spiritual action. The
higher dignity of the latter is in that case a consequence

of the natural preponderance of the progress it promotes. Thus, the practical sphere of religion is the perfecting the human order—first physical, then intellectual, lastly and chiefly moral. Different as the three aspects are, their close connection forbids their ever being separated, and it must be respected more even for action than for speculation. As for the external order, its direct and special improvement concerns not religion : it forms the proper province of politics or industry. Still, religion indirectly finds an important though general share in the work, by virtue of the great influence which the state of the human agent necessarily exerts on the actual results of his effort. In all practical work, success requires as its first condition that each co-operator should be honest, intelligent, and courageous. But it is only in this sense that religion takes part in the fundamental constitution of each special industry.

The Woman.—So, my father, morals, as an art, differs from all others by its complete generality. It is the only art which all without exception must learn, since all human beings equally stand in constant need of it. Its unsystematic study then is for all, in proportion to their natural ability and the light they derive from experience. But its systematisation must be left to the priesthood, as a consequence of the priesthood's necessary connection with the whole body of scientific theory. It is in this way that morals seem to form the essential domain of religion, first as science, then even as art.

The Priest.—You ought, my daughter, to complete such a view by taking into account the special participation of the Positive priesthood in each industry as a whole, on the ground that it alone knows all the essential laws of the external order. Although these theoretic notions can never dispense with practical studies, as scientific pride often dreams, they must subserve them as basis and even as guide. After first learning from the priesthood the more important laws of the phenomena to be modified, each practician connects with them all the special developments to which the inductions of his experience lead him. When the progress of his own labours makes him feel the want of new general ideas, it is to the priesthood he must again go for them, instead of disturbing his industrial action by a vain scientific cultivation.

The Woman.—From this explanation as a whole, I think, my father, of the fundamental separation of the priesthood and the government as resulting above all from the necessary division between theory and practice. But the foregoing appreciation essentially relates to progress only, that is to say, to the activity. Now to place so capital a principle on a solid foundation, it would still be necessary, it seems to me, to connect it directly with order properly so called, that is to say, with conservation. If in the social harmony the proletariate should naturally in the main be progressist, my sex, by its passive position, has for its principal function to conserve.

The Priest.—Duly to satisfy you, it is enough, my daughter, to consider the human order from the statical point of view. Study in it existence and not motion, and you will soon arrive at the separation of the two powers, as the all-pervading basis of the social order; your starting-point being the single principle of co-operation, on which Aristotle founded the true theory of the city association resulting from the concert of families. For each servant of Humanity must always be looked at under two distinct but co-existent aspects, first as regards his special office, then in reference to the general harmony. The first duty of every social organ is, without doubt, the right discharge of his own function. But good order also requires that each assist, as far as he can, all others in the discharge of theirs. Such assistance becomes even the chief characteristic of the collective organism, as a consequence of all its agents being intelligent and free.

Now, from their nature these two offices of each human functionary, the one special, the other general, are in more and more marked opposition to each other. For, as the first becomes more special in proportion as co-operation is developed, it fosters intellectual dispositions, and even moral tendencies, which are more and more adverse to generality of conception, in itself also become more and more difficult. Such is the true elementary point of view of the general theory of government, first temporal, then spiritual.

As no function, even vital, and still more social, can be rightly performed unless through a special organ, the humblest co-operation of man requires a force specially charged to bring back to general views and feelings agents whose constant tendency is to abandon them. It must unceasingly restrain their divergences and foster their convergences. From another point of view, this indispensable power is a natural outgrowth of the inequalities always attendant on human advance.

Deep as is the sympathy which constitutes the simple association of the family, even when reduced to the original pair, it is yet never exempt from this necessity. It is there that we can best appreciate this great axiom : *There exists no society without a government.*

In the civic order, each combination of families for a given end soon throws up a practical leader whose authority is limited naturally by the amount of the operations which either his ability, or still more his capital, enables him really to conduct. In such chiefs is vested the true temporal power, which can equally impel or hold back as need directs. All power on a larger scale necessarily has a spiritual origin. The several practical chiefs have, however, a tendency to mutual co-ordination on the basis of a hierarchy determined by the natural relations of their several departments. This instinctive concert establishes then a kind of government, but more general, always reduced to its material power,

N

more qualified for resistance than direction. Its several
members are usually unable to grasp the whole system
in which they move, though each is competent as regards
one of the component systems.

Solidarity alone then would suffice, if not too restricted,
to indicate the inadequacy of the practical power, and
the need of a theoretic authority, which, renouncing all
special action, has to secure the constant supremacy of the
general harmony. But continuity, on which the human
order more and more depends, places this necessity beyond all dispute. These empirical powers, whilst aspiring to direct the present, know neither the past which
governs it nor the future which it is preparing. Their
interference is therefore blind and often disturbing, when
they do not submit it to the advice of the priesthood.
At the same time, they cannot dispense with the influence of the priesthood, as alone able to give an adequate
sanction to their temporal ascendency, almost always
liable to be jealously disputed. Each consecration consists in representing the power sanctioned as the minister of a higher power which all respect—God under the
provisional regime, Humanity in the final. Now this implies always, but more particularly as regards this final
state, that the present is duly connected with the past
and with the future. The priesthood, which alone can
establish this twofold connection, thus becomes the necessary consecrator of all human powers, without needing
for itself any consecration from an external power, since
it is the immediate organ of the supreme authority.

Here we see the source of this second axiom : *No
society can be maintained and developed without a priesthood in some form or other.* Equally indispensable to all
for education and counsel, this theoretic power is alone
competent to consecrate the governors and protect the
governed. It is the normal moderator in public life, as
women are in private life ; not forgetting, however, that
both these forms of existence demand the continuous con-

currence of moral influence and intellectual power. You
may condense all the social attributes of the priesthood
by adopting the biblical name, *Judge*. For, its threefold
office of adviser, consecrator, and regulator, is discharged
always by judging, that is to say, on the basis of an
appreciation which commands respect.

The Woman.—Catholicism had fortunately prepared
me, my father, to apprehend aright this fundamental
principle, disregarding the popularity of the Protestant
and deistic sophisms, aimed, with a blind fury, against
the chief construction of the Middle Ages. But I do not
quite see why Positivism, whilst it consolidates and
carries farther this grand but inchoate conception, ad-
heres to expressions which at first sight seem only refer-
able to its theological origin, though susceptible of a
purely natural sense. Over and above the just respect
inspired by this historical nomenclature, I suppose that it
also rests on dogmatical grounds, though I do not discern
them.

The Priest.—They are especially derived, my daughter,
from the want of homogeneity traceable in these two
expressions, which thus by their contrast recall the two
principal characteristics of the great social division, instead of merely pointing to one. In terming the theoretic
power *spiritual*, we make it clear that the other is purely
material. Thereby we indirectly indicate the best point
of comparison between them socially, which consists in
looking at them as disciplining, one wills, the other acts.
Conversely, to call the practical power *temporal*, is to suggest with sufficient force the eternity which is characteristic of the theoretical power. By the aid of these
distinctions, we define satisfactorily their respective provinces ; on the one hand the present, on the other the
past and future : the one specially establishes solidarity,
the other continuity ; to the one belongs above all the
objective, to the other the subjective life. Now, these
two essential attributes, simultaneously indicated by the

very discordance of the names in use, concur in recalling
also the last contrast between the two human powers,
namely, as to their respective extent. For the theoretical
power, whether as spiritual or as eternal, by its nature
admits of complete universality; whilst the practical, as
material and temporal, must always be local. From this
last contrast, if drawn out to its full consequences, the
separation follows.

The Woman.—My old Catholic habits lead me, my
father, to condense all the essential attributes of the
spiritual power in the systematic direction of the common education, where its exclusive competence admits of
no dispute.

The Priest.—Such is, in fact, my daughter, the fundamental office of the priesthood, which, when it discharges
worthily this main duty, necessarily derives from it great
influence over the whole of human life. Its other social
functions are but the natural consequences or the necessary complement of this characteristic destination. First,
preaching becomes a necessary continuation of it, in order
duly to recall the principles of the general harmony, which
our action in detail often inclines us to forget. Again, it
is on this ground that the spiritual power acquires its
competence to consecrate functions and organs, in the
name of a doctrine which all regard as having permanently to regulate human existence. Similarly it draws
from it its consultative influence on all the important acts
of life, private and public, wherein each man often feels
the need of having recourse voluntarily to the enlightened
and kind advice of the sages who guided his systematic
initiation. Lastly, the education enables the priesthood
to become, by common consent, the regular arbiter in
industrial disputes, by virtue of the equal confidence with
which it naturally inspires superiors and inferiors.

The Woman.—I am thus led, my father, to ask you in
what consists, in the Positive regime, this paramount
function of the religious power. Already I feel that the

education should especially qualify to live for others, in order to live again in others by others, a being naturally inclined to live for itself and in itself. This great change demands the close union of the woman and the priest, acting duly on the heart and the intellect. But I need a more accurate conception of their respective offices.

The Priest.—For that, my daughter, look first on education in its strict sense as naturally ended at the age of emancipation, when each, after receiving the third social sacrament, becomes at length a direct servant of Humanity, which previously kept him as was fit in pupilage. Next break up this preparation of twenty-one years into two main parts, the one unsystematic, the other systematic, the second lasting only half the time of the first. You thus mark off the successive rule of the affective sex and the theoretic power in the whole of human initiation, which is begun by the heart and completed by the intellect, though both always take a share in it.

The first phase, lasting till the age of puberty, must be subdivided into two periods of equal length, separated by the true dentition. Till that period, the mother has the sole direction of an education, which is entirely spontaneous, whether for the body, the intellect, or the moral nature. Though the development of the body should then take the first place, the heart soon plays a capital part, and its action will make itself felt throughout life. The upgrowth of home affections leads the child at this early stage of his existence to the first rudiments of Positive worship, through the adoration of its mother, who necessarily is for him the representative of Humanity ; her distinct predominance, however, being brought within his reach by the institution of language. At the same time, the intellect collects from experience notions of all kinds, which later will supply the materials for the true systematisation. If these natural exercises of the senses and muscles are wisely guided, without ever impairing their spontaneity, the life of thought and the life of action will be judiciously begun, whilst they are in constant subordination to the life of affection. But the mother alone can rightly combine these three aspects. She will urge the child, especially if patrician, habitually to accomplish some practical task, so that he may better understand the difficulty of carrying on the most unimportant work to its natural end, and be in more sympathy with the classes engaged in such labour. These exercises will give accuracy and clearness to his intellect, as well as tenderness and humility to his heart.

From dentition to puberty, we begin to systematise the education in the family, by introducing gradually a series of regular studies. Still, the direction rests always with the mother, who can easily guide purely æsthetic studies, when she herself has received in the needful degree the education which all are to receive. Till that time, all study properly so called should have been carefully eschewed, even reading and writing, allowing for what the child acquires absolutely by itself. But in this period there is born the habit of intellectual exertion, by the development under regulation of the faculties of expression, the culture of which is peculiarly suited to this second phase of childhood. Such a study, in the main kept clear of all rules, consists solely in æsthetic exercises, in which readings in poetry are wisely combined with singing and drawing. Whilst the moral growth continues of itself, the worship soon develops in this period, in proportion as the child gains fresh means of giving better expression to his affections. He should, in fact, sum up all his exercises in a song and a portrait in honour of his mother. At the same time, he acquires a more complete sense of Humanity, as he becomes familiar with the great masterpieces in every art; provided that his taste and his morality are not both at once lowered by an admixture of mediocre productions.

The Woman.—These two periods of the home education convey to me, my father, no sense of serious difficulty except as to religion. Though you may then dispose the child favourably towards it by the heart, no attempt can be made to give him any dogmatic teaching, from the want of the scientific bases, reserved for his last preparatory period. Yet it is not possible to avoid his thinking and inquiring on the subject.

The Priest.—Remember, my daughter, that the growth of each individual must in all essential features spontaneously reproduce the initiation of the race. You will then see that, on this point, the child must be left to follow unchecked the general laws of our intellectual growth. Till dentition he will naturally be fetichist, and then polytheist till puberty. He will be led by these two philosophical states, as the race was, to develop more fully first the power of observation, then the artistic faculties.

As for the questions he may ask his parents, if he perceives that they do not think as he does, the profoundly relative nature of Positivism will always allow them to answer without hypocrisy. Enough if they frankly tell him that the opinions he now holds are natural at his age, but warn him that he will change them soon, by a law which they themselves formerly obeyed. If made to observe that he has already of himself passed from fetichism to polytheism, he will easily believe in further changes, which, it may be added, need not be hastened by artificial means. His intellect is thus diverted from the absolute, whilst his heart sympathises better with the populations which represent these preliminary states.

The Woman.—This point clear, I may now, my father, proceed to the examination of the systematic education. Though always under the guidance of the priesthood, the continuous ascendency which Positivism assigns to the heart over the intellect already warns me that it will never withdraw the adolescent from his family ties. Their daily influence becomes even more needful for him when his scientific studies will be tending to dry up his feelings and foster his pride. I know your profound dislike to our scholastic conventual establishments, where moral corruption grows faster even than stupidity.

The Priest.—Yes, my daughter, it is under the constant superintendence of his mother that the adolescent, after receiving the sacrament of initiation, goes, each week, to the school adjoining the temple of Humanity, to hear from the priesthood one or two lectures on the doctrine. Moreover the chief fruit of this outside teaching depends on the work done in connection with it at home. For the true influence of teaching is to qualify for active thought, rather than to dispense with it.

The general plan of this systematic study of the doctrine of Positivism is naturally pointed out by the encyclopedic hierarchy which delineates the universal order. Its seven primary degrees correspond to as many years of an intellectual noviciate, a quarter of each year being reserved for examination and rest. The number of yearly lessons is thus reduced to forty, one per week, which is sufficient for the philosophical study of each science. Only in mathematics, the extent and peculiar difficulty of the training, which will always be in a scientific point of view the most important, require two lectures a week during the first two years, when the practical apprenticeship is less engrossing. It is thus that, from geometry up to morals, every adolescent must, in seven years, systematically accomplish the objective ascent which exacted from Humanity so many centuries of spontaneous effort.

During this scientific initiation, a monotheism, gradually becoming simpler, offers the adolescent, as the race, a general transition towards Positivism as the goal. The normal uniformity of the Western priesthood will render such study quite compatible with the most useful travels of our proletaries. During the course of these studies, the natural prolongation of the æsthetic training will support the mother's influence in preventing or remedying their moral degradation. At first limited to our living languages, the poetical readings of the Western nations will then take in the Greco-Roman sources of our intellectual and moral development, always, however, without any special master.

After having developed his private worship, and learnt to feel the charm of family worship, the future citizen enters on the direct and systematic adoration of the true Great Being, whose principal benefits he can then worthily appreciate. As the result of this system of preparations the young Positivist deserves the sacrament of admission, when his intellect is at length competent to serve the Family, the Country, and Humanity, without his heart ceasing to love them.

The Woman.—During this last initiation the superintendence of the mother, as it seems to me, my father, will have seriously to consider the deviations from right conduct to which the passions expose the adolescent at that age. The language of physicians on this point has often alarmed me, by making me fear lest the natural laws of our bodily development render these vices as a general rule unavoidable. I should need to be reassured on this particular danger, in regard to which the moral disturbance may besides compromise the intellectual development.

The Priest.—You would, my daughter, attach much less weight to these assertions of medical men, if you knew how profoundly incompetent are those who make them. Though professing to study man, physicians, whether theoretical or practical, especially in modern times, are far from being able to know his nature. For they confine themselves essentially to what we have in common with the other animals; so that their proper name would be veterinary surgeons, were it not that, in the best of them, practice makes up, in some small degree, for the defects of their scientific instruction. Since man is of all living beings the most indivisible, whoever does not study in him body and mind together can form only false or superficial notions of him.

The materialism of our schools of medicine cannot then prevail as against a large and decisive experience, fully explained by the true theory of human nature. This alleged sexual necessity was overcome commonly, during the whole of the Middle Ages, by all those who submitted duly to the discipline of Catholicism and chivalry. Even in the midst of modern anarchy, many individual instances still prove that it is possible to remain really pure until marriage. A life of labour, and above all the uninterrupted play of the family affections, are generally sufficient protection against such dangers, which only in very rare cases become insurmountable, cases erroneously treated as typical by physicians unversed in moral struggles. Our young disciples will be accustomed, from childhood, to look on the triumph of the social over the personal feelings as the grand object of man. They will train themselves to overcome one day the sexual instinct by early struggling with that of nutrition, which it must be remembered is closely connected with it by virtue of the juxtaposition of the respective organs. Lastly you are aware that a deep affection was always the best preservation against libertinage. Thus, the mother will complete the protection of her son against the vices you fear, by leading him to centre on a worthy object the personal affections which are to determine later his home destiny, instead of waiting till such affection come abruptly from chance contacts.

The Woman.—This valuable explanation leaves me, my father, as regards the whole system of Positive education, in want of no other important elucidation except as concerns my own sex in particular. I feel already that, for mothers to direct the initiation of the family, they must themselves in due measure have shared in the encyclopedic instruction from which, with rare exceptions here and there, none must be excluded. In

default of this complete universality, the Positive faith
could never gain the systematic ascendency requisite for
its social mission. Besides, the mother would be unable
to retain in sufficient degree the moral superintendence
of human education, if her ignorance exposed her to the
ill-concealed contempt of a son often puffed up with the
pride of knowledge. Still I doubt as to women, whether
they are to follow the same course of studies as men and
under the same masters, though at separate times.

The Priest. — You have your answer already, my
daughter, from the great Molière, who prescribes to your
sex a general insight, *clear ideas on all subjects.** For,
in fact, our encyclopedic instruction has no other aim.
It is quite free from the character of specialism, which is
justly repugnant to you in the existing education, as little
suited, as a general rule, for men as for women. To this
common stock, the theoretical or practical man must
afterwards, by himself, apply for the further knowledge
which his function demands, not as a general rule needing any private instruction, unless he have but imperfectly profited by the common teaching.

Our general plan of the systematic noviciate really
admits, in the case of your sex, of no other reduction
than halving the number of the weekly lectures which
distinguishes the first two years. Not mixing in active
life, women should confine themselves, in mathematics,
to a logical rather than a scientific training, and for this
one lecture a week is enough, as in all the rest of the
seven years' course. This simplification only requires
greater philosophical efforts from the professor.

As for a difference of professors, it would tend to discredit equally teacher and pupil. Not to say that it
would be contrary to the profoundly synthetical nature
which should be the characteristic of the Positive priesthood. The more entirely to exclude dispersive tendencies,
it is important that each priest teach in succession the

* See p. 49.

seven encyclopedic sciences. A further result of this
should be the great social advantage of fostering, during
this long initiation, unbroken relations with the same
pupils, who will thus be indebted to him for the whole
of their instruction in science. This permanence will
greatly facilitate the after influence of our priesthood
on the whole of active life.

Now, on similar grounds, the two sexes must draw
their systematic education from the same sources. If the
High Priest of Humanity do not change too frequently
the stations of the priests, all family disputes will be
more easily settled through this personal subordination
of the several members of the family to the same masters.
Priests who should only speak to one sex would be
rendered incompetent for their social office, besides being
so intellectually to begin with.

The Woman.—Now, my father, I fully grasp the social
influence which the priesthood of Positivism will derive
naturally from the adequate discharge of its fundamental
office. Still, I am not clear that, on this basis alone, it
will acquire sufficient authority. I beg you then to explain directly the various general means it has at its disposal to secure, as far as possible, the constant harmony
of the whole.

The Priest.—They must all be derived, my daughter,
from the educational system. The better to estimate
them, we must remember that the Positive noviciate ends
in a year entirely devoted to moral science. This last
branch of instruction will be always divided into two
equal portions, one theoretic, the other practical. In the
first, all the essential laws of our nature will be solidly
based on the whole system of our conceptions relating to
the world, to life, and to society. This basis will enable
us to establish definitively real demonstrations as regards
the general rules of conduct applicable to each case,
individual, domestic, or civic. In them there will be
specified all the duties of each of the four powers indis-

pensable to the human providence. These final deter-
minations, which condense the Positive education, may
have a great power, by virtue of the moral disposition
of the taught, as yet kept free from the aberrations
attendant on active life.

The system of these practical rules fulfils for each the
twofold purpose of guiding his own conduct and judging
that of others. This second application of it is better
secured than the first against the disturbing action of the
passions, which seldom prevent us from appreciating the
faults of others, however blind they make us to our own.
An egoist is the last person to tolerate egoism, as it raises
all around him unmanageable competitors.

We must thus distinguish two general modes in the
spiritual discipline, the one direct, the other indirect.
The priesthood's main effort is to change the guilty
person, by acting first on his heart, then on his intellect.
This is at once the purest and most efficacious method,
though the least apparent. It will always remain the
only method perfectly consonant with the nature of the
spiritual power, which should constantly discipline the
will by persuasion and by conviction, with no coercive
influence. But its wise and prolonged use is often inadequate. In such cases the priesthood, not able to
correct the internal tendencies, proceeds indirectly against
them, by an appeal to outside opinion.

Without converting the criminal, it controls him by
the judgment of others. That this indirect mode of
action is perfectly legitimate cannot be denied, as it rests
in all cases on a simple examination of the conduct of
each. No one can bar such a judgment, in which every
one takes part as regards others, and which rests on a
doctrine which has the free assent of all. Yet the
criminal, who does not allow that he is wrong, or whose
will has undergone no change, is thus subjected to the
pressure of a real coercive force. But he cannot object,
as it remains purely moral. If others abstained from

judging, it is they who would be the oppressed party, and
that without having in any way deserved it. Legitimate,
however, as this indirect method evidently is, we must only
have recourse to it when all direct means are exhausted.

When necessary, it admits of three degrees in succession. The priesthood employs first a simple remonstrance
in the family, before the relations and friends called
together for the purpose; then a public censure, pro-
claimed in the temple of Humanity; lastly, excommunication from society, either for a time or for ever. Without
outstepping its just authority, the spiritual power may, in
fact, go so far as to pronounce, in the name of the Great
Being, the absolute unworthiness of a false servant, thus
rendered incapable of sharing in the duties and benefits
of human society. But, if the priesthood abused this
power, either to gratify unjust animosity, or even from
a blind or mistaken zeal, it would be speedily punished
for its fault. For the whole force of excommunication
depending on the free sanction of the public, the neutrality
of the latter would make the blow fail, and by failing it
would tend to discredit its authors. When the general
opinion strongly supports the priesthood in its condemnation, this spiritual discipline will be efficacious to a degree
of which we can form no conception from the past, for
such a concert could not in the past be fully established,
in the absence of Positive education.

Then, however rich or powerful the criminal may be,
he will, at times, without any loss of property, see himself gradually abandoned by his dependants, his servants,
and even his nearest relatives. In spite of his wealth,
he might, in extreme cases, be reduced to provide himself his own food, as no one would serve him. Though
free to leave his country, he will only escape the condemnation of the universal priesthood by taking refuge
with populations not as yet acquainted with the Positive
faith, which will ultimately spread over the whole human
planet. Fortunately this extreme development of religious

discipline will always be exceptional. But its distinct appreciation is necessary here to indicate more clearly the efficacy of our regime.

The Woman.—Whatever be this moral power, I should find it difficult to think, my father, that it ever entirely superseded the recourse to temporal repression, whether directed against property, or even against the person.

The Priest.—In truth, my daughter, legislation properly so called will always be necessary, to make up for the inadequacy of mere moral force as regards the more urgent social needs. Conscience and opinion would be often powerless against daily violations of right, were not the temporal power to apply physical repression in the most ordinary cases. Besides these frequent yet slight deviations, due mainly to the inactivity of the good instincts, the same protection is more suitable to the more serious transgressions resulting directly from the predominance of the bad instincts. There are, in fact, in our species, as in the others, thoroughly vicious individuals, for whom true correctives are useless or undeserved. In the case of these exceptional organisations, society in its own defence will never fail to be driven to the destruction by a solemn act of every vicious organ, when his unworthiness has been sufficiently proved by decisive acts. It is only a false philanthropy that can lead us to lavish on criminals a pity and a care which would find better objects in so many honest victims of our imperfect social arrangements. But, although capital punishment and, still more, total or partial confiscation, can never entirely be given up, their employment will become less and less frequent as Humanity advances. The continuous upward growth of feeling, intelligence, and activity tends more and more to place spiritual discipline above temporal repression, though we can never dispense with this last.

The Woman.—This general glimpse of the regime of man seems, my father, to omit the cases in which the moral perversion should originate with the priesthood itself.

The Priest.—Then, my daughter, the spiritual discipline takes a similar course, though somewhat less regularly. For our moral system is of universal application, and demonstrates the duties of the priesthood as much as those of any other class ; nay, it even brings them into stronger light, seeing their paramount importance. Moreover, the public censure tends by preference to assail these judges of the rest, secretly hated by the patricians, coldly respected by the proletariate, and arousing no deep sympathy, in general, anywhere but in women. Finally, the Positive faith is, by its nature, always open to discussion, which prevents it from creating any prestige strong enough to bar criticism when become really necessary.

Whatever the veneration with which the priesthood of Humanity is habitually regarded, it never has any other source but the adequate discharge of a well-defined office. The intellectual and moral conditions which the spiritual power imposes on all in the name of the common faith may be turned against it, in the same name, when it fails to fulfil them.

If, on the commonest hypothesis, the perversion is partial, the priesthood is competent to meet it by its own internal discipline. But, in case of its neglect, reparation may at any time be freely called for by any believer whatever. The fulness and precision which characterise the Positive faith allow each individual to exercise, for himself, on his own responsibility, this irregular priesthood, which becomes efficient if sanctioned by opinion. Finally, if the corruption were to become general in our priests, a new clergy would soon arise to meet the general wish, fulfilling better the conditions imposed by a doctrine not liable to adulteration, and always superior to its organs, whoever they may be.

The Woman.—I am thus led, my father, to ask you to end this general survey by pointing out the true constitution of the Positive priesthood.

The Priest.—You will easily see, my daughter, that the

first condition required by its fundamental object is a complete renunciation of temporal power, and even of mere wealth. This is the primary engagement which every aspirant to the priesthood must solemnly contract, when he receives, at the age of twenty-eight, the sacrament of destination. Our priests do not even inherit from their families, whether to keep clear of deviations in the temporal direction, or to leave capital to those who can use it. The contemplative class should as a body be always maintained by the active; at first through the free contributions of the believers, afterwards by aid from the public treasury, when the faith is unanimously accepted. It must not then possess anything as its own, land, houses, nor even annuities; allowing for its annual budget, always settled by the temporal power. The generality of views and the generosity of feeling which should always distinguish the priesthood are absolutely incompatible with the ideas of detail and the disposition to pride inherent in all practical power. If you would restrict yourself to advice, you must always be unable to command, even by wealth : otherwise our poor nature remains inclined often to substitute force for demonstration. This condition of the priesthood was felt in its sublimest exaggeration by the admirable saint who, in the thirteenth century, endeavoured, but in vain, to regenerate exhausted Catholicism. But he forgot, when prescribing to his disciples an absolute poverty which they soon evaded, that he was distracting them from their proper office by the daily cares for their subsistence.

The better to define the befitting moderation, I think I should name the yearly stipends of the several ranks of the priesthood, adapting them to the actual rate of expenditure usual in France, which is a mean, on this point, between the different Western nations. This summary statement will, moreover, give you the internal organisation of the Positive clergy, already sketched in outline in the exposition of the worship.

o

Generally it is composed of three successive orders, the aspirants admitted at twenty-eight, the vicars or substitutes at thirty-five, and the priests proper at forty-two.

Though the first, whose number has no natural limit, are already considered as having a real priestly vocation, they do not as yet belong to the spiritual power, and exercise none of its functions. Their free renunciation, therefore, of all inheritance remains simply provisional, as is their stipend, fixed at 3000 francs (£120). Without any clerical residence, they are yet under regular surveillance, as to their work and conduct.

The vicars are irrevocably members of the priesthood, though limited as yet to the functions of teaching and preaching, allowing for special delegation in cases of urgency. Besides their definitive renunciation of property, their admission is conditional on a worthy marriage. They live with their families, but apart from the priests, in the philosophical presbytery annexed to each temple of Humanity, parallel to the Positive school. The class which directs in all other classes the influence of the heart upon the intellect, should itself furnish the best masculine type of moral elevation, by the full development of the family affections, without which the love of the race is an illusion. Though marriage is left optional for other citizens, it becomes then obligatory for the priests, whose office cannot be worthily performed without the persistent influence, it may be objective or subjective, of woman on the man. The better to test them on this point, the Positive religion requires even simple vicars to fulfil this condition. This second rank, which, with exceptions for failure, always leads to the third, secures a yearly stipend of 6000 francs (£240).

During the seven years which separate him from full priesthood, every vicar has taught all the encyclopedic sciences, and duly exercised his powers of preaching. Then he becomes a true priest, and may discharge, in the family or the city, the threefold office of adviser, con-

secrator, and regulator, which is the social characteristic
of the Positive clergy. In this final state, his annual
payment rises to 12,000 francs (£480), besides the
expenses of visiting his diocese.

Every philosophical presbytery is composed of seven
priests and three vicars, whose residences may always be
changed, such change never taking place, however, without really serious justification. The number of these
priestly colleges is two thousand for the whole West:
which gives a spiritual functionary for every six thousand inhabitants; whence we get one hundred thousand
for the whole earth. The rate may appear too low, but
it is really adequate for all the services, from the nature
of a doctrine which seldom demands systematic explanations, almost always replaced by the unprompted intervention of women and proletaries. It is important to
limit as far as possible the priestly corporation, both to
avoid superfluous expense, and still more to secure the
better composition of the clergy.

The Woman.—In this statement I do not see, my
father, the head which is to direct this vast body.

The Priest.—Though its doctrine and its office tend,
my daughter, to give it a self-direction with the aid of
public opinion, it really does require a general head.
This supreme power is vested in the High Priest of
Humanity, whose natural residence will be Paris as the
metropolis of the regenerated West. His income is five
times that of ordinary priests, over and above the expenses necessitated by his vast administration.

He governs alone the whole Positive clergy, ordain-
ing, changing their residence, and even cashiering, on his
moral responsibility, any of its members. His chief care
is to maintain the priestly character in its integrity as
against the various temporal seductions. Any servile or
seditious priest, who should aim at temporal power by
flattering the patriciate or the proletariate, would be ultimately excluded from the priesthood, though in certain

cases finding a place amongst its pensioners, supposing him to have sufficient scientific merit.

In the general discharge of his functions, the supreme head of Western Positivism has the aid of four national superiors, whose income is half the amount of his. Under his direction, they guide the four classes of churches, Italian, Spanish, English, and German.* As for France, there the High Priest is in place of the national superior, though he may be taken from any one of the five Positivist populations. The regular mode of replacing him is, as in the temporal order, his own nomination, but sanctioned in this case by the unanimous assent of the four national superiors, and even, when there is division of opinion, in accordance with the wish of the senior priests of the two thousand presbyteries.

CONVERSATION X.

PRIVATE LIFE.

The Woman.—At the close of the foregoing conversation, I did not ask you, my father, what would be the proper subject of each of the two other conferences on the life. I quite felt that the two halves of the practical domain of our religion must have essentially the same subdivisions, always taken from the existence which they are respectively to idealise and guide. The study of the worship, then, indicated the plan which suits that of the regime, first private, then public life. In that which is our subject to-day, I also feel that you are going to distinguish similarly the individual existence and the family life.

The Priest.—For the first, which becomes the normal basis of all human conduct, its regeneration by Positivism

* See *Pos. Pol.,* iv. p. 426.—*E. Tr.*

consists, my daughter, in placing it on a social footing. This radical transformation, at all times denied to theologism, monotheistic more than any, but constantly anticipated and demanded more and more loudly by the public instinct, is not now the product of any sentimental exaggeration. It rests solely on an accurate appreciation of the real facts, which in the human order, more synthetical than any other, looks to the whole before the parts.

Although every human function is necessarily discharged by an individual organ, its true nature is always social ; since the share of the individual agent in it is always subordinate to the indivisible contribution of contemporaries and predecessors. Everything we have belongs then to Humanity; for everything comes to us from her—life, fortune, talents, information, tenderness, energy, etc. A poet never suspected of subversive tendencies put into the mouth of Titus this decisive sentence, a sentence really worthy of such a mouthpiece :

> So che tutto è di tutti ; e che nè pure
> Di nascer meritò chi d' esser nato
> Crede solo per se.
> —METASTASIO, *Clem de Tito*, Act ii. Sc. 10.

I know that all is from all ; and that not even did he deserve
To be born, who thinks himself born for himself alone.

Similar anticipations might be found in the oldest writings. Thus, Positivism, when condensing all human morality into *living for others*, is, in reality, only systematising the universal instinct, after having raised the scientific spirit to the social point of view, unattainable by the synthesis of theology or metaphysics.

The whole of the Positive education, intellectual as well as affective, will familiarise us thoroughly with our complete dependence on Humanity, so as to make us duly feel that we are all necessarily meant for her unintermitting service. In the preparatory period of life, when incapable of useful action, every one owns his powerlessness as regards his chief wants, the habitual supply of which he sees to come from others. At first he believes himself indebted for it to his family only, which feeds, cares for, instructs him, etc. But before long he discerns a higher providence, of which his mother is for him merely the special minister and the best representative. The institution of language alone would be enough to reveal it to him. For its construction is beyond any individual power, and is solely the result of the accumulated efforts of all the generations of men, notwithstanding the diversity of idioms. Moreover, the least gifted man feels himself continually indebted to Humanity for quantities of other accumulations, material, intellectual, social, and even moral.

When this feeling is sufficiently clear and vivid during the preparation, it is able later to resist the sophisms of the passions to which real life, theoretic or practical, gives occasion. The exertions we habitually make then tend to make us ignore the true providence, whilst overrating our own value. But reflection can always dispel this ungrateful illusion, in those who have been properly brought up. For it is enough if they observe that their success in any work whatever depends mainly on the immense co-operation which their blind pride forgets. The most skilful man with the best directed activity can never pay back but a very slight portion of that which he receives. He continues, as in his childhood, to be fed, protected, developed, etc., by Humanity. Only, her agents are changed, so as no longer to stand out distinct to his view. Instead of receiving all from her through his parents, she then conveys her benefits through a number of indirect agents, most of whom he will never know. To live for others is seen to be, then, for all of us, the everduring duty which follows with rigorous logic from this indisputable fact, the living by others. Such is, without any exaltation of sympathy, the necessary conclusion from an accurate appreciation of reality, when philosophically grasped as a whole.

The Woman.—I am happy, my father, to find thus systematically sanctioned a disposition for which at times I reproached myself as due to an exaggeration of my feelings. Before I became Positivist, I used often to say : " *What pleasures can be greater than those of devotedness to others ?* " Now I shall be able to defend this holy principle against the sneers of egoists, and perhaps raise in them emotions which will prevent their doubting it.

The Priest.—You have, my daughter, unaided anticipated the chief characteristic of Positivism. It consists in finally condensing, in one and the same formula, the law of duty and the law of happiness, hitherto asserted by all systems to be irreconcilable, although the instinct of men always aimed at reconciling them. Their necessary harmony is a direct consequence of the existence in our nature of the feelings of benevolence, as demonstrated by science, in the last century, on a survey of the whole animal world, where the respective participation of the heart and the intellect is more easily traced.

Besides that our moral harmony rests exclusively on altruism, altruism alone can procure us also life in the deepest and truest sense. Those degraded beings, who in the present day aspire only *to live*, would be tempted to give up their brutal egoism had they but once really tasted what you so well call the pleasures of devotedness. They would then understand that to live for others affords the only means of freely developing the whole existence of man ; by extending it simultaneously to the present in the largest sense, to the remotest past, and even to the most distant future. None but the sympathetic instincts can have unimpeded scope, for in them each individual finds himself aided by all others, who, on the contrary, repress his self-regarding tendencies.

This is how happiness will necessarily coincide with duty. No doubt, the fine definition of virtue, by a moralist of the eighteenth century (Duclos), as *an effort over oneself in favour of others*, will always remain applicable. Our imperfect nature will indeed always need a real *effort* to subordinate to our sociality the personality which is constantly stimulated by the conditions of our existence. But the triumph once gained, it tends of itself, not to mention the power of habit, to gain strength and to grow by virtue of the incomparable charm inherent in sympathy whether of feeling or in act.

It is then felt that true happiness is above all the result of a worthy submission, the only sure basis of a large and noble activity. Far from grieving over the sum of the fatalities to which we are subjected, we exert ourselves to strengthen the order they form by imposing on ourselves rules of our own creation, which may more successfully contend with our egoism, the main source of human misfortune. Where such rules are freely instituted, we soon find, according to the admirable precept of Descartes, that they deserve as much respect as the laws not within our choice, which have less moral efficacy.

The Woman.—Such a view of human nature makes me at length see, my father, that it is possible to give an essentially altruistic character even to the rules which concern our personal existence, rules hitherto always grounded on selfish prudence. The wisdom of antiquity summed up morals in this precept : *Do to others as you would be done unto.* However precious at the time this general rule, all it did was to regulate a purely personal calculation. This character recurs if you sift it in the great Catholic formula : *Love your neighbour as yourself.* Not only is egoism thus sanctioned and not compressed, but it is excited directly by the motive on which the rule is based, *the love of God*, without any human sympathy, not to say that such *love* was generally but another expression for fear. Still, when we compare the two precepts, we see in them a great advance. For the first only bore upon acts, whereas the second presses

on to the feelings which direct them. Still, this moral
improvement remains very incomplete, so long as love in
the theological sense retains its stain of selfishness.

Positivism alone becomes at once both noble and true,
when it calls on us to *live for others*. This definitive
formula of human morality sanctions explicitly only the
instincts of benevolence, the common source of happiness
and of duty. But implicitly it sanctions the personal
instincts, as necessary conditions of our existence, provided they are subordinated to the former. With this
sole limitation, their continuous satisfaction is even enjoined on us, so as to fit ourselves for the real service
of Humanity, whose we are entirely.

Thus I understand the strong reprobation with which
I always saw you visit suicide, previously, as it seemed
to me, condemned only by Catholicism. For our life is
less even than our fortune or any of our talents at our
arbitrary disposal; since it is more valuable to Humanity,
from whom we hold it. But, on the same principle, the
Positive religion also condemns, though often due to
respectable motives, that kind of chronic suicide, at least
social suicide, which the Catholic system too often encouraged. I remember that the daily abuse of bodily
discipline had so completely reduced the hermits of the
Thebaid, that their abbots were at length obliged to authorise them to pray sitting, or even lying down, because
they were unable to remain long enough on their knees.

The Priest.—Besides that we ennoble the just satisfaction of the personal instincts by ever subordinating
it to its social purpose, observe, my daughter, that this
necessary subordination becomes the only possible basis
of really unassailable prescriptions on the subject. Without this unique principle, the simplest rules relating to
our individual existence necessarily retain a character of
instability, unless connected arbitrarily with supernatural
ordinances, valid only for certain times and within limits,
with a validity which is now exhausted.

If our sobriety rests solely on personal prudence, it is
often exposed to the sophisms of greediness, which are
even not to be refuted in the case of many individuals,
who can commit excesses for a long time with real
impunity physically. But the social point of view at
once dispels all uncertainty, prescribing for each an
amount of food almost always less than that which he
might take without physical risk. For beyond the very
moderate limits set by our service as regards the Family,
the Country, and Humanity, we are thus consuming provisions which in moral fairness belonged to others. At
the same time the reaction of this bodily regimen on
the brain tends necessarily to degrade our feeble intelligence in science, art, or industry. Images become habitually more indistinct, induction and deduction harder
and slower : all is weakened, even to the faculties of
expression.

But it is the moral influence of the slightest daily
intemperance that is its chief danger, as more difficult to
avoid and more corrupting. For, in thus indulging the
most personal of our acts beyond what is required really
for our support, we are cultivating, as far as possible,
egoism at the expense of altruism ; since we even overcome our involuntary sympathy for those who are at the
time in want of food. Moreover, the close connection in
the brain of the several egoistic instincts soon propagates
to all the others the strong, even if passing, excitement
of any one of them. The admirable painter of human
nature to whom we owe the unrivalled poem of the
Imitation, felt profoundly this normal connection, when
he tells us (book i., chap. xix., § 4) : *Frena gulam, et
omnem carnis inclinationem melius frenabis.—Bridle thy
appetite, and thou shalt the easier bridle all fleshly desires.*
If you read daily this inexhaustible treasure of true
wisdom, substituting therein Humanity for God, you will
soon feel that this final change gives great strength to
such a precept, as to most others.

The wholesome restraint of the instinct of nutrition is still very far short of the systematic extension which it will gradually receive from the Positive religion. For the sophisms of our sensuality continue to treat as essential wants many material stimulations which are rather hurtful than beneficial. Such is especially the use of wine, the Musulman prohibition of which was general and sincere during the centuries in which Islam best displayed the kind of bodily activity for which in particular we think wine indispensable. When we scrutinise as they deserve the admirable designs of the great Mohammed, we soon come to see that by this prohibition he wished radically to improve the whole nature of man, first in the individual, then in the race, by the law of hereditary transmission. This noble attempt has not really failed any more than all the other efforts of the monotheism of the Middle Ages, Eastern no less than Western, to further our highest improvement. Only, as they, it requires to be systematised by Positivism, which will know how to strengthen and develop it, without detriment to the progress of industry. Even at the present day, this salutary abstinence, already so common with your sex, at least in the South, may gradually extend to all the advanced organs of human progress. As Positivism shall prevail, women and priests will freely, throughout the West, allowing for exceptional cases, renounce the habitual use of this stimulant, the more fatal inasmuch as it often leads to many other excesses.

The Woman.—I understand, my father, why you have laid so much stress on the Positive discipline of the nutritive instinct. For, besides its predominance directly and its indirect reaction, it stands here as the sufficient type of all the other restraints we must regularly place on the personal appetites. These rules as a whole give systematic expression, in both sexes, to true *purity*, the first basis of an unshakeable morality. In fact, this precious term must not be confined to the two adjacent organs on

which depends the conservation of the species and of the
individual.   We must make it include also the whole of
the seven personal instincts, which we always have to
purify to a considerable extent, on the ground of their
normal subordination to the unintermitting service of
Humanity.

The Priest.—This great principle, my daughter, will
always be able to surmount all honest doubts on the point,
and even to solve the most captious sophisms.   The heart
of the true Positivist should, in the within, always reject arbitrary wills, as his intellect rejects them in the
without.   Our humble Goddess is, in truth, exempt from
the various caprices attendant on her omnipotent precursor.
All her acts follow intelligible laws, more and more revealed to us by the Positive study of her nature and her
destiny.   By subordinating ourselves to them as much
as possible, we shall without ceasing advance in an inexhaustible progress towards peace, happiness, and dignity.

The Woman.—These indications when combined seem
to me, my father, to delineate clearly the regimen of
individual life in Positivism.   With the cerebral table in
our hand, we might, in reference to each of the egoistic
instincts, carry out a study equivalent to that which we
have just made of the most important, so as to determine
their suitable repression.   As for the means of developing
the several sympathetic instincts, our worship has already
pointed out those which are not a consequence of their
direct action.   All these detailed explanations would
exceed the limits of our present exposition, and would
even divert it from its main object.   When the Positive
faith shall be accepted, it will be time to compose a new
Catechism, more closely resembling those of the Catholics,
to give in detail these different practical rules, the general
bases of which will then be familiar to the true believers.   But this first Catechism is, on the contrary,
especially meant to lay down these essential bases, only
considering their applications so far as they are indispens-

able to the establishment of the principles. I beg you then, without dwelling any longer on personal morality, to pass on to the second part of the private life, and describe the Positive regeneration of family life.

The Priest.—It depends essentially, my daughter, on the constituting on an altruistic basis human marriage, which has hitherto been made to rest on a purely egoistic principle, as the legitimate satisfaction of the sexual instinct, tending to the reproduction of the species. This coarse view was naturally adopted on system, so long as the prevalent theory ignored the benevolent instincts. But the instinct of mankind never ceased to protest against it, and at all times evoked efforts of an empirical character, each stronger than the last, to which were due the successive improvements of the marriage institution. Positivism alone comes forward at length to institute, on this fundamental point, a noble harmony of theory and practice, in reliance on the chief discovery of modern science, as to the innate existence of the altruistic instincts.

This great conception, the full bearing of which is yet so imperfectly understood, leads at once to the regeneration of human marriage, by conceiving of it henceforward as having for its special object the mutual perfecting of the two sexes, putting aside every sensual idea. It shows by direct proof the twofold affective superiority of woman, from the less intensity of the personal instincts, especially the lower ones, and the greater energy of the sympathetic. Hence follows the Positive theory of marriage, in which your sex raises mine, by disciplining the animal desire without which the moral inferiority of man would hardly ever allow him sufficient tenderness. But this fundamental relation is fortunately aided by all the other differences in the cerebral organisation of the two sexes. The superiority of man is indisputable in all that regards the character properly so-called, the chief source of command. As for the intellect, on the one side, it is stronger and of wider grasp; on the other, more accurate and penetrating. Everything then combines to show the mutual efficacy of this close union, which constitutes the most perfect friendship, embellished by an incomparable mutual possession. In all other human ties, possible if not actual rivalry always checks the fulness of confidence which can only exist between those of different sex.

In this view the sexual appetite has no other purpose than to originate or to sustain, more particularly in the man, the impulses calculated to develop tenderness. But for that object it must be gratified very moderately. Otherwise its profoundly egoistic nature tends, on the contrary, to stimulate self almost as much as excess in food, and often with even more serious results, as the woman is odiously sacrificed to the brute passions of the man. When my sex becomes sufficiently pure, as yours is generally, for tenderness to have a due hold without this coarse stimulant, the true influence of marriage is much better brought out.

So it will be in the normal case of the chaste union sanctioned by our worship to meet the wants of those who are disqualified for contributing to the propagation of the species. Many diseases are transmitted, and even aggravated, by inheritance; so that thousands of children are born in a wretched condition to die early, their life never having been anything but a burden. In modern civilisation, where all births equally are protected, these sad results are far more frequent than with the ancients who destroyed as a general rule their offspring when weak. A thorough sifting of this important question would perhaps show that a fourth of the population in the West would be wise to abstain from having children, to concentrate the function where the parents are properly qualified. When there shall be paid the same attention to the propagation of our species as to that of the more important domestic animals, there will be a recognition of the necessity of thus regulating

it. But that can only come from the voluntary adoption
of chaste marriages, in accordance with the Positive
theory of the marriage union, in which the sexual relation is not directly necessary. For to forbid marriage
by law in the case of hereditary disease, as physicians
have often urged, would be a remedy as odious as it
would be illusory. The influence of Positive religion on
private and public life can alone give birth, on this point,
to resolutions which if not absolutely voluntary fail in
efficacy as much as in dignity. In these exceptional
unions, the true nature of marriage will be more appreciable, when the two souls are rightly organised. An
extension of the practice of adoption will even allow free
scope in such marriages to the other family affections,
besides relieving the pairs on whom it devolves to have
children.

The Woman.—This theory, my father, is adequate to
express the true idea of marriage, independently of its
bodily results, which are at times not attained. The
moral amelioration of man is then the principal function
of woman, in this unrivalled union instituted for the
mutual perfecting of both sexes. As for the functions of
the mother, you have already defined them, as consisting
especially in directing the whole human education, so that
the heart may therein always prevail over the intellect.
So, by virtue of the succession which is normal for these
two offices of woman, your sex is ever under the affective
providence of mine. Such a mission at once indicates
that the marriage tie must be exclusive and even indissoluble, so that the family relations may attain the completeness and stability required for their moral efficacy.
These two conditions are so consonant with human nature
that illicit unions instinctively tend towards them. Still
I believe that divorce ought not to be absolutely pro-
hibited.

The Priest.—You are aware, my daughter, that St.
Augustine, overcoming, by his own reason, the necessarily

absolute character of his theological doctrine, opens his
chief work by remarking that murder may be often excusable, and sometimes praiseworthy. The same may
be said of falsehood, and of almost everything else that
generally deserves reprobation. But whilst extending
the exception to divorce, we must not impair the fundamental indissolubility of marriage. There is in truth but
one case in which the marriage union should be dissolved
by law, the condemnation of one or other of the parties
to any degrading punishment which carries with it social
death. In all other disturbances, the long continuance of
unworthiness can merely determine the moral disruption
of the union, resulting in separation, but without allowing a second marriage. Positive religion imposes on the
innocent in such cases a chastity compatible, be it remembered, with the deepest tenderness. If the condition
seems to him hard, he should accept it first in the interest
of the general order, then as a just consequence of his
original mistake.

The Woman.—I know already, my father, the holy law
of eternal widowhood, by which Positivism at length
completes the great institution of marriage. My sex will
never raise an objection on this point, and you have
taught me how to refute the various sophisms, even the
scientific, which might yet come from yours. Unless
so completed, monogamy becomes illusory, since the new
marriage always creates a subjective polygamy, unless the
first wife is forgotten, which can be but small comfort to
the second. The mere thought of such a change is enough
greatly to impair the existing union, as the event of death
is always possible. It is only by the assurance of an
unchangeable permanence that the ties of intimacy can
acquire the consistence and completeness which are indispensable for their moral effect. The most contemptible
of the ephemeral sects sprung from modern anarchy seems
to me that which wished to make inconstancy a condition
of happiness, as the want of fixity in occupations a means

of improvement. I read, in the *Positive Politics*, a remark on this point which struck me greatly : " Between two beings so complex and so different as man and woman, the whole of life is not too long to know each other fully and to love each other worthily." Far from taxing with illusion the high estimate which a true husband and wife often form of one another, I have almost always attributed it to the deeper insight only to be gained by complete intimacy, which, moreover, developes qualities which escape the indifferent. It is even to be considered as very honourable to our species, this strong mutual esteem which its members inspire when they study each other carefully. For hatred and indifference alone would deserve the reproach of blindness which a superficial judgment brings against love. We must consider then as in full conformity with human nature the institution which prolongs beyond the tomb the identification of a noble married pair. No intimacy can stand a comparison with theirs ; since, between the mother and son, the disparity of age, and even a just veneration, are always a bar to entire harmony.

The Priest.—Besides, my daughter, widowhood can alone give woman's influence its main efficacy. For, during the objective life, the sexual relation impairs to a great degree the sympathetic influence of the wife, by mixing with it something coarsely personal. This is why the mother is then our chief guardian angel. Angels have no sex, as they are eternal.

But when the subjective existence has purified the higher intimacy which distinguishes the wife, she definitively becomes our highest moral providence. One single year of a true marriage is enough to procure for the longest life a source of happiness and amelioration which time never ceases to nourish, purifying it constantly in proportion as, imperfections being forgotten, the excellences come into fuller light. Thus, without the subjective union which is a consequence of widowhood, the moral

P

influence of the woman on the man would be extinguished
at the very moment when its main results should become
visible, perfected as it is and purified by death.   When
this complement of marriage shall be adequately appreciated, it will furnish one of the best practical distinctions
of the Positive religion, from the evident incompatibility
of such an institution with the principle of theology.

The Woman.—To complete my understanding of the
constitution of the family, my father, I need but knowledge of its material conditions.

The Priest.—They follow, my daughter, from its social
and moral destination.   The two fundamental functions
of woman, as mother and as wife, are, for the family, the
equivalent of the spiritual power in the State.   They
require then the same exemption from active life and the
like renunciation of all command.   To stand aloof from
both is still more indispensable for the woman than for
the priest, in order to preserve that superiority in affection in which her real merit consists, and which is less
qualified than superiority of intellect to resist the influences of action.   Every woman, therefore, must be
carefully secured from work away from home, so as to
be able to worthily accomplish her holy mission.   Remaining willingly within the sanctuary of home, she
there freely devotes herself to the moral improvement of
her husband and children, from whom she there receives
gracefully their just homage.

This constitution of the family rests from the material
point of view on this fundamental rule, systematically
formulated by Positivism alone, but of which the general
instinct always had a presentiment—*Man must support
woman.*   The obligation is equivalent to that of the active
class towards the contemplative class, allowing for the
essential difference in the mode of discharging it.   The
maintenance of the priesthood remains purely a social
duty, and can only become an obligation for individuals
in very exceptional cases.   Precisely the reverse is the

case with woman, from the difference in the moral influences, on the one hand domestic, on the other general.
At first maintained by her father or brothers, each woman
is subsequently supported by her husband or sons. In
default of these special supports, the obligation of the
active sex towards the affective becomes general, and the
government must provide for its discharge, on the representation of the priesthood. Such is the first material
basis of the true constitution of the family.

But the fulfilment of this condition necessitates at once
another institution, the renunciation by women of all inheritance. This voluntary renunciation rests on grounds
as valid as in the case of the priesthood, be it to prevent
a corrupting influence, or in order to concentrate human
capital in the hands which are to direct its employment.
Wealth is even more dangerous to your sex than to the
priesthood, as more detrimental to moral superiority than
to intellectual. Lastly, the renunciation of inheritance
by women provides the only means of abolishing the
custom of dowries, so injurious to so many families, and
directly contrary to the true objects of marriage. Then
the marriage union will issue from a worthy choice, freely
made without restriction of class, from the uniformity
between the classes due to the common education, despite the necessary inequalities of power and wealth.
But, to give all these conjoined reasons their full validity,
women's disinheritance must remain absolutely voluntary,
and never be the result of a legal enactment.

The Woman.—The Positive religion will have little
difficulty, my father, in getting women to adopt this
resolution, when their material existence shall be duly
guaranteed on the security of private duties enforced by
the general convictions. Regret has often been expressed
for the caprices produced by idleness and wealth in women
who wish to command by wealth instead of loving. But
the moral degradation has seemed to me still greater when
woman grows rich by her own labour. The hardness of

continuous money-making robs her then even of that instinctive kindness which the other type keeps in the midst of its dissipation. There can exist no worse industrial chiefs than women.

The Priest.—In order to complete this general glimpse of the family constitution peculiar to Positivism, it remains for me, my daughter, to point out an institution which is indispensable for the full efficacy of such a renovation. It consists in giving perfect freedom of devising, adding to it freedom of adopting; but under the moral responsibility of the head of the family, always submitted to the due examination of the priesthood and the public. The next conversation will show you the social value of these two institutions, as remedies, so far as possible, for the main inconveniences attending the hereditary transmission of property. But for the present you should only look at their power to purify and strengthen all the elementary ties, by clearing them from the mean desires which at present sully them. It is the only means to make the affection of sons for their fathers, if not as tender, yet as noble as that of wives for their husbands. Fraternal affection will be thus more secure than under the revolutionary system of equal division, or even under the feudal subordination to the elder. Amongst the rich, no one will expect anything from his family beyond the assistance required for his education and his establishment as a social functionary. Then all without check will give themselves up to the full cultivation of the best affections. If fathers have not worthy sons, they will remedy it by wise adoptions.

Such are the families amongst which a priesthood, the object of the free veneration of all, will unceasingly exert itself to anticipate or to repair the contests occasioned by bad passions. It will in such a milieu make women feel the merit of submission, by drawing out to its consequences this admirable maxim of Aristotle : *The greatest strength of woman lies in overcoming the difficulty of obeying.* Their education will have prepared them to understand that all power, far from really raising, necessarily degrades them, by vitiating their highest claim, as expecting from strength the ascendency which is due only to love. At the same time, the priesthood will protect them against the tyranny of their husbands and the ingratitude of their sons, judiciously reminding both of the precepts of Positive religion as to the moral superiority and social office of the affective sex. It is mainly by the powerful reaction on it of public life that private life was gradually raised in the past. The fostering this preponderating influence is by the final regime vested in the priesthood of Humanity, which alone can enter on a right footing the circle of the family, in order to ennoble and to strengthen all the domestic affections by connecting them constantly with their social destination.

CONVERSATION XI.

PUBLIC LIFE.

The Woman.—On approaching the higher portion of Positive morals, I must, my father, ask for three preliminary explanations.

The first refers to the metaphysical objection often made to Positivism that it admits no kind of *rights*. If it is so, I am more inclined to congratulate you on it than to complain. For the interposition of *right* has almost invariably seemed meant to supersede reason or affection. It is fortunately not allowed women, and they are all the better for it. You know my favourite maxim : *Our species more than the others needs duties to engender feelings.*

The Priest.—It is true, my daughter, that Positivism

recognises no other right for any one but the right always to do his duty. To speak more accurately, our religion imposes on all the obligation to help each one to discharge his proper function. The idea of *right* has to disappear from the political, as the idea of *cause* from the philosophical domain. For both notions refer to wills above discussion. Thus, all rights whatever imply of necessity a supernatural source, for no other can place them above human discussion. Whilst concentrated in the governors, they could have a real social efficacy, as the normal guarantees of an indispensable obedience, so long as the preparatory regime lasted, based on theology and war. But since the decay of monotheism spread them among the governed, in the name, more or less distinctly, of the same divine principle, they have become as anarchical on the one side as retrograde on the other. As such they lead to nothing, on either side, but to prolong the disorder attendant on the revolution ; so that they should entirely disappear, by the common consent of the honest and the sensible men of whatever party.

Positivism never admits anything but duties, of all to all. For its persistently social point of view cannot tolerate the notion of *right*, constantly based on individualism. We are born loaded with obligations of every kind, to our predecessors, to our successors, and to our contemporaries. Later they only grow or accumulate before we can return any service. On what human foundation then could rest the idea of *right*, which in reason should imply some previous efficiency ? Whatever may be our efforts, the longest life well employed will never enable us to pay back but an imperceptible part of what we have received. And yet it would only be after a complete return that we should be justly authorised to require reciprocity for the new services. All human rights then are as absurd as they are immoral. As divine right no longer exists, the notion must pass completely away, as relating solely to the preliminary state, and directly incompatible with the final state, which admits only duties, as a consequence of functions.

The Woman.—Now, my father, I would know if, over and above the general relation between public and private life, the latter does not call into existence dispositions calculated to fit us individually for the former.

The Priest.—Those which arise from our individual existence have their chief sphere, my daughter, in the private worship which answers to that existence. It is not merely adapted to solidify and develop all private virtues. It finds its most important application in public life, where our three guardian angels should at once turn us from evil and urge us to good, through short special invocations to meet the various conjunctures of import-ance. The power of such assistance was rightly felt in the noble beginning of the worship of woman which was essayed by the admirable chivalry of the Middle Ages. So well had these eminent natures harmonised private and public life that the beloved image often arose to animate and embellish their warlike existence, giving rise to the tenderest emotions in the very midst of desolation or terror. If then the softer affections could be familiarly combined with destructive activity, a similar combination should more easily issue from labours directly bearing on the happiness of man, and free from any painful con-sequence to any one. The holy canticle which ends the most beautiful of poems is still more suited to the new than to the old worship :—

> Donna, se' tanto grande, e tanto vali
> Che qual vuol grazia e a te non ricorre
> Sua disianza vuol volar senz' ali.
>   La tua benignità non pur soccorre
> A chi dimanda, ma molte fiate
> Liberamente al dimandar precorre.
>   In te misericordia, in te pietate,
> In te magnificenza, in te s'aduna
> Quantunque in creatura è di bontate.
>   —DANTE, *Parad.* xxxiii. 13-21.

So mighty art thou, lady, and so great,
That he who grace desireth, and comes not
To thee for aidance, fain would have desire
Fly without wings. Not only him who asks
Thy bounty succours, but doth freely oft
Forerun the asking. Whatsoe'er may be
Of excellence in creature, pity mild,
Relenting mercy, large munificence,
Are all combined in thee.—CARY'S *Translation.*

More than any other class should the priesthood of
Humanity avail itself of such aid. Its social struggles
cannot but largely develop in it courage, perseverance, and
even prudence. But they will often tend to impair its
moral purity by the seductions of ambition, the more formidable as they will seem to spring from a holy zeal. Our
priests will then frequently feel the need of tempering
afresh their true dignity in a noble intercourse, at first
subjective, then even objective, with the loving sex.

As for the dispositions emanating from family life, it
will always offer in special degree the best apprenticeship in this fundamental rule which each should freely
bind on himself, as the personal basis of public life :
Live openly. To hide their moral misconduct, our metaphysicians secured the adoption of the shameful legislation which still forbids us to scrutinise the private
life of public men. But Positivism, giving due systematic
expression to the common instinct, will always court a
careful examination of the personal and domestic as the
best guarantee of the public life. As no one should wish
for the esteem of any but those who inspire him with
esteem, each does not owe to all without distinction a
constant account of all his actions. But, however limited
may become, in certain cases, the number of our judges,
it is enough that we always have judges for the law of
living openly not to lose its moral efficacy, impelling us
constantly to do nothing but what we can avouch. Such
a disposition involves at once undeviating respect for
truth and the scrupulous performance of every promise.

In these two general duties, nobly introduced in the
Middle Ages, is condensed all public morality. They show
you the thorough soundness of that admirable judgment
in which Dante, unconsciously representing the spirit of
chivalry, assigns to traitors the worst hell. In the very
midst of modern anarchy, the best poet of chivalry was
heard to proclaim nobly the grand maxim of our heroic
ancestors :—

> La fede unqua non deve esser corrotta,
> O data a un solo, o data insieme a mille ;
>
> .   .   .   .   .   .
> Senza giurare, o segno altro più espresso,
> Basti una volta che s'abbia promesso.
> —ARIOSTO, *Orlando Furioso*, xxi. 2.

> Faith never must be broken,
> Be it given to one, or to a thousand at once ;
>
> .   .   .   .   .   .
> Without oath, or other more distinct sign,
> Enough that once the promise have been given.

These strengthening presentiments of sociocratic manners
are definitively systematised by the Positive religion,
which represents falsehood and treason as directly incompatible with all human co-operation.

The Woman.—I have, my father, lastly to ask you if
public life does not admit of a general division analogous
to that of private life, founded on the inequality in
extent of the two concerned. Neither the heart nor
even the intellect can properly rise from the Family to
Humanity without the intermedium of the Country. If
so, public life seems to me necessarily to present two
very distinct degrees, when we take first the relations of
citizens, then the relations of men.

The Priest.—As a fact, my daughter, this distinction
determines the general plan of the present conversation.
But before applying it, we must give it the requisite
accuracy and consistence, by limiting the sacred idea of
Country, which has in modern times become too vague
and consequently almost barren, as a result of the exor-

bitant extension of the Western States. Following out the indication roughly stated in the study of the doctrine, you should here look on the republics of the future as much smaller than is foreshadowed by the revolutionary prejudices of the day. The gradual break-up of the colonial system since the independence of America is, at bottom, only the beginning of a final disruption of all the overgrown kingdoms which arose on the dissolution of the Catholic union.

In the final arrangement the normal extent of the Western States will not be larger than that which we now see in Tuscany, Belgium, and Holland, and shall soon see in Sicily, Sardinia, etc. A population of one to three millions, at the average rate of one hundred and fifty per square mile, is really the extent suited to States enjoying true freedom. For we can so designate States only those of which all the parts coalesce, without any violence, from the instinctive sense of a practical community of interest. The continuance of peace in the West, by dispelling all serious fear of foreign invasion and even of a reactionary coalition, will soon awaken a general feeling that it is desirable by peaceful means to break up factitious aggregates which for the future have no real justification. Before the end of the nineteenth century, the French Republic will of its own free will be divided into seventeen independent republics, each comprising five of the existing departments. The approaching separation of Ireland will naturally lead on to the rupture of the artificial bonds which now unite Scotland, and even Wales, with England proper. A similar process of decomposition taking place in all the States which are overgrown, Portugal and Ireland, granting they remain entire, will be, at the beginning of next century, the largest republics of the West. It is to countries with these limits that we are to apply here the normal examination of public life. Then the national feeling becomes a true intermedium between the family affection and the love of the race.

The Woman.—With this valuable simplification of
Positivist policy, I hope not to find, my father, any serious
difficulty in your direct explanation of our public life.

The Priest. — It consists wholly and entirely, my
daughter, in the due realisation of these two maxims :
*Devotion of the strong to the weak ; veneration of the weak
for the strong.* No society can last if the inferiors do not
respect their superiors. The strongest confirmation of
this law is the existing degradation, wherein, in default
of love, each obeys force only ; though our revolutionary
pride laments the so-called servility of our ancestors, who
were able to love their chiefs. The second then of these
two conditions of society is common to all times. But
the first really dates its introduction from the Middle
Ages ; since all antiquity thought otherwise, with here
and there a happy exception, as its favourite aphorism
witnesses : *Paucis nascitur humanum genus. Mankind is
born for the few.* Thus the social harmony rests on the
combined activity of the two best altruistic instincts, respectively adapted to the inferiors and superiors in their
relations with one another. Still, this concurrence can
only come into existence and be permanent in minds
prepared for it by a sufficient habitual exercise of the
most energetic, though the least eminent, of the three
sympathetic instincts, as a consequence of the legitimate
development of the domestic affections.

Such a solution depends entirely on the fundamental
separation of the two powers, the spiritual and the temporal. To secure the devotion of the strong to the weak
there must arise amongst the strong a class which can
attain social ascendency solely by devoting itself to the
weak, as a return for their veneration freely given. It
is thus that the priesthood becomes the soul of the true
sociocracy. It is of course implied, however, that it
always limit itself to counsel, without ever being able to
command.

This is why I laid such stress on its complete renuncia-

tion of power, and even of wealth. The better to secure
it, the priests must also abstain from deriving any material
profit from any works, books, or lectures; so as always
to subsist solely on their annual stipends. The central
budget of the priesthood will, with certain exceptions,
provide for the printing of all their writings, requiring
only the signature of the authors, and leaving them their
distribution, as naturally the best judges, and so constantly responsible. The priest who should sell his books
or his lectures would then be severely punished, even to
the loss of his position on the third offence.

Still more completely to purify the priesthood, it must
also be prevented from crushing any teaching contrary to
its own. This is why the Positivist regime will always
require full liberty of exposition, and even of discussion,
as is but fitting where the doctrines are throughout
demonstrable. The only normal restrictions of this
fundamental liberty must come from public opinion,
which, by virtue of a sound common education, will of
itself reject doctrines contrary to its convictions. We
may even now understand this by the unconscious
discipline which upholds the Positive faith, without
any material constraint, as regards the leading doctrines
of modern science. Provided there never be any legal
prohibition of opposition, no one can complain reason-
ably of the aversion he excites in the public. Such a body
of conditions will always compel the priesthood to per-
suade or convince in order to exert a real influence on
high and low equally.

The Woman.—Its interference in civic life being
directed mainly to regulate aright the habitual relations
of the patriciate and proletariate, I ask you, my father,
to delineate in particular its office on this essential point.

The Priest.—For that, my daughter, I must first give
in more detail the normal constitution of modern industry.
It rests on two general conditions, already perceptible at
the close of the Middle Ages, and in constant growth

ever since ; the distinction between capitalists and workmen ; and the internal hierarchy of the patriciate, whence
we get that of the proletariate. The subordination of the
country districts to the towns completes this organisation.

On the abolition of serfage, industry became sufficiently
strong to dispense with working to order ; it anticipated
the public demand. In consequence of this change, the
masters proper (*entrepreneurs*) soon separated from the
simple workmen. Their separate upgrowth gradually
worked out, from the nature of their occupations, the
normal hierarchy already indicated in our worship. It
rises from the agriculturist to the manufacturer, from him
to the merchant, the last step being the banker, basing
each class on the one that precedes it. Operations more
indirect, entrusted to agents more carefully selected and
fewer, require, it is found, more general and more abstract
conceptions, as also a greater responsibility. This spontaneous classification, systematised by Positivism in
accordance with our hierarchical principle, makes the
normal co-ordination of industry the natural continuation of the co-ordination applicable first to science, then
to art.

For this industrial hierarchy to have social efficacy it
is presupposed that the patriciate is so far concentrated
that each patrician administers all that he can really
superintend, so to lessen as much as possible the expenses
of management and the better to ensure responsibility.
Here the true interest of the inferiors entirely coincides
with the natural tendency of the superiors. For great
duties demand great powers. Our existing disorders are
most aggravated by the jealous ambition of the smaller
capitalists and their blind contempt of the people.
When the conduct of this class shall be 'in sufficient
degree regenerated, under the joint stimulus of circumstances and convictions, its heads will be absorbed into
the patriciate and its mass into the proletariate, so doing
away with the middle classes properly so called.

The Woman.—This necessary concentration of wealth is even now, my father, desired by the proletaries of our large towns, as a real social benefit, though our country population clings too strongly to its almost indefinite dispersion.   But such concentration must largely depend on the hereditary transmission of property.   The hints given in outline on this point in the exposition of the worship not appearing to me adequate, I beg you to complete them here.

The Priest.—We must, my daughter, connect it with the more general principle which regulates the normal succession for all functionaries whatsoever.   The method of election was only introduced as a protest, long necessary, against the caste system, finally become oppressive. But, in itself, all choice of the superiors by the inferiors is thoroughly anarchical : it has never been of use but to break up gradually a defective order.   The final state must, in this respect, differ from the primitive state only in substituting for the heredity of theocracy, resting solely on birth, the heredity of sociocracy, in all cases dependent on the free initiative of each functionary.

All the social complications originating in distrust end after all in irresponsibility.   Perfect confidence and full responsibility, such are the two characteristics of the Positive system.   The worthy organ of any function whatever always comes to be the best judge of his successor, submitting, however, his nomination of him to his own superior.   In the spiritual order alone is the choice always vested in the supreme head, so as to obtain the requisite concentration of so difficult an office.

For the highest temporal functions, the control of the superior finds a natural substitute in the examination of the priesthood and the public.   This is why the chief must solemnly nominate his successor on receiving, as you are aware, the sacrament of retirement, at an age when his choice may still be modified on suitable advice. In exceptional cases, the priesthood might then, by refusing this sacrament, prevent in a degree this last act of an unworthy or incapable power.

Wealth being from the social point of view an authority, must pass by the same general rules. This free choice of an heir, involved in the full liberty of devising and adopting, offers the best remedy against the ordinary abuses of property. Indeed, each one then becomes responsible for an unworthy successor, who now can be no reproach to him. There is little need to fear that the inheritance will generally fall to one of the sons, if all are really incapable. For the tendency of the industrial chiefs to perpetuate their *houses* in proper hands makes them often disposed to choose their successors outside of their own family, which at the present day they can only do by sacrificing their daughters. Thus sociocratic heredity, far from lessening the power of the wealthy, is found more favourable to it than theocratic, at the same time that it largely increases their moral responsibility.

The Woman.—Such an explanation sufficiently completes, my father, my knowledge of the temporal constitution of the Positive regime. You may then directly consider the interposition in general of the priesthood of Humanity in the more important civic disputes.

The Priest.—The better to describe this capital function, I think I should, my daughter, begin by giving you the statistics of the patriciate when regularly organised for the whole West. Two thousand bankers, a hundred thousand merchants, two hundred thousand manufacturers, four hundred thousand agriculturists, in my judgment provide enough industrial chiefs for the hundred and twenty millions who form the population of the West. With this small number of patricians will be concentrated all the capital of the West, of which they will have to direct in freedom the active employment, under a constant moral responsibility, and in the interest of a proletariate of thirty-three times their number.

In each separate republic, the government properly so

called, that is to say the supreme temporal power, will be vested naturally in the three leading bankers, respectively taking by choice the operations of commerce, manufactures, and agriculture. It is then to these two hundred triumvirs in especial that the Western priesthood, under the direction of the High Priest of Humanity, will have to refer in due form the legitimate claims of an immense proletariate. The exceptional class, which habitually contemplates the future and the past, then concentrates its care on the present, speaking to the living in the name of those who have lived and in the interest of those who shall live.

The Woman.—This language, my father, seems to me never to depart from a sound estimate of the several divisions of human existence. By raising all citizens to social functionaries, their respective offices being really useful, Positivism ennobles obedience and strengthens government. Instead of a simple private aim, each form of activity feels honoured by its due participation in the public welfare. Now, to effect this wholesome change, the priesthood need never evoke an exceptional enthusiasm. Enough if it always secure an accurate judgment of the ordinary realities of life.

The Priest.—Our basic principle of the necessary gratuitousness of human labour gives us, my daughter, powerful means for better developing the feelings and convictions which are suited to each class of society. When wages are no longer looked on as paying the value of the functionary, but merely the material he consumes, the merit of each individual stands out more clearly in the eyes of all. The priesthood can then more easily discharge its chief social duty, which consists in always contrasting in a right spirit the abstract classification, founded on the intellectual and moral appreciation of the individuals, with the concrete classification drawn from the subordination of the functions. If properly drawn out, this contrast will recall the superiors to a better disposition towards their inferiors, when they shall see that their own elevation depends more on position than on merit. Though the subjective life alone can really insure the preponderance of the personal classification without exciting any subversive tendency, still this contrast emanating from religion will place in a truer light the official classification, whilst upholding the respect which is its due.

But, at the same time, the priesthood will make the proletaries deeply conscious of the real advantages of their social condition. To minds prepared by a wise education, and under the constant influence of home affections, it will have no difficulty in proving the thorough reality of that admirable maxim of the great Corneille—

On va d'un pas plus ferme à suivre qu'à conduire.

(in paraphrase of the *Imitation*, i. 9, 51)—

With firmer step we follow than we lead.

The happiness springing from a noble submission and from a just freedom from responsibility will be unceasingly appreciated by them, when the family life shall have been properly organised in the class best qualified to enjoy it rightly. Then the proletariate will feel that the main office of the patriciate is to secure to all the peaceable enjoyment of these home satisfactions, in which our true happiness chiefly lies. Their less attainment by the spiritual or temporal rulers of society, who are ever under the sense of a vast responsibility, will make their exalted position generally more an object of pity than of envy, having for sole compensation a larger share in promoting the public welfare. But this noble reward is only fully tasted by the higher minds, who are very rare at all times in the patriciate, and even within the limits of the priesthood. There must be left, then, a fair course for the ordinary gratifications of pride or vanity, as alone able on the average to sufficiently stimulate the zeal requisite for command and counsel.

Q

The Woman.—I would, my father, know with more
precision this essential function of the free administrators
of the capital of the race which aims at ensuring the proletaries a due development of their domestic existence,
the first normal guarantee of civil order.

The Priest.—Limit yourself, my daughter, to looking
on each first as possessing property, then as receiving
wages.   Every proletary should own in property all the
materials of exclusive and constant use, either for himself,
or for his family.   This rule, evidently feasible, can alone
ensure order in practical life.   But we are far from its
satisfactory attainment.   Many estimable men are yet
without property in their furniture in most common use ;
and some do not even own the clothes they wear.   As for
the dwelling, you know that most proletaries are still
rather encamped than housed in our anarchical towns.   It
would be enough, however, to sell by apartments the houses
that are sold, as we see done in some towns, for each
family of the people, on payment of a slightly increased
rent for some years, to own in property its lodging.

The private worship and private life fix with sufficient
precision the normal extent of such domicile, and show the
importance of its fixedness, without which we may say
that the first revolution in man's existence, the passage
from the nomad to the sedentary life, remains incomplete.
It ought even to react on the outward stability of industrial relations, by suppressing as a natural consequence a
noxious vagabondism.   Whilst sanctioning the full liberty
of human co-operation, the Positive religion prescribes it
as a duty for each never to change his inferiors or superiors
without serious reasons.   The capricious change of the
shops we deal with is itself blameable, tending as it does
to disturb the general economy of their operations, which
presupposes the requisite steadiness in their customers.

As for the wages paid at fixed periods, they must be
regularly divided into two unequal parts, one independent
of the actual labour and attached to the service performed,

the other dependent on the results obtained. It is the only means of securing the workmen against the stoppages for which they are not responsible, without, however, ceasing to allow the chiefs due scope for the various in-dustrial improvements, especially in machinery. The extension of machinery, which raises the moral dignity of the human workman and gives him increased efficiency, may then go on freely, open to no objection on social grounds. But the proportion between the fixed and the variable portion of the workman's wages will differ in different industries, in obedience to laws which the patri-ciate alone can settle.

The Woman.—In spite of the healthful influence of this normal order, I feel, my father, that the instinct of de-struction, stimulating the other egoistic propensities, will always occasion conflicts in the Western populations even when regenerated. I should then ask you what will be the interference of the priesthood in these unavoidable disputes.

The Priest.—It will endeavour at first, my daughter, to prevent them as far as possible, by a wise use of its spiritual discipline. This differs from the temporal mainly in that it evokes the good instincts rather than contends with the bad. Its method is then positive rather than negative, correcting by comparison rather than by compression, rewarding the one rather than punishing the others ; though at need it can be severe, as I have already explained.

The combination of these means will often prevent, or will soon repair, the civic conflicts resulting from the practical activity, under the natural play of the egoistic passions. The whole of Positive religion tends to incul-cate the truth, that, society resting always on free co-operation, the only lasting arrangements and legitimate modifications are those which result from a voluntary assent of the several co-operators. The greatest of social revolutions, the gradual abolition of Western slavery, was effected, in the Middle Ages, without a single insurrection.

Still, as the imperfection of our brain will not always allow the priesthood to secure due respect for the wills of man, it must ultimately apply itself to moderate the contests it cannot prevent.   Its general rule, in accordance with the nature of modern civilisation, is to brand as radically wrong, as equally anarchical and retrograde, all recourse to force on the one side or the other.   In the industrial society, material contests, when inevitable, must be decided by wealth, concentrated or dispersed, never by personal violence, which is to be reserved for criminals in the strict sense.   For we ought to repress by force only such acts as are unanimously disapproved, even by those who commit them.

The destructive instinct is always susceptible of this change, one already almost complete as regards chronic violations of order, even by bodies of men, and which it only remains to systematise by extending it to acute disturbances.   Already persecution which is the habit of men, and which formerly attacked life, respects even liberty, confining itself to property, so as to be more easily avoided and remedied ; as, with criminals, murder has given way to theft.   There is ground for hope, then, that the Positive religion will bring men to settle their most violent disputes without any war properly so called, even between fellow-citizens.   The normal restriction of the several republics should greatly facilitate this final transformation, by increasing simultaneously the power of the patriciate and the independence of the proletariate.

The Woman.—However precious the conversion thus effected in material contests, it seems to me, my father, more advantageous to the superiors than to the inferiors. In renouncing habitually all use of force in the strict sense, to limit themselves to a struggle of purses, the workmen seem to me to be doing an act of great social generosity, not but that there is ample reason for it. But I fear lest by thus suffering the dispute to be transferred to the peculiar domain of the masters, they often fall victims to the selfishness of the rich, even when they shall have everywhere obtained the just permission to form coalitions at their pleasure without any violence. For, whatever social power the plebeians may derive from their just refusal, as a body, of industrial co-operation, the immense capitals of our patricians will perhaps enable them ultimately to triumph over the most legitimate resistance. Though the priesthood will give great strength to the unions of workmen when it sanctions them, I still dread the abuse of the paramount power of wealth.

The Priest.—To reassure you, my daughter, consider first the habitual influence of the priesthood on the patriciate through their close personal relations. By our statistical statement, the regular number of bankers in the West is the same as that of the Positivist temples, each of which will be under the temporal protectorate of the adjacent banker, commissioned by the national triumvirate to be the channel of all sacerdotal payments. It follows that there will be frequent intercourse between the priests and the principal industrial chiefs ; so as to rekindle specially in the latter the veneration engendered by their own education and prolonged by that of their children.

The Woman.—Allow me, my father, to interrupt you a moment as to this last influence. As our encyclopedic instruction is never to be compulsory, the rich perhaps will be deterred, by a foolish pride, from letting their sons share in it, and still more their daughters, renouncing of course the sacraments which will follow it, and even the social weight it will carry. If so, the personal influence you speak of would be essentially nothing more than the involuntary deference everywhere gained by ability and virtue.

The Priest.—Your incidental objection has more force in it, my daughter, than you think ; and yet I shall not find it difficult to set aside. In fact, attendance in our Positivist schools will not be necessary for admission to our social sacraments, or even to our public examinations, where no question will be asked as to whom the instruction comes from, provided it be real and adequate. Only, when it does not come from the priesthood, our priests will have to take greater pains in getting the information as to moral character which will always be as indispensable as the judgment on intellectual ability.

Notwithstanding this full liberty of teaching, which will have the further result of increasing the zeal of our professors, the official schools will never be deserted by the rich, unless the priesthood degenerate. For they will not like their children to be in instruction below the people, and yet they will not be able to get them its equivalent, even at a great cost, in private. Indeed, the priesthood will naturally absorb the best professors, always diverted by their other functions from giving private instruction, to say nothing of its being, as you know, strictly forbidden. The private masters will be recruited then from those who are incapable of becoming priests or even vicars ; so that their lectures will be in permanent disrepute.

The Woman.—Your explanation quite sets me at ease, my father, as to the aristocratic dislike to our common education. So I beg you to resume your important appreciation of the influences attaching to the priesthood of Positivism, as regards the industrial chiefs, to prevent or remedy the effects of the more serious practical disputes.

The Priest.—Over and above its personal relations with the highest patrician class, which can act so powerfully on the rest, it will find everywhere, my daughter, special allies, by virtue of a befitting reorganisation of the voluntary protectorate. The institution of chivalry is in no way peculiar to military existence, the rough principle of which must, on the contrary, have greatly shackled its admirable development in the Middle Ages. It is more adapted, under better forms, to the Positive regime, where the protection, though in the main given in the form of money, will often call forth a devotion less striking, but more effectual and moreover better regulated. Many industrial chiefs, especially amongst the bankers, will, from early life, enrol themselves as members of the free association which, having at its disposal enormous wealth, will, either on its own impulse, or on an appeal from the priesthood, generously interfere in the more important contests. Its noble protection will not be limited to oppressed proletaries; it ought also to secure the priests against temporal tyranny.

The Woman.—This valuable institution seems to me to complete, my father, the sum of the means at the disposal of the priesthood of Humanity for duly regulating civic relations. You may then explain to me its normal intervention in the widest human relations.

The Priest.—We must, my daughter, in them distinguish two classes, according as they concern Positivist populations, or peoples still unacquainted with the true religion.

The first case simply requires the enlargement of the preceding considerations; and may therefore be readily apprehended. Nay, the influence of the priesthood becomes then at once more easy and more decisive. For after the approaching break-up of the existing States, the great Western Republic will be divided into sixty independent republics, which will have really in common only their spiritual organisation. There will never arise in it a temporal power with a possibility of universal dominion, such as the phantom emperor of the Middle Ages, who was therein, for Catholicism, nothing but a disturbing relic, an empirical offshoot of the Roman order. All collective action, for the rest purely temporary, will be always directed by the national triumvirates acting for the time in concert. As for the practical institutions which ought to become really universal, their very object reserves them always for the priesthood, for it alone can override national rivalries sufficiently to secure their free adoption by all. The several governments should only interfere to aid in their foundation by finding the requisite money. It is only in this way that monies, weights and measures, etc., can readily and peaceably become truly universal.

Thus, the sixty republics of the regenerated West will have no other habitual bond than a common education, community of manners and customs, and common festivals. In a word, their union will be religious and not political ; allowing for the historical relations resulting from previous aggregations, and soon to disappear in the new connection, unless when they rest on community of language. The High Priest of Humanity will be, more truly than any mediæval pope, the only really Western chief. He will be able then, at need, to concentrate the whole priestly action in order to repress any tyrannical triumvirate, calling also on the neighbouring knights for aid, and even on the neutral governments for peaceful mediation. If, however, the industrial contests are found to be unavoidable, his well-weighed sanction will be able to secure for the combinations of the workmen an extension which must decide the issue, by inducing all their fellow-workmen in the West, even when not belonging to the industry threatened, to take part in them. But, conversely, when the priesthood shall blame the conduct of the workmen, or only refuse its approval, the capitalists will easily overcome any unwarranted demands.

The Woman.—We have now only, my father, to determine the systematic relations of the Positivist population with the nations that have not yet embraced the Religion of Humanity.

The Priest.—By virtue of the close connection originating in the Catholic-feudal initiation, which followed everywhere on the Roman incorporation, you may conceive, my daughter, that the new faith will prevail simultaneously in the whole of the European West, including therein its various colonial appendages, especially the

American. The convergences due to the growth of the Positive spirit in science, art, and industry, are, in many ways, far more powerful than the divergences caused by the disruption of the Catholic bond, and even by a faulty excess of nationalism. But this vast spiritual republic hardly comprises more than the fifth of the whole human population. It is important then to consider, in the general, how the West when regenerated should gradually bring into communion with it all the inhabitants of our planet.

When the reorganisation of the West shall be fairly secure, this noble missionary proselytism will become the principal collective occupation of the Positive priesthood. No claim of the temporal power is valid against its exclusive prerogative in respect to such a function. If the priesthood is even now alone competent to regulate properly the mutual relations of the several Western nations, for still stronger reasons can it have no competitor in regulating the widest social relations. Under and despite ephemeral and disastrous attempts at domination, it is to advances in science or industry that is really due all the beneficial and permanent intercourse of the West with the rest of the globe. The persistently relative character of Positivism adapts it exclusively for true missions, calculated gradually to bind all populations whatever to its characteristic unity, which is alone worthy to embrace all.

The Woman.—This immense conversion, indispensable to the full organisation of Humanity, will have to follow, my father, a natural course ; I should like to know its essential features.

The Priest.—It depends, my daughter, on the decreasing affinities of Western Positivism with the several populations outside its pale ; first monotheistic, then polytheistic, and lastly fetichist. But the cases that seem most unfavourable, from a less degree of spontaneous preparation, allow, on the other hand, more systematic interference, if we rightly apply the general theory of human transitions. The whole conversion may be in principle satisfactorily effected in three generations, one for each of the main phases, leaving it to the next century to develop the various bases of uniformity laid down by a numerous and zealous priesthood, if properly aided.

The first case is that of the monotheists of the East, first Christian, then Musulman, or Russia and Turkey with Persia. In both cases the populations may be raised to the definitive level of the West, without requiring from them a servile and hazardous imitation of the stormy and difficult course exacted by the original evolution. Even at the present day, by its historical theory, Positivism will offer valuable guidance to the noble governments which are exerting themselves to direct this necessary ascent whilst guarding it from Western disturbance. Russia which. in the last century, guided itself by France, is at present led to hold aloof from her systematically. The change is a very wise one, since the old policy of imitation would henceforth expose the Slav populations to very great disturbance, without offering to them any real intellectual or social progress.

But, when regenerated Paris shall cease to present a completely revolutionary type, it will be able to furnish the Czars who are worthy of their station with ideas and assistance such as may second systematically their admirable instinctive zeal for the peaceable amelioration of their vast States. Instead of urging them to imitate a past which can never be repeated, Positivism will soon exhort them to appreciate more justly their peculiar advantages. For instance, the break-up of the great feudal fortunes was necessary in France as a step to the advent of a new patriciate under the ephemeral ascendency of the middle classes. In Russia, on the contrary, it is important at the present day to maintain the concentration of wealth which is required by the final state, and which we shall have great difficulty in reconstituting in France. The whole effort of a wise autocrat should then be limited to the substitution of the industrial for the military character, the foundation of which transformation is already laid by the permanence of general peace, for the future perfectly secure.

The Woman.—Such an influence of Positivist advice seems to me, my father, confined to Russia, from its resemblance to the West in religion. But Turkey and Persia perhaps afford much less scope for intervention, as they have not yet reached even monogamy.

The Priest.—Polygamy is at present, my daughter, often more real at Paris than at Constantinople. Besides that Islam has undergone the same dissolving process as Catholicism, we form, in general, very exaggerated ideas of the difference of manners and opinions between the Eastern and Western nations; witness the instinctive tendency of the Musulmans to take us as guides.

When rejecting the separation of the two powers, the better to constitute his military theocracy, the incomparable Mohammed had a presentiment that this enormous improvement of the social order was as yet premature, as being incompatible with the theological principle. He naturally at that time looked on such an attempt as peculiar to the West, where its ultimate failure would long give rise to serious dangers. If Islam deprived the Easterns of the admirable progress effected under the impulse of Catholicism in the Middle Ages, it preserved them, afterwards, from the anarchical transition from which we have suffered these five last centuries, and which is now the origin of so many obstacles. Thanks to their regime, Musulmans are in the main exempt from metaphysicians and even lawyers. Positivism, whilst dissuading them from a disastrous imitation, will enable them fully to appreciate this capital advantage, which may powerfully aid their final regeneration.

The Woman.—I understand, my father, this relation, though I had missed the principle on which it rests, from defective knowledge of your historical theory. But for the polytheists, who are nearly half the human race, it

would surprise me much if our faith were equally susceptible of an immediate efficacy, as the distance between us
and them is too great.

The Priest.—On the contrary, my daughter, we may
be much more useful to the polytheists than to the monotheists, by sparing them a longer and more difficult transition. Their unaided ascent would perhaps take them first
through some monotheism or other; although they are but
little disposed thereto by observing the complete discredit
which attaches to it, for a century at least, in the West
and even in the East. But the Positive religion will relieve
them from this empirical course, by a special management of their direct passage to the final religion of man.
Monotheism is really indispensable only in the original
evolution. Many of our adolescents will unconsciously
overleap it in their encyclopedic novitiate. Much more
certainly will the rational zeal of the Western priesthood
be able to preserve the existing polytheists from it, for
their leading doctrines are transformable into Positive
conceptions, covered merely with a species of theological
illumination, which would soon disappear.

The Woman.—As for the fetichists, who are moreover
few in number, their state seems to me, my father, so distant from ours that I cannot conceive the possibility of
bringing them rapidly to the ultimate level of the West.

The Priest.—Though few in number, my daughter,
they occupy, in the centre of Africa, a vast region still
wholly out of the reach of our civilisation, which can only
penetrate there by the sustained impulse of the priesthood of Positivism. Our noble missionaries will find in
Africa the case best adapted to stimulate their intellectual
efforts and their practical zeal, when they set before them
the spreading among these simple populations the Universal Religion, without requiring of them any monotheistic or even polytheistic transition. The feasibility
of such success is a consequence of the profound affinity
of Positivism for fetichism, which differs from Positivism,

in point of doctrine, only in that it confuses activity with life, and, for the worship, in that it worships materials instead of products.

In every human initiation, unaided or guided, fetichism is the only form of the fictitious regime which is really unavoidable, because both for the race and the individual it comes at a period when they are incapable of reflection. Each of the other two preliminary phases may be spared where the evolution is completely systematic. If we clung to preserving our children from polytheism, we could do so by prolonging the fetichist state till, by gradual modifications, it issued in Positivism. But this effort would then be unseasonable, not to speak of its tendency to disturb the natural development of the human imagination. It is quite otherwise with the evolution of the nations of central Africa, where such transformations may have the most wholesome results, not merely local but for the whole of mankind.

The Woman.—I have, my father, but one last remark to make to you on these vast intellectual and social metamorphoses, which give such an interest to the most extended relations of men, heretofore always stained by egoism and empiricism. Without in any way sharing the barbarous prejudices of the white against the black, I scarcely venture to hope that the universality of the Positive faith will not be hampered to an indefinite extent by the difference of race.

The Priest.—The true biological theory of the races of men, my daughter, follows from the conception of Blainville, which represents these differences as varieties due to the environment, but become fixed, even hereditarily, when they had reached their greatest intensity. On this principle, we may subjectively construct a theory in essential agreement with the only differences established by objective study, which really admits but three distinct races, white, yellow, and black.

In fact, it has not been possible for essential and per-

manent differences to be developed except as regards the
relative preponderance of the three ultimate divisions of
the brain, its speculative, active, and affective parts. Such
are then our three necessary races, each of which is
superior to the other two, either in intelligence, or in
activity, or in feeling, as all sound observations combine to show. This final judgment should turn them
from all mutual contempt, and make them all equally see
the power there lies in their close union, to complete the
constitution of the true Great Being.

When our labours shall have made our planet uni-
formly healthy, these organic distinctions will tend to
disappear, by virtue even of their natural origin, and
especially of proper intermarriages. The increasing
fusion of the races will, under the systematic direction
of the universal priesthood, procure us the most precious
of all improvements, that which concerns our cerebral
constitution as a whole, thus become more apt to think,
to act, and even to love.

Conclusion.

— ⚬ —

GENERAL HISTORY OF RELIGION.

CONVERSATION XII.

THE FETICHIST AND THEOCRATIC PERIOD COMMON TO ALL PEOPLES.

The Woman.—These last conversations have a strong antecedent attraction for me, my dear father, from the want I have often felt of such an historical complement of the triple exposition you have just completed. I have already understood, in many cases, that the final state regulated by the Religion of Humanity had always to be preceded by a long and difficult initiation, especially indispensable to every original evolution. But these partial glimpses excite, rather than satisfy, my desire to know the outlines of the historical theory which enables you to appreciate the past, so as to determine the future, with a view to clearly delineate the present.

The Priest.—Its main foundation, my dear daughter, is in the two laws of mental evolution with which you are now familiar. You already know how there follows from them the general division of the preparation of man, begun by fetichism, carried on by polytheism, and completed under monotheism. However, before we proceed

further, you must for a short time return on this fundamental principle, to convince yourself in regard to it that
the course which at first seemed merely inevitable was
really indispensable.

Attend particularly to the intellectual necessity of such
an initiation, as it is less understood than any other. If
every true theory necessarily rests on observed facts, it is
not less certain that any connected observation demands
a theory. Originally, then, the human mind could find
no outlet but in a purely subjective method, by drawing
from the within the means of connection which the without would only supply after long study. Then feeling
makes up for the weakness of the intelligence, by supply-
ing it with a principle for all explanations, in the similarity of the affections of all beings, instinctively assimi-
lated to the human type. But this primitive philosophy
is necessarily fictitious, and consequently merely provisional. It establishes, between theory and practice, a
constant antagonism, which, gradually modified by the
increasing influence of the activity on the intellect, continues during our whole preparation, and ends only in
the Positive state. Whilst speculation was attributing
everything to capricious wills, action always assumed
invariable laws, the knowledge of which, less and less
empirical and more and more extended, has at length
reorganised the human intellect.

The Woman.—I needed, my father, this explanation,
to understand the philosophical mission of the initial
regime, though I had already quite felt its poetical power.
But the necessity for it morally seems to require no
explanation. Whoever has studied children to any
purpose, or who has even seen through the accounts
of travellers and formed a true idea of savages, must
look on this external support as indispensable for our
original weakness. The fictitious regime is still more
adapted to develop our tenderness, for which the Positive state can only offer an equivalent nurture when

it reaches its full maturity. Thus suited to our three-fold individual nature, the primeval religion must be equally applicable to our social existence, which at first could find no other source of common opinions or of guiding authority.

The Priest.—To complete this basic theory of the human evolution, all that is left for me to do, my daughter, is to point out the law which governs our temporal advance. It presents, as does the spiritual advance, and for similar reasons, the necessary succession of three distinct states : the first purely provisional, the second simply transitional, and the third alone definitive, in correspondence with the several modes of our activity. Man's existence begins, in fact, by being essentially military, to become ultimately completely industrial, passing through an intermediate stage in which conquest is transformed into defence. Such, clearly, are the respective characteristics of the civilisation of antiquity, of modern society, and of the transition peculiar to the Middle Ages.

This course of our activity, as that of our intellect, is due to the impossibility of any other at the beginning. The social state cannot, doubtless, gain strength and develop but through labour. But, on the other hand, the growth of labour as much implies the pre-existence of society as that of observation demands the impulse of theory. The unravelling of this difficulty is then again effected by a spontaneous evolution, which supersedes any complex preparation. Now, war is the only activity which fulfils this condition, considering the natural preponderance of the destructive over the constructive instinct. Effective only through collective action, war is peculiarly adapted to create strongly cemented and permanent associations, in which the sympathy becomes very intense though very limited, by virtue of a strong solidarity. Lastly, war alone can determine the formation of large States by a gradual incorporation, which

R

restrains military restlessness everywhere but in the
ιuling people, where it takes a higher character from a
noble destination.   There exists no other general means
of overcoming the aversion man originally feels for all
regular labour.

When this rule founded upon war attains a sufficient
extension, the primitive regime tends to transform itself
of itself, because defence becomes more important than
conquest.   Then we pass to the intermediate stage,
during which the predominance of war prepares the way
for industrial existence, which soon remains the only one
susceptible of uninterrupted progress.

The Woman.—The evolution of activity seems to me,
my father, easier to grasp than that of the intelligence.
But I am surprised at your thinking that the two in
combination are a sufficient basis for the theory of history.   True, there is a natural correspondence between
them ; for the fictitious synthesis harmonises with war as
Positive religion with industry ; one feels even that metaphysics would naturally prevail whilst war was in the
main defensive.   Nevertheless this dynamical conception
of Humanity seems to me not sufficiently in consonance
with the statical conception of our nature, in which
feeling towers above both the intelligence and the activity.   After the two laws of the spiritual evolution,
and that which governs the temporal evolution, I expected an equivalent statement as to the affective life,
without which motion and existence are to me equally
unintelligible.

The Priest.—You forget, my daughter, that the chief
region of the brain is not, as the two others, in direct communication with the outer world, which cannot then act
on feeling except through the medium of the intellect or
the activity.   It is true that the organs of affection are
immediately connected with the viscera of organic life.
But the moral influence of these last, to say nothing of
its depending on laws imperfectly known, is only to be

taken into account in the individual existence. As regards society we may neglect it, as a consequence of the neutralisation it there spontaneously undergoes amid the variety of cases, co-existent or successive. Our opinions then and our circumstances constitute the only normal sources of the variations our feelings undergo, in the different phases of the human evolution, especially of the collective evolution. But the general course of these indirect changes conforms, moreover, to that of the direct changes on which they depend. For if we can sum up the speculative evolution and the active by considering them as tending to make us more synthetical and more disposed to co-operation, we equally recognise that our affective evolution consists above all in our becoming more sympathetic. As the grand characteristic of our existence is unity, the great object of our growth is to develop human harmony. Thus, the whole history of Humanity is necessarily condensed in that of religion. The general law of the human movement, whatever the point of view chosen, consists in this, that man becomes more and more religious. Such is the ultimate result of the whole body of dynamical conceptions, thus in perfect consonance with the statical : the education of the race, as that of the individual, trains us gradually to live for others.

The Woman.—By this last explanation, I feel now, my father, no serious difficulty as to the theory of evolution which serves as base to the true philosophy of history. You may proceed then at once to explain in outline the principal phases of Humanity.

The Priest.—To make the study easier, I urge you, my daughter, to consult frequently the table I subjoin (*Table D*), taken from the fourth edition of *The general system of public commemoration adapted for the organic transition of the Western Republic.*

The first point that will strike you in it will be the entire absence of any notice of fetichism, which yet constitutes our primeval state, and still exists in vast populations. But this inevitable omission is solely a consequence of the concrete character of this synopsis, not able to include a phase of history which threw up no name that abides. Fetichism can only receive its due honour in our abstract worship, where you know how fully we shall glorify it.

Its intellectual value consists above all in its spontaneously originating the subjective method, which, at first absolute, directed the whole of the race's preparation, and which, become relative, will more and more preside over our normal state. The true logic, in which feelings take precedence of images and signs, has then its origin in fetichism. When any strong emotion impels us to seek for the causes of phenomena of which we know not the laws, in order first to foresee and then to modify them, we attribute directly to the beings with which we are concerned human affections, instead of subjecting them to external wills. Fetichism is then more natural than polytheism.

Its moral efficacy is beyond dispute, by virtue of its tendency to give spontaneously the predominance to the human type. It inspires us with deep sympathy for all forms of existence, even the most inert, for it always represents them as essentially analogous to our own. And therefore this primal state of humanity awakes keener regret than any other in those who are rudely torn from it ; such is the daily experience of the unhappy Africans carried far from their homes by Western barbarity.

Even under the social aspect, less favourable to fetichism, we owe to it important services which the Positive worship will duly honour. So long as man's existence remains nomad, it moderates, by its tendency to the worship of external objects, the vast destruction, necessary, it is true, but blind, which the hunter or the pastoral tribes then inflict on animals or plants, in order to prepare the scene of man's action. But its highest service is its unconscious guidance of the first social revolution, that which serves as the basis for all the others, the passage to sedentary life. This great change, of which we misjudge the difficulty no less than the importance, certainly belongs to fetichism, as a consequence of the deep attachment it fosters for our native land.

The chief imperfection of this spontaneous regime lies in its only allowing very tardily the rise of a priesthood, qualified to direct man's future progress. For this cult, even when highly developed, requires at first no priest, as it is by its nature essentially a private worship, which permits each to worship without a mediator beings almost always within his reach. Ultimately, however, a priesthood arises in fetichism, when the stars, long neglected, come to be the principal fetiches, and as such common to vast populations. Their inaccessibility being clearly recognised, it gives rise to a special class, whose duty is to transmit homage and interpret their will. But, in this its last stage, fetichism borders on polytheism, the origin of which in all cases was astrolatry ; as is still shown by the names of the greater gods, always borrowed from the stars most adapted to perpetuate the fictitious synthesis.

The Woman.—Although this passage cost no effort, it seems to me, my father, the most difficult of the preliminary revolutions of our intelligence. For we have then to pass by an abrupt transition from activity to inertia in our general conception of matter, so as to give a reason for the influence of the gods.

The Priest.—Still, my daughter, external agents come in without effort when the human mind, reaching the second period of childhood, rises from the contemplation of beings to that of events, the only possible basis for scientific meditations. Carrying on the original method, the phenomena, considered simultaneously in many bodies, are then attributed to more general wills, wills necessarily of external origin. This intellectual transformation should become familiar to us, as we have frequent opportunities of observing it, at the corresponding period in the individual evolution.

Be this as it may, it is chiefly on polytheism that depends the whole preparation of man, his social evolution most, but also his mental. In the first place it alone completes the primitive philosophy, by extending it to our highest functions, which shortly give occasion for the favourite occupation of the gods. For fetichism, in the main relating to the material world, could not distinctly take in our intellectual and moral nature, whence, on the contrary, were drawn all its physical explanations. But when we introduce supernatural beings, we can adapt them to this new sphere, and it soon becomes the chief one. At the same time, polytheism necessarily gives rise to a priesthood in the strict sense, or rather consolidates and develops that which astrolatry had originated.

In the midst of the varieties of the polytheistic regime, we trace two closely connected institutions, common to all its modes : the radical confusion of the spiritual and temporal powers ; the slavery of the labouring population.

On the intellectual, and still more on the social ground, all combines without effort in the explanation of the first. In the first place, you cannot confine yourself to advice when you speak in the name of an authority without limits, all the suggestions of which naturally become absolute commands. In the second place, our preliminary regime had above all to develop the several powers of man, reserving for the final state their wise regulation on the basis of such apprenticeship taken as a whole. In it then all powers had to be extensively combined, so as to overcome in due degree the indiscipline natural to primitive man. The separation of the two human powers would have radically hampered the active mission of polytheism, by thwarting the progress of conquest. Lastly, the complete divergence of scientific conceptions and practical notions made it at that time imperative that these two orders of thought should equally engage the attention of the brain, in order that their respective defects might be sufficiently neutralised therein. On the other hand, this indispensable concentration was a spontaneous result; as is shown by the then inability to conceive a real separation of counsel from command, even in the philosophers who were best prepared for it.

A similar remark is applicable to the slavery of antiquity, always considered necessary to the social order, till the times bordering on the final emancipation. The slave, as we are reminded by the Latin etymology (*servus*), was originally a prisoner of war, saved to labour, instead of being killed or eaten. By virtue of the conciliatory character of polytheism, he could keep his own worship, in subordination of course to the religion of his conqueror, now become his spiritual and temporal leader. This social status to which all were more or less liable, considering the vicissitudes of war, was at that time so natural as to be often accepted without any reference to war, which, however, was always its chief source.

The institution of slavery was in two ways the basis of ancient civilisation, first as indispensable to the progress of conquest, then in order to accustom man to labour, which thus became the only means of personal improvement, after having been the pledge of life. Under all these aspects, it is impossible to compare it with the ephemeral and monstrous form thrown up by modern colonisation.

The Woman.—After this general glimpse of the polytheistic regime, I need, my father, a knowledge in outline of its principal forms.

The Priest. —The most fundamental consists, my daughter, in theocracy properly so called. This conservative polytheism constitutes the only really complete order attainable throughout the whole preparation of man, all its other phases offering but destructive modifications of this primitive regime, the sole source of their partial consistence.

It rests on two closely connected institutions, the heredity of all professions, and the universal supremacy of the priestly caste. The first supplies the only means for preserving the advances made, and for allowing slowly secondary modifications; so long as education took the form rather of imitation than of instruction, there being no separation of theory from practice. But this necessary system would break up the population into completely independent castes, did not the uniform supremacy of the priesthood intervene to organise the state, by offering to all the castes a bond which they revered, and which is naturally susceptible of a wide extension.

This primitive constitution is so natural that it still subsists, in the largest existing populations, in spite of immense disturbances. Though universal, it could only attain such durability in countries where the development of intelligence and industry preceded that of the military activity. This last, indeed, always acts as the spontaneous solvent of theocracy, by its tendency to raise the soldier above the priest. Great as were the efforts of the priestly policy to divert the military energy on distant expeditions, always followed by permanent colonisation, the theocracy in all cases issued in the supremacy of the military patriciate, but without losing the old manners and customs. Its power in this last respect, a convincing evidence of the tenacious character of the regime, enables us at the present day to study it in existence, greatly altered though it be, even in China and India, so better to understand ancient Egypt, the venerable mother of all the civilisation of the West. We can then appreciate, on a large scale, the social office of the priesthood, as at once counselling, consecrating, regulating, and lastly judging. But we also see, at the same time, to what an extent the exercise of this fundamental function was vitiated by the command and wealth which necessarily sullied the original interference of the intellect in the domain of feeling and activity.

It naturally surprises you that such a regime finds so small a place in the Table I have given you. This depends chiefly, as for fetichism, on the concrete character of this historical composition, esthetic rather than scientific. Still, in regard to a system which leaves so many memorials of all kinds, this general explanation requires a fuller treatment. Such treatment leads us to observe one of the noblest characteristics of the true theocracy, where the government of man is vested in vast and permanent corporations, whilst the services rendered can scarcely ever be connected with individual names. Had there not been this tendency to absorb the individual, the various priestly colleges would often have been disturbed by the natural rivalries of the gods of polytheism. It is only when the theocracy, by what is happily a solitary exception, is founded on monotheism, that an extreme concentration brings into full light the highest names. And so the concrete character of our Table necessitated the choice of Moses as the personal type of the initial regime, though he but very imperfectly represents an organisation which is essentially polytheistic.

The Woman.—This thoughtful admiration for theocracy makes me judge more soundly, my father, the profound unfairness of the blind reproaches it is yet exposed to from most of those who claim to be advanced thinkers. It would seem from them that the organisation from which all springs, and which lasted longer than any other, was always oppressive and degrading ; so that it would be beyond comprehension whence the progress made could take its rise.

The Priest.—All these criticisms of theocracy should be regarded, my daughter, as equally frivolous with the reproaches levelled by St. Augustine against the whole of polytheism and the attacks of Voltaire on Catholicism. No regime could deserve such blame except in its decay. It would never have risen or prevailed if the greater part of its supremacy had not been to a considerable extent in

agreement with our nature, and even largely favourable
to our progress.

The oppressive tendencies towards stagnation are only
developed really in the latest stage of theocracy.   They
are there a consequence of the inevitable degradation
of the priestly character through command and wealth.
But after all, the unchangeableness of theocracy has been
greatly exaggerated, from judging it by the contrast
offered by the greater rapidity which marks the Western
movement.   Apart from any external interference,
decisive and numerous indications attest, and that far
back, the spontaneous movement of theocratic civilisation.   For instance, Bouddhism, though crushed at its
centre, soon led in Thibet to great modifications of the
theocratic system, which were carried farther in China
by the adoption of the examination system.

When it shall be incumbent on Positivism to make its
way to these immense populations, then will be the time to
study carefully the natural progression by which of themselves they would ultimately have risen to the definitive
level of the West, by a distinct but equivalent course.
For it is with these instinctive tendencies that we shall
have wisely to connect our systematic acceleration, elimi-
nating all the violent disturbing influences imported by
monotheism, first Musulman, then Christian.   Nevertheless, reserving this important question, we should for the
present concentrate our historical studies on the immediate ancestors of Western civilisation.   We are thus
led to give precedence to the examination of the populations in which the establishment of theocracy was barred
by the precocious growth of military activity.

But this progressive polytheism appears under two very
different forms, the one mainly intellectual, the other
eminently social.   The first is found when local and
political circumstances prevent war, although very largely
encouraged, from organising a real system of conquest.
Then its latent reaction is to impel all the higher minds

to mental cultivation, which has also become the chief object of public attention, and thus is detached from the sacerdotal discipline.   When, on the contrary, war is free to tend to universal empire, the intellect subordinates itself to activity, and all citizens, as a rule, are absorbed in social cares, at home as abroad.   These two forms of progressive polytheism were, each according to its nature and in its time, equally indispensable to the great Western movement which followed on the spontaneous throwing off of the yoke of theocracy.

Ultimately no theocracy escapes the social ascendency of the soldier over the priest.   Even in Judea, despite its exceptional concentration, theocracy underwent this change, when the kings took the place of the judges, six centuries after its foundation.   But it is important to distinguish the cases where this change is not effected till after the theocratic manners have acquired great consistence, and those where its rapid introduction precedes such settlement, which consequently is essentially a failure. Our Western evolution depended mainly on this last impulsion, which, however, would never have answered the purpose without the germs judiciously borrowed from the pure theocracies.

The times sung by Homer mark distinctly the beginning of such sequence.   For there had then elapsed two generations at most since the soldiers began to overbear the priests among our Grecian ancestors.   The primeval theocracy still manifests itself there in numerous and respected, though dispersed oracles, which lasted longer in Greece than elsewhere.

The Woman.—Starting from this era in the West, you told me, my father, that the human evolution forms in reality an immense transition, admitting no real organisation.   One feels strongly the accuracy of such a judgment, when one contrasts the short duration of the several states of society which from that time forth follow one another, either with the previous persistence of the theocracy which succeeded fetichism, or with the magnificent future of the Positive order. But I should like now to understand the general outline of this indispensable transition.

The Priest.—Such a preparation, accurately represented by our concrete Table, is in relation, my daughter, as is the whole of human nature, first with intelligence, then with activity, in order to arrive ultimately at feeling. The initial theocracy cultivated simultaneously these three aspects of our existence, thus brought under a complete system of rules, though one too little favourable to our continuous advance. But this discipline was so surely the only one adapted to theologism that it was never possible to find any durable substitute so long as the fictitious synthesis prevailed. The rate of progress was only quickened by breaking up such harmony, in order to develop in succession each part of man's existence at the expense of the two others. This marked character of incompleteness distinguishes clearly first the Greek intellectual evolution, then the Roman preparation, lastly the Catholic-feudal initiation.

The order of these three partial evolutions is at once determined by their common destination. For it was then the first object to develop the powers of man, without attempting as yet to discipline them, otherwise than through their spontaneous antagonism. Every premature attempt to regulate the whole of human life tended to re-establish a theocracy which was always imminent, and became adverse to the partial growth it was wished to promote. This is why feeling, the chief source of human discipline, was naturally long despised, so as only to prevail when the intellectual and practical development should be sufficiently advanced. For the due growth of our powers, intelligence must precede activity. For, as our activity at that time tended to unite all the progressive polytheists under one dominion, it would have become incompatible with the full liberty required for the speculative evolution, had this latter not been previously accomplished.

———

CONVERSATION XIII.

THE TRANSITION OF THE WEST.

The Woman.—I understand thus, my father, the nature and the succession of the three great phases which belong to the necessary transition which separates us from the Homeric times. But I need a clearer understanding of their course and their connection, beginning with the Greek evolution.

The Priest.—Its imperishable brilliancy should not prevent you, my daughter, from regretting the contrast it offers in the general to the Roman evolution, as to the respective influence of each on its nation. In Rome, we are in contact with a collective construction, in which all free men must always take an active part, or the failure would be complete. In Greece, the people is in the main passive, and forms a kind of pedestal for some thinkers of real eminence, the total number of whom is not above one hundred, in art, philosophy, and science, from Homer and Hesiod to Ptolemy and Galen. On the one side, the high community of action stamps on the whole nation a nobleness of which the traces are yet distinguishable. But, on the other, the monstrous preponderance allowed to speculation over action issues in the degradation, too perceptible at the present day, of a population sacrificed to it which ended by assigning the first place to the gift of expression. Their conquest by Rome alone preserved the Greek cities from succumbing in every case to the despicable tyranny of some rhetorician.

These overpraised tribes were really incapable of more than one fine phase of social existence, lasting with difficulty for two centuries, often, too, interrupted by their

wretched disputes. That phase was due to their admirable struggle, defensive at first, then offensive, against the
forcible compression with which the Persian theocracy
threatened this precious nucleus of freethinkers, at that
time charged with the intellectual destinies of Humanity.
But, even there, it is mainly to some citizens of pre-
eminent merit that the chief successes are due : for each
population is seen often ready to sacrifice the national
defence to mutual jealousies.

In this long intellectual elaboration, we must distinguish three periods of unequal length, faithfully represented in our Calendar. The movement begins with art,
and Homer is for all time its representative. It was quite
necessary that poetry, at once more independent and more
fettered, should be the first to detach itself from the
theocratic stem, so to begin the Western emancipation.
It prepares the advent of philosophy which, first outlined
by Thales and Pythagoras, finds its impersonation at
length in the incomparable Aristotle, so far above his age
that it was not till the Middle Ages that he could be
appreciated. Under his immortal elaboration, this second
movement attains sufficient distinctness to make true
thinkers soon feel the impossibility of outstripping it
without a long scientific preamble which should adequately
develop its primary Positive basis. Then true science,
admirably represented by Archimedes, became, in its
turn, the chief object of Greek genius, its capacity for art
and its philosophical power being irreparably exhausted.

The Woman.—As for the Roman preparation, I have
always found it, my father, much easier to appreciate,
owing to the homogeneous and strongly marked character which distinguishes this admirable gradual ascent to
universal empire. Bossuet's greatest work contains, on
this point, some remarkable hints, which I have long
known. This political system is so within grasp that it
could be adequately presented in a few matchless lines,
which were once explained to me (Virgil, *Æn.* vi., 848–

854). Though they bear only on Rome's external mission, they make us feel how intimate is its connection with the internal constitution.

The Priest.—You have only now, my daughter, to complete this whole by distinguishing its two main phases. So long as the Roman incorporation did not include the greater part of the West, Rome's warlike energy was naturally directed by the senatorial caste, strong in its theocratic ascendency, by virtue of which the common advance was sufficient restraint on the jealousy of the plebeians. But this military constitution had to change when the dominion became so extended and so consolidated as no longer to absorb the attention of the people, of whom the emperors became the true representatives as against patrician tyranny. Virgil defined the policy of Rome, personified in the incomparable Cæsar, at the very time when that policy was undergoing, unknown to the tender poet, this decisive change, the first symptom of its inevitable decline.

These two nearly equal phases, the one eminently progressive, the other essentially conservative, had each a powerful social influence on the whole preparation of the West. If to the first we owe the salutary sway which everywhere put a stop to fruitless and yet continuous wars, we are indebted to the second for the civil benefits of this political incorporation, by virtue of the uniform propagation of the Greek evolution. In conquering Greece, Rome always paid her a noble tribute, and devoted her influence to spread results in art, in philosophy, and in science, which, unless so disseminated, would not have fulfilled their highest purpose.

When the last movements peculiar to antiquity, the one intellectual, the other social, had thus fused irrevocably, the preparation of man at once set towards its last necessary phase. The development, theoretically and practically, of our chief powers soon awoke a deep consciousness of the need of their regulation. For the spontaneous discipline which resulted from a temporary end was altogether broken up on the attainment to a certain extent of that end. Then the intellect and the heart gave themselves over to an unparalleled dissipation, in which all our intellectual and material wealth was wasted in ignoble gratification of unbridled selfishness. At the same time that regeneration was becoming indis-. pensable, the whole of our Græco-Roman antecedents seemed to supply it with a systematic basis, through a combination of the intellectual superiority of monotheism with the social tendency towards an universal religion.

Thus arose Catholicism to satisfy this great want of complete discipline, under the impulse, an impulse too little recognised, of the incomparable St. Paul, whose sublime self-abnegation facilitated the growth of the new unity, by accepting a founder who had no claim. But the profoundly self-contradictory nature of this construction was in itself an indication that this last transition would be more rapid and less extensive than its predecessors. For its chief end could be attained only through the radical separation of the two human powers, a separation, it is true, spontaneously issuing from a state of things in which monotheism was slowly growing under the political supremacy of polytheism. Still, such a division always remained incompatible with the necessarily absolute character of theologism, which, especially in its mono-theistic concentration, only allows its priesthood to con-fine itself to counsel so far as it cannot grasp command.

This inevitable contradiction is best drawn out by two general contrasts, the one social, the other intellectual. The only possible foundation at that time for human dis-cipline is the future life, to which the new priesthood gives an importance previously unknown, even in Judea, in order to have in it an exclusive domain. But such a form of discipline became unfit to regulate real life, for it dissuaded each believer from society in order to impel him to a solitary asceticism. Under another aspect, the complete disunion between theory and practice, which was masked, and even atoned for, whilst the two powers remained fused, became quite evident on their separation. The monotheistic concentration drew out most strongly the inherent opposition between arbitrary wills and immutable laws. For the ingenious reconcilement of the two which Aristotle had prepared was only available for the later phase when the Positive spirit should be first tending towards its final ascendency under the guardianship of theology.

On combining these points of opposition, we need feel but little surprise that the Catholic movement was long rejected as purely retrograde by the most eminent philosophers and statesmen of the Roman empire. These great chiefs had been gradually prepared, since Scipio and Cæsar, for the direct advent of the kingdom of Humanity, under the simultaneous predominance of the Positive spirit and the industrial life. But they had not perceived the necessity of one last social preparation, essentially relative to feeling, for the introduction of the final regime by the twofold emancipation reserved for the Middle Ages as to woman and the labouring classes.

The Woman.—This great result seems to me, my father, here referred at the outset to Catholicism solely with the view of bringing out more clearly its historical filiation, by representing it as a possible outcome of the regime of antiquity under the new religious impulsion. But it was very greatly aided, and even much accelerated, by the influence of feudalism. Catholicism, which once had my belief, must always have my reverence. And yet I could never prevent myself from secretly preferring chivalry, the noble condensation of which I hear echoing still in the sixteenth century: *Fais ce que dois, advienne que pourra. Do thy duty, come what may.*

The Priest.—I need, my daughter, but complete your just estimate by showing you that feudalism, erroneously attributed to the German invasions, was itself a necessary consequence of the Roman system, which at its close tended spontaneously towards it. For the extension of the empire soon·substituted defence for conquest. Now, the two other political characteristics of the Middle Ages are necessary results of this leading change. On the one hand, it gradually transformed slavery into serfage, after having naturally limited the slave trade to the interior of the Roman world. At the same time, it more and more broke up the central power into local authorities, each charged with a part of the common defence, and it was their hierarchical subordination that constituted feudalism properly so called. All that Catholicism did was implicitly to sanction these three political tendencies, by recommending peace, emancipation, and submission. But it was at that time the worthy exponent of the feelings called forth by the circumstances of the West, nor are we bound to attribute them to its doctrine, which often served later to sanction dispositions of an entirely opposite kind, by virtue of its vague and even anti-social nature. It contributed much less than feudalism, either to the abolition of Western slavery, first in the towns, then in the country ; or to the emancipation of women, in respect of which we owe it the prerequisite of purity, but in no wise the final aim, tenderness, ever of chivalric origin. Throughout the Greek Church, it still sanctions the seclusion of women and the serfage of the worker, which the Czars alone modify nobly.

The Woman.—Sufficiently prepared, my father, for this general estimate of the Middle Ages, it remains for me only to know the chief division of this last organic transition.

The Priest.—It is taken, my daughter, from the two systems of defensive wars which naturally absorbed at that time the collective action of the West, whilst the great social revolution which I have just delineated was in process of gradual accomplishment. A first phase, beginning with the opening of the fifth and ending with the seventh century, is occupied by the primary settlement, where, under the invasions which admitted of lasting success, we trace all the proper characteristics of the Middle Ages, with the exception of language. In this period independence takes precedence over concert. In a second period of equal length, concentration becomes the paramount want, in order to repel the unsettling invasions of the populations which were ready for incorporation into the West, so easy was their conversion from polytheism to Catholicism. This collective action of the West was directed especially by the dictatorship of the incomparable Charlemagne, worthily carried on by his German successors.

Thus is founded the Western Republic, in which the commonalty of antiquity, due to forcible incorporation, is transformed into a voluntary association of independent States, whose only direct bond is a common spiritual regime, concentrated in the papacy. Even at its commencement this change tends, notwithstanding the influence of the church and political memories, to displace the social centre of the system, removing it from Rome to Paris, where, by the end of the Middle Ages, it was irrevocably fixed, as more in conformity with geographical relations.

But during this second period, the East experienced a vast convulsion, which soon reacted deeply on the whole West, first by prolonging its Catholic-feudal regime, then by beginning its irreparable dissolution.

The want of a really universal religion had been long felt by the greater part of the white race, including even that portion which, though adjacent to the Roman empire, had escaped its dominion. Now, this universality, the appeal to which is at once the chief merit and the best test of Catholicism, can in no wise belong to theologism, and is exclusively the apanage of Positivism. Monotheism, however, approaches it more nearly than polytheism. This last was always an essentially national religion, though very compatible with the incorporation by war. Monotheism, on the contrary, may be the rallying-point for quite independent nations, though it has never practically been so except in the West during the mediæval period. It was natural then for the East also to aspire to a monotheistic belief, but one entirely incompatible with the faith of the West, owing to the difference in their social missions.

In fact, Islam directed principally the military development of another noble portion of the white race, aspiring, in its turn, to become the central nucleus of the true Great Being. This is why the fusion as in antiquity of the two powers was retained perforce, and even carried farther by Islam, as a result of its monotheistic concentration. Thus become more consonant with the natural genius of theologism, monotheism could, and must even in the East, attain a simplicity of doctrine inadmissible for it in the West. For, with us, the factitious separation of the two powers had compelled the real founder of Catholicism to complicate its dogma, by adding as complement to the revelation, with which no monotheism can dispense, the godship of the reputed founder. Hence other secondary complications, which, to the honour of Islam, it also rejected, the better to secure the predominance of its military character against the degeneracy of the priesthood in the person of its supreme head. The independence of the clergy was, in fact, the real ground of these subtle refinements of Catholicism, which, judged historically, deserve the respect of the philosopher, however repugnant they may be to our reason.

At the very beginning of this struggle between two irreconcileable monotheisms, an unprejudiced thinker might have foreseen that it would shortly end in discrediting both equally, by showing the thorough futility of their common claims to universality. This vast contest fills the last period of the Middle Ages, beginning with the eleventh century and ending at the close of the thirteenth. Then first was established feudalism in the strict sense, in which independence and concert, which prevailed in turn, were at length admirably combined, so as to inspire even then an anticipation of the final sociocracy. This admirable institution became, in the twelfth century, the general basis for those heroic expeditions in which the Western Republic, consolidated and developed by collective action, finally dispelled all anxiety as to a Musulman invasion. As early as the next century, the Crusades, as essentially deprived of any social purpose, were soon perverted and discredited. The whole of the Roman world was from that time divided between two incompatible monotheisms, each of which tended at once to its inevitable decline, which was only delayed, in either case, by the difficulty of substituting a new system.

The Woman.—This general theory of the Middle Ages, my father, makes me at length understand Catholicism in its entirety, as an intellectual and social system : I apprehend its necessary advent, its temporary mission, and its irremediable decay. But such an insight shows more clearly how unjust Catholicism was towards the intellectual creation of Greece and the Roman incorporation, the spontaneous combination of which had determined its own formation. After cursing its parents it was in its turn cursed by its children. Though the first wrong excuses not the second, it explains it by manifesting the breach in human continuity.

The Priest.—As a fact, my daughter, this continuity had been respected in the preceding revolutions. At the outset polytheism had almost insensibly supplanted fetichism, by a spontaneous incorporation of it into itself. When the primitive theocracy gave place to the military regime, there was still no breach of social antecedents, which always retained their honour. So it is when Rome absorbs Greece, making it her glory to continue its evolution. But the advent of Catholicism has, on the contrary, an anarchical character. The future and the present are conceived of and directed by it as though the Greco-Roman past had never existed. Nay, the Christian injustice extends even to its Jewish antecedents, notwithstanding the importance unwisely attached to them.

This rude disruption of continuity, which Islam exerted itself to avoid, greatly weakened the general consciousness of social progress, the first inchoate notion of which was a spontaneous outcome of Catholicism, by virtue of the real superiority of its system to its predecessor. It is important to rightly judge such a rupture of historical tradition. First of all it explains the profoundly contradictory position, intellectually and morally, in which is soon placed a doctrine which, the child of discussion, subsequently wished to stifle it, and which claimed from its children the respect it refused its parents. But above all we must see in it the true origin of the most serious tendency which attends on modern anarchy. The anti-historical feeling and spirit, the prevalence of which is now the greatest obstacle to the regeneration of the West, thus date as far back as the rise of Catholicism. Positivism alone can overcome this enormous difficulty, as alone able to do equal justice to all the phases, social or intellectual, of the human evolution.

Still, here as everywhere else, we must acknowledge that the Catholic priesthood by its remarkable wisdom long neutralised the main defects of its deplorable doctrine. By adopting the language of Rome, when it ceased to be the language in common use, it preserved as a natural consequence all the intellectual treasures of antiquity, even its beautiful theology. The touching legend, so well immortalised by Dante, of the successful intercession of a sainted pope on behalf of Trajan, were enough to indicate to what an extent nobler Catholic spirits regretted that their doctrine in its blindness prevented their honouring their best ancestors. But the general respect for the Greek and Roman antecedents was most developed in the temporal chiefs, despite their frequent ignorance. Throughout we meet the same contrast. An admirable discipline is then applied to the whole range of human feelings, though it rests on an immense egoism, the preponderance of which alone could overpower in the beginning the ordinary selfishness. The tenderness of chivalry finds its way prepared by, its sanction in, the faith the most adverse to women which ever held supremacy. By its institution of the celibacy of the clergy, which destroys all sacerdotal heredity, the most signal blow struck, in the West, at the system of caste comes from a doctrine by its nature favourable to theocracy, the ultimate aim of the papacy in its degeneracy. Monotheism, which ultimately became thoroughly hostile to all intellectual progress, prepared the way for its general advance, by completing the elaboration of human logic. Founded by fetichism on the feelings, it owed to polytheism the introduction of images. But its spontaneous growth was only completed under monotheism, by the habitual aid of signs. This result, essentially common to Islam and Catholicism, appertains more to Catholicism, considering the habit of discussion to which its separation of the two powers gave rise, amongst all classes.

All these contrasts should greatly increase the admiration and respect of true philosophers for those beautiful priestly natures which, during several centuries, found such powerful resources in a faith which was radically defective, though the only one suited to this transition. Still, let us never forget that the progress made in the Middle Ages was always due to the necessary concert of the two heterogeneous elements which we must ever combine in our view of them, Catholicism and feudalism.

Over and above its immediate services, this admirable transition called into existence once for all the essential germs of the final state. Nay, it initiated, under each great aspect, the true human order, at once temporal and spiritual, as far as was possible with the then belief and circumstances. And so Positivism has now but to take up its programme as a whole in order to carry it out worthily, on the groundwork of a better faith combined with a more propitious form of activity. But the influence of feudalism, at the present time without special advocates, is unjustly sacrificed, in these historical estimates, to that of Catholicism, the only one studied by the retrograde school. A searching examination, however, shows the reaction of chivalry even on the little understood modifications which the last provisional belief then underwent. After inaugurating admirably the worship of Woman, the necessary prelude to the Religion of Humanity, the feudal feeling really brought about, in the century of the Crusades, the change which Western monotheism underwent when the Virgin tended to take in it the place of God.

But in assigning to their true authors the results of the Middle Ages, we feel more clearly the profoundly precarious constitution of the Catholic feudal system, the latest form of the theological and military regime.   If it was the priesthood alone that compensated the imperfections of its doctrine, its power to do so could only endure so long as its social and moral mission made it keep a progressive character   Now, the very fulfilment of such a mission impelled the West towards progress incompatible with the Catholic faith, and at variance with the ultimate constitution of its clergy in its retrograde state ; as is shown by the admirable but unsuccessful attempt at regeneration in the thirteenth century.   In a word, all the results of the Middle Ages imperatively called for a new system, from the moment that Islam and Catholicism finally neutralised one another.   For instance, the emancipation from theology, long limited to certain individuals, spread widely in consequence of the Crusades, under the impulse of the Knights Templars, who were in better contact with the Musulmans.

With the fourteenth century then begins the vast

revolution in the West, which Positivism comes forward at the present day to close. At that date the whole human movement becomes profoundly hostile to the earlier order, though the new system can as yet in no way be seen. For, after Catholicism, no theological organisation was possible ; just as after its feudal constitution no modification of the military system was possible. The West was beginning to realise the too precocious anticipations of Cæsar and of Trajan as to its direct tendency to accept definitively the supremacy of a Positive faith and a peaceful activity. But to attain this end it was still required that science, industry, and even art should undergo a long elaboration, which in the main must be one of detail and dispersive, so as to mask its social bearing. Hence are derived these two characteristics of the last human transition, which is one of growing anarchy as regards the whole, though also more and more organic as to its elements.

The Woman.—Since it is thus, my father, that the present is directly tied to the past, I need to know the general course of this movement, to be able to follow in it the simultaneous advance of anarchy and reorganisation.

The Priest.—In the negative progress, more distinctly marked than the other, we must, my daughter, above all distinguish two necessary phases ; according as decomposition remains purely spontaneous, or becomes more and more systematic. The first embraces the fourteenth and fifteenth centuries, the other the three following. These two periods differ similarly as concerns the Positive movement, though the difference is less marked. The whole West partakes in the spontaneous decomposition, whereas the systematic negation triumphs only in the North.

From its commencement, the direction of the revolutionary movement was always in the hands of two closely connected classes, originally emanating from, and soon rivals of, the old powers. They are the metaphysicians and lawyers, who constitute the spiritual and temporal element in this negative regime, most traceable, particularly in France, in the universities and the parliaments. But the second class is more entitled to respect than the first, because the spirit which actuates both was modified in the legists under the wholesome influence of social considerations. Whilst the metaphysicians never were anything, as regards theology, but inconsistent destructives, the lawyers, and above all the judges, not to mention their temporary or special services, always tended to construct, on the vestiges of Rome, a purely human morality.

During the first modern phase, the whole mediæval regime was in a state of utter disorder from the internal conflicts between its component parts, its doctrines remaining intact. The chief struggle was naturally that between the temporal and spiritual powers, whose precarious harmony had always oscillated between the theocracy and the empire. . The vain efforts of the popes in the thirteenth century to establish their absolute dominion were succeeded generally, and in France more than elsewhere, by the successful resistance of the kings, who in the course of the next century annihilated beyond hope of recovery the power of the papacy in the West. This decisive revolution was completed, in the fifteenth century, by the subordination of every national clergy to the temporal authority, leaving only a delusive appearance of influence to the central head, thus degenerating into an Italian prince. With its independence the priesthood loses also its morality —its public morality first, then even its private. To ensure its material existence, it places its teaching at the service of all the strong.

At the same time, the struggle, begun in the Middle Ages, between the local and central constituents of the temporal order, continues on a larger scale. Everywhere the power which was originally weaker gets the upper hand, by the instinctive aid of the classes thrown up by the abolition of serfage. In the normal case, royalty prevails over aristocracy. The contrary result is to be looked on as an exception, of which Venice was the first instance, England the most complete.

In both forms alike, the combination of this political concentration with the humiliation of the priesthood inaugurates, in every Western state, a true dictatorship, which could alone keep in bounds the temporal anarchy arising from the spiritual disorganisation. The eminent Louis XI. was the best type of this exceptional magistracy ; he alone rightly discerned and wisely guided the whole of the modern movement.

As for the positive progression, its most important feature during this first period is the upgrowth of industry. Prepared by the twofold organisation of the labouring classes in the Middle Ages, it then develops under the stimulus of three capital discoveries, the occurrence of which has nothing fortuitous in it. First, the invention of gunpowder comes to perfect the transitional institution of standing armies, so relieving the Western nations from a military education opposed to their new form of activity. Then printing connects science with industry, by allowing the gratification of the intellectual fervour which was becoming universal. Lastly, the discovery of America and a sea passage to India offer a wide field for the decisive extension of commercial relations, so giving shape and solidity to the new Western life. The intellectual movement becomes at that time remarkable only in poetry, beginning the fourteenth century with a peerless epic, and producing, in the fifteenth, an admirable mystical composition. But the growth of science is being prepared by the accumulation of useful materials of all kinds.

This simultaneous progress of the intelligence and activity throws into stronger relief the lamentable neglect of moral improvement, which in all classes constituted the chief merit of the Middle Ages. The twofold ardour which then prevails in the West rests mainly on an universal and ill-regulated development of pride and vanity, often in conjunction with the most ignoble egoism. The esthetic development, it is true, despite its revolutionary tendencies, spontaneously keeps alive better sentiments. But moral culture is more and more centred in the affective sex, which, unaffected by the impetus of science and action, alone, amid modern anarchy, hands down the more important results of the Middle Ages, in spite of the increasing aversion they awakened. This holy providence cannot, however, prevent the gradual weakening of the true principle of all human discipline from coinciding with the special development of the new forces, spiritual and temporal, peculiar to the final state of the West.

The Woman.—The initial stage of the two modern movements being adequately delineated, I beg you, my father, to give me a similar view of its systematic period.

The Priest.—Hitherto unassailed, the doctrines of the old regime were then, my daughter, directly attacked by purely negative principles. That the anarchy should so spread was as indispensable as inevitable, in order to evidence the need of a real reorganisation, masked by the appearance of life which was still worn by a system of which all the social bases were irrevocably destroyed. But to form a sound judgment on its mission, we must divide this period into two parts, the first of which, beginning with the sixteenth century, ends at the retrogradation of the French monarchy, coinciding with the triumph of the English aristocracy. The second brings us, a century after, to the actual commencement of the revolutionary crisis, which still, after two generations, inflicts on the West its deplorable vicissitudes.

This necessary distinction is traceable especially to the increase of system introduced into the negative doctrine, which at first seems compatible with the fundamental conditions of the theological regime, whilst later it becomes evidently contrary to them. We should demarcate these two successive degrees of the negative movement by the respective names of Protestant and deist. Infinitely varied as are the sects of Protestantism, their common adherence to the Christian revelation suffices to separate them all from the more complete emancipation which distinguishes deism.

At the very commencement of the second modern phase, the negative doctrine broaches directly its anarchical principle, by asserting absolute individualism, which it does by its allowing to every one, without any conditions of competence, the decision of all questions. Then all spiritual authority is utterly broken up. The living rise in complete insurrection against the dead ; witness the blind reprobation of the whole mediæval period, a reprobation but ill compensated by an irrational admiration of antiquity. Thus is widened, under the influence of Protestantism, the fatal breach which Catholicism instituted in the continuity of the race.

The Woman.—Allow me, my father, for a moment to interrupt you that I may express the profound dislike which was always aroused in me by Protestantism, which professed to reform Western monotheism by stripping it of its best institutions. Thus it suppresses the dogma of purgatory, the worship of the Virgin and of the Saints, the system of confession, and perverts the mysterious sacrament which supplied to the hearts of the Western nations a sublime condensation of their whole religion. Hence it was that my sex, which of old had aided so powerfully the rise of Catholicism, remained almost completely passive in a reformation in which for the rejection of its tenderness it was offered as sole compensation the permission to interpret books which are unintelligible and dangerous. Protestantism would have grievously lowered the institution of marriage in the West by re-establishing divorce, had not modern habits and feelings always instinctively rejected so retrograde a movement, even where it was accepted officially.

The Priest.—Your just repugnance explains of itself, my daughter, the extreme disagreement of the West in regard to a purely negative doctrine, which soon divided nations, cities, nay, even families. Its partial success must, however, then have met some important wants, intellectual and social. Despite its anarchical character, the principle of Protestantism aided at first the progress of science and the development of industry, by stimulating individual efforts and setting aside oppressive rules. We owe to it the two preliminary revolutions directed, in Holland, against foreign tyranny, and, in England, to internal reform. Though the second, as too premature, was doomed ultimately to fail, it gave even then an indication, under the admirable dictatorship of Cromwell, of the inevitable tendency of the Western movement.

Then the requirements of order and of progress, both equally imperative, became absolutely irreconcilable, and the Westerns ranged themselves apart accordingly as they felt more strongly the one or the other. There was imminent danger of universal oppression had Protestantism nowhere obtained the ascendant, because a retrograde clergy was everywhere awakening the anxious attention of the older powers in opposition to a movement of which the tendency was no longer doubtful. But we should rather congratulate ourselves that the greater part of the West was preserved from the ascendency of Protestantism. For its universal acceptance, which would have been deemed generally the legitimate issue of the common revolution, would have everywhere completely masked all the essential conditions of human regeneration, by proclaiming the permanent fusion of the two powers. By these two judgments, we find ourselves led to sympathise equally with the great spirits who fought nobly in that immense struggle, the necessary preliminary to a true reorganisation.

In spite of the obstacles arising from the Protestant

agitation, the second period of modern history perfected the temporal dictatorship which issued from the first. Its rise coincides with the formation of the great nationalities, a provisional result of the disruption of the Western union which marks the Middle Ages. But this political anomaly has really a high social value, one moreover necessarily temporary, only for the central population. More and more charged, since Charlemagne, with the general direction of the Western movement, France needed to become a very compact power, large enough to give a decisive impact and overcome all reactionary aggression. Everywhere else, such concentration was but a blind and perilous imitation of this exceptional policy.

In this second phase, the Positive movement developed most of all its scientific character and philosophical tendency. Cosmology makes a capital advance by establishing the doctrine of the earth's motion, soon completed by the systematisation of celestial geometry and the foundation of celestial mechanics. Then the scientific spirit becomes radically at variance with all theology and metaphysics. The direct tendency to a thoroughly Positive philosophy finds visible expression, under the joint impulse of Bacon and Descartes, which indicates even then the preparation demanded by such a synthesis. During this decisive movement, the general and the special arts pursue worthily the course of evolution which the preceding period owed to the Middle Ages. Notwithstanding the absence of philosophical guidance and of social purpose, the poetry of the West produced, in five centuries, more real masterpieces than we derive from the whole of antiquity. As for the growth of industry, its extension becomes then increasingly the object of the attention of governments, though they still subordinate it to warlike aims. But it already displays the tendency of the masters to separate themselves from the workmen, so to gain admission into the degenerate aristocracy.

The Woman.—I would now, my father, form an idea of the character and object of the last modern phase.

The Priest.—It was rendered necessary, my daughter, by the general result of the preceding. Abandoning all idea of universal supremacy, Protestantism and Catholicism divided the West definitively between them, as the Roman empire was divided formerly between the Koran and the Bible. In the more important cases, this division of the West coincides naturally with the distinction, henceforward more marked, between the two forms, aristocratic and monarchical, taken by the temporal dictatorship everywhere thrown up by the preceding phase.

Both forms equally had become hostile to the radical emancipation which threatened them alike. Progressive so long as it had a powerful opposition to overcome, royalty, in France especially, displayed its retrograde tendencies, as soon as it no longer feared resistance. As early as the second half of the reign of Louis XIV., it gradually rallied round it all the fragments of the older order, to arrest in union with them a social movement which it could not but consider as simply anarchical. But the aristocratical and Protestant dictatorship became at that time, especially in England, a still more formidable enemy to the Western movement than the monarchical and Catholic, because it found more aid from the people. Protestantism, which, so long as it had to struggle, favoured liberty, as soon as it was established officially, exerted itself to check emancipation, as is the tendency of every system which rejects the separation of the two human powers. It set up, in England, an all-pervading system of hypocrisy, more skilfully organised and more pernicious than that with which it taunted Jesuitism, the latest form of expiring Catholicism. But the most corrupting influence of such a regime lay in the full development of the system of national selfishness, which in Venice had not been able to be more than inchoate, and which, too cordially welcomed by the whole British population, tended to isolate it from the West.

Such a state of affairs rendered as indispensable as inevitable the negative explosion of the eighteenth century, without which it was impossible to work out, nay, even to imagine, a true re-organisation. The critical doctrines, which had their original source in their fundamental principle under the two Protestant revolutions, were already sufficiently co-ordinated by the metaphysicians who succeeded Bacon and Descartes. They were then spread broadcast by the assiduous exertions of a class hitherto subaltern, the *littérateurs* properly so called, which thus took the place of the mediæval doctors in the direction of the revolutionary movement, in which the lawyers soon supplanted the judges. Two generations exhausted the preliminary ascendency of these inconsequent schools, who wished to destroy the altar and maintain the throne, or conversely. But the eighteenth century will never be represented philosophically by pure destructives, such as Voltaire and Rousseau, nearly forgotten at the present day. Its great school, that of Diderot and Hume, of which Fontenelle is the precursor and Condorcet the complement, accepts the total work of destruction only to gain as clear a conception as possible of the final regeneration, of which Frederick the Great was the precursor among the statesmen. For, from that time forward, it was only the narrower minds that could hope by any conceivable modification of the older order to meet the wants of the modern renovation.

During this final phase, the Positive movement completed cosmology by the foundation of chemistry. With this signal advance end the services of the analytical spirit and of the academical regime, the blind predominance of which became at once an obstacle of growing importance to labours which were bound to be essentially synthetic. In the industrial progress, we see then the class of bankers rising to its natural supremacy, which alone can reduce to system material activity. At the same time war becomes the minister of industry, the colonial disputes furnishing the occasion. The capital extension of machinery gives its last characteristic to modern industry. But it also fosters the lamentable neglect of the masters as regards the social conditions proper for the workmen, who became more and more a mere source of profit instead of being governed.

We thus understand the necessarily stormy character of the vast revolution which was the final issue of the whole five centuries which lie between us and the Middle Ages. It is the result of a fatal want of harmony between the two progressions which together make up the whole Western movement, in which the positive advance was unable to meet the demand for organisation created by the negative. Whilst this last was destroying all general conceptions, the former could only substitute for them special notions. The leadership in the modern regeneration, at the time of its greatest difficulty, had devolved on the most incompetent class, the class of mere writers, whose sole aspiration was the metaphysical pedantocracy dreamed of by their Greek masters, in order to centre all power in themselves.

The Woman.—Although these hints explain clearly enough the revolutionary crisis as a whole, I should like, my father, to know in outline its general course, so as to rightly estimate its actual state, the last object of this concluding conversation.

The Priest.—In it you must, my daughter, observe first the necessary abolition of the French monarchy, in which had centred the whole of the decaying regime. The funeral of Louis XIV. might have led men to foresee it, had there been at that time a true theory of history to interpret it aright as indicating at once the irremediable degeneracy of the government and the rooted antipathy of the people.

After some years of metaphysical hesitation, a decisive

shock overthrew for ever this retrograde institution, the last vestige of the caste system, according to the theocratic consecration given it by the servility of the modern clergy. But the glorious assembly, the only really popular assembly in France, which had thus to prelude the social regeneration, could not make good the intellectual deficiencies of the Western movement. Not in possession of any real organic doctrine, whilst directing in an heroic spirit the defence of the republic, it could only vaguely state the modern programme under cover of a metaphysical philosophy ever incapable of any construction.

The thoroughly subversive tendencies inevitably brought to light by the political triumph of this negative doctrine soon led to a retrograde reaction. Begun by the ephemeral ascendency of a bloodthirsty deism, it took its largest proportions on the official restoration of Catholicism under the military tyranny. But the basic tendencies of modern civilisation repelled from it alike theologism and war. Though every egoistic instinct was at that time stimulated in an unparalleled degree, the military spirit could not help resting, in its last orgies, on a system of compulsory recruitment, the universal adoption of which presages the proximate abolition of standing armies, to be replaced by a police force. No one of the retrograde expedients since introduced to avert such a result has been able to revive the corpse of war any more than that of theology, even under the plea of progress, and despite the absence of such convictions in the public as should reprobate this conduct. In reference to the most immoral of these expedients, I venture here to avow the wish which I solemnly express, in the name of true Positivists, that the Arabs may forcibly expel the French from Algeria, if the latter cannot bring themselves to restore it nobly. It will always be a matter of pride to me that, in my childhood, I ardently wished success to the heroic defence of the Spaniards.

This retrogression, which drew its apparent strength

solely from war, issued in a complete failure as a result of the definitive advent of peace in the West. But the continued absence of all organic views then led metaphysical empiricism to try to put forward as a solution for universal adoption a futile imitation of the parliamentary system peculiar to the English transition. Its official supremacy during a single generation really had no other result for that generation than to give regularity to a lamentable series of oscillations between anarchy and reaction, where the sole merit of either party lay in saving us from its rival.

During this long fluctuation, which more and more displayed the equal powerlessness of all the doctrines in vogue, the spiritual anarchy reached its height, all previous convictions, revolutionary as well as retrograde, being in a state of languor. No partial discipline can be real and lasting. Now the sole principle of an universal discipline—the constant supremacy of the heart over the intellect—had fallen into more and more discredit since the close of the Middle Ages, notwithstanding the holy resistance of women, who were less and less respected by the insanity of the West. This is why, even in the scientific evolution, the provisional order which Bacon and Descartes had tried to institute soon disappeared under the upgrowth on empirical grounds of dispersive specialisms, which rejected blindly all philosophical control. Instead of reducing each encyclopedic phase to what was required for the introduction of the next above it, every exertion was made to develop it indefinitely, by isolating it from a whole which was more and more lost sight of. This tendency became as retrograde as anarchical, in that it threatened to destroy even the leading results of former labours, under the increasing sway of academical mediocrities. But anarchy and reaction are still more rampant in art, the eminently synthetical nature of which rejected analytical empiricism more absolutely. Even in poetry itself, the degradation has become so great that the literary world can appreciate nothing but style ; so far as often to place real masterpieces below compositions not less mediocre than they are immoral.

The Woman.—In this sad picture, whose accuracy I cannot dispute, I do not see, my father, whence could come the final solution set forth in this Catechism.

The Priest.—It had its origin, my daughter, in the accomplishment in fair degree of the immense objective introduction which, beginning with Thales and Pythagoras, was carried on during the whole of the mediæval period, and did not cease to advance in defiance of modern anarchy. At the beginning of the French Revolution, it was adequate only in cosmology, owing to the recent creation of chemistry. But the decisive rise of biology, begun by Bichat and completed by Gall, soon achieved the supply of a scientific basis for the total renovation of the philosophical spirit. The whole Positive movement then issued in the advent of sociology, already heralded by Condorcet's immortal though abortive attempt to bring the future into systematic subordination to the past, in the face of a most anti-historical spirit.

The human point of view prevailing universally, a subjective synthesis could thus at length construct a philosophy really proof against all objections, and that led to the foundation of the final religion, as soon as the moral development had completed the regeneration of the intellect. Henceforward, the mediæval period was admired, at the same time that antiquity was better appreciated. A radical reconcilement was effected between the culture of feeling and that of the intelligence and the activity.

All noble hearts and all great intellects, henceforward always convergent, accept this termination of the long and difficult initiation through which Humanity had to pass, under the constantly declining sway of theologism and war. The modern movement loses its radically disparate character. Under its Positive aspect it at length shows itself able to meet all the demands, intellectual and social, made by its negative advance, and that not solely as regards the future, but also for the present, though I was not bound to take it into account here. Everywhere the relative definitively takes the place of the absolute, and altruism tends to bear down egoism, whilst a systematic method takes the place of a spontaneous evolution. In a word, Humanity definitively substitutes herself for God, without ever forgetting his provisional services.

There, my beloved daughter, you have the last explanation I owed you as to the triumphant advent of the Universal Religion, the aspiration, during so many centuries, of the West and the East. Though it be yet very greatly hampered, especially at its centre, by the prejudices and passions which, under different forms, reject all wholesome discipline, its efficacy will soon be felt by women and proletaries, chiefly in the South. But its best recommendation must come from the exclusive competence of the Positive priesthood to rally everywhere the honest and the thoughtful, nobly accepting the whole inheritance of mankind.

TABLES, &c.

TABLE A.

SYSTEM OF SOCIOLATRY,

Love for Principle
and Order for Basis;
Progress for End.

or

SOCIAL WORSHIP,

Live for Others.
(The Family, Coun-
try, Humanity.)

Embracing in a Series of Eighty-one Annual Festivals the Worship of Humanity
under all its aspects.

THE FUNDAMENTAL SOCIAL RELATIONS.

1st Month. HUMANITY.
- New Year's Day...... { Synthetical Festival of the Great Being.
- Weekly Festivals of the Social Union. { religious. historical. national. municipal.

2nd Month. MARRIAGE.
- complete.
- chaste.
- unequal.
- subjective.

3rd Month. The PATER-NAL RELATION ......
- complete............. { natural. artificial.
- incomplete........... { spiritual. temporal.

4th Month. The FILIAL RELATION.............. Same subdivisions.

5th Month. The FRA-TERNAL RELATION.. Same subdivisions.

6th Month. The RELA-TION OF MASTER AND SERVANT........
- permanent........... { complete. incomplete.
- temporary............ Same subdivision.

PREPARATORY STATES.

7th Month. FETICHISM.
- spontaneous { nomad ...... Festival of the Animals. sedentary ....Festival of Fire.
- systematic .. { sacerdotal. ...Festival of the Sun. military......Festival of Iron.

8th Month. POLYTHE-ISM....................
- conservative ..Festival of Castes.
- intellectual.. (Salamis) { esthetic..Homer, Æschylus, Phidias. scientific and philoso-phic. { Thales, Pythagorus, Aristotle, Hippocrates, Archimedes, Apollonius, Hipparchus.
- social..Scipio, Cæsar, Trajan.

9th Month. MONOTHE-ISM ....
- theocratic ....Abraham, Moses, Solomon.
- catholic.............. { St. Paul. Charlemagne. Alfred. Hildebrand. Godfrey of Bouillon. St. Bernard.
- Islamic (Lepanto) ......Mahomet.
- metaphysical .... { Dante. Descartes. Frederic II.

NORMAL FUNCTIONS.

10th Month. WOMEN ....
Moral Providence.
- mother.
- wife.
- daughter.
- sister.

11th Month. The PRIEST-HOOD...................
Intellectual Providence.
- incomplete ....Festival of Art.
- preparatory ....Festival of Science.
- definitive { secondary. principal. Festival of Old Men.

12th Month. The PATRI-CIATE...................
Material Providence.
- banking................Festival of the Knights.
- commerce.
- manufactures.
- agriculture.

13th Month. The PRO-LETARIATE............
General Providence.
- active. Festival of Inventors: Gutenberg, Columbus,
- affective. [Vaucanson, Watt, Montgolfier.
- contemplative.
- passive ....St. Francis of Assisi.

COMPLEMENTARY DAY ....Festival of all the DEAD.
The additional Day in LEAP YEARS ....General Festival of HOLY WOMEN.

Paris, Saturday, 7 Archimedes, 66. (1 April 1854.)
Pol. Pos., iv. p. 141, E. Tr. Positivist Catechism, p. 100.

TABLE B.

THEORETICAL HIERARCHY OF HUMAN CONCEPTIONS,
OR SYNTHETICAL VIEW OF THE UNIVERSAL ORDER,
In an Encyclopedic Scale of Five or Seven Degrees.

POSITIVE PHILOSOPHY, OR SYSTEMATIC KNOWLEDGE OF HUMANITY.

	HISTORICAL DIVISION.	
	NATURAL PHILOSOPHY, or PRELIMINARY SCIENCE. (The Order of the External World.)	FINAL SCIENCE, or MORAL PHILOSOPHY. (Social and Moral Order.)

STUDY OF THE EARTH, or COSMOLOGY.

- Abstract, or Fundamental Study of the form of Existence common to all things (*Number, Extension, Motion*). — I. MATHEMATICS 1
- Concrete, or Direct Study of the Laws of Matter ...... II. PHYSICS
  - Celestial, or .... ASTRONOMY ... 2
  - Terrestrial { General, or PHYSICS (Proper.) ... 3
  - { Special, or CHEMISTRY 4
- Preliminary, or General Study of the Laws of Life. III. BIOLOGY 5

STUDY OF MAN, or SOCIOLOGY.

- Final, or Direct Study of Man; or of Social and Moral Laws ......
  - In Society. IV. SOCIOLOGY (Proper.) 6
  - Individual. V. MORALS 7

DOGMATICAL DIVISION.

Paris, 10 Dante, 64. (Saturday 24 July 1852.)

Positivist Catechism, p. 131.

TABLE C.

POSITIVE CLASSIFICATION

OF THE EIGHTEEN INTERNAL FUNCTIONS OF THE BRAIN,

OR

SYSTEMATIC VIEW OF THE SOUL.

LIVE FOR OTHERS.

HUMANITY.

TO THINK, TO ACT,
AFFECTION, THINK TO ACT.

	IMPULSION. (THE HEART.)	COUNSEL. (THE INTELLECT.)
	Decrease of energy, increase of dignity, from the back of the head to the front, from the lower part to the higher, from the sides to the middle.	Knowledge, or vision, for the sake of prevision, with a view to provision.

PRINCIPLE.

10 AFFECTIVE MOTORS. Propensities, when active; feelings, when passive.

7 PERSONAL.

INTEREST — Instincts of Preservation
- 1 of the Individual, or *nutritive Instinct*.
- 2 of the race, or.... *sexual Instinct.* / *maternal Instinct.*

INTEREST — Instincts of Improvement
- 3 by destruction, or *military Instinct.*
- 4 by construction, or *industrial Instinct.*

AMBITION
- 5 Temporal, or Pride, desire of power
- 6 Spiritual, or Vanity, desire of approbation

3 SOCIAL. (General — Special)

- 7 ATTACHMENT
- 8 VENERATION
- 9 BENEVOLENCE or Universal Love (sympathy), *humanity*
- 10

MEANS.

5 INTELLECTUAL FUNCTIONS.

CONCEPTION
- Passive, or Contemplation, hence objective materials.
- Active, or Meditation, hence subjective constructions.

EXPRESSION
- Mimic, oral, written, hence *Communication*

COUNSEL (THE INTELLECT):
- 11 Concrete, or relative to Beings, essentially *synthetical.*
- 12 Abstract, or relative to Events, essentially *analytical.*
- 13 Inductive, or by comparison, hence *Generalisation.*
- 14 Deductive, or by co-ordination, hence *Systematisation.*
- 15

RESULT.

EXECUTION.
(THE CHARACTER.)

ACTIVITY.. { Courage	16	
Prudence	17	
FIRMNESS, hence *Perseverance*	18	

3 PRACTICAL QUALITIES.

(TO LOVE, ACT FROM

SUMMARY OF THE CEREBRAL THEORY.

These eighteen organs together form the cerebral apparatus, which, on the one hand, stimulates the life of nutrition, on the other, co-ordinates the life of relation, by connecting its two kinds of external functions. Its speculative region is in direct communication with the nerves of sensation, its active region with the nerves of motion. Its affective region has no direct communication except with the viscera of organic life; it has no immediate correspondence with the external world, its only connection with which is through the other two regions. This part of the brain, the essential centre of the whole of our existence, is in constant activity. It is enabled to be so by the alternate rest of the two symmetrical parts of each of its organs. As for the rest of the brain, its periodical cessation of action is as complete as that of the senses and muscles. Thus, our harmony as living beings depends on the principal region of the brain, the affective; it is from this that the two others derive their impulse, and in obedience to this impulse, the two others direct the relations of the animal with the external agencies which influence it, whether such relations be active or passive.

(*Positivist Catechism*, p. 179.)

TABLE D.

POSITIVIST CALENDAR.

TABLE

POSITIVIST

ADAPTED TO ALL

CONCRETE VIEW OF THE PREPARATORY

ESPECIALLY INTENDED FOR THE FINAL PERIOD OF TRANSITION THROUGH WHICH THE WESTERN REPUBLIC
OF THE FIVE LEADING POPULATIONS, THE FRENCH,

		FIRST MONTH. MOSES. THE INITIAL THEOCRACY.	SECOND MONTH. HOMER. ANCIENT POETRY.	THIRD MONTH. ARISTOTLE. ANCIENT PHILOSOPHY.
Monday...	1	Prometheus............*Cadmus.*	Hesiod.	Anaximander.
Tuesday...	2	Hercules................*Theseus.*	Tyrtæus.... ....*Sappho.*	Anaximenes.
Wednesday	3	Orpheus................*Tiresias.*	Anacreon.	Heraclitus.
Thursday..	4	Ulysses.	Pindar.	Anaxagoras.
Friday	5	Lycurgus.	Sophocles.............*Euripides.*	Democritus...........*Leucippus.*
Saturday ..	6	Romulus.	Theocritus..............*Longus.*	Herodotus.
Sunday	7	NUMA.	ÆSCHYLUS.	THALES.
	8	Belus................*Semiramis.*	Scopas.	Solon.
	9	Sesostris.	Zeuxis.	Xenophanes.
	10	Menu.	Ictinus.	Empedocles.
	11	Cyrus.	Praxiteles.	Thucydides.
	12	Zoroaster.	Lysippus.	Archytas..............*Philolaus.*
	13	The Druids...............*Ossian.*	Apelles.	Apollonius of Tyana.
	14	BOUDDHA.	PHIDIAS.	PYTHAGORAS.
	15	Fo-Hi.	Æsop....................*Pilpay.*	Aristippus.
	16	Lao-Tseu.	Plautus.	Antisthenes.
	17	Meng-Tseu.	Terence..............*Menander.*	Zeno.
	18	The Theocrats of Thibet.	Phædrus.	Cicero........*Pliny the Younger.*
	19	The Theocrats of Japan.	Juvenal.	Epictetus.................*Arrian.*
	20	Manco-Capac ......*Tamehameha.*	Lucian.	Tacitus.
	21	CONFUCIUS.	ARISTOPHANES.	SOCRATES.
	22	Abraham................*Joseph.*	Ennius.	Xenocrates.
	23	Samuel.	Lucretius.	Philo of Alexandria.
	24	Solomon.................*David.*	Horace.	St. John the Evangelist.
	25	Isaiah.	Tibullus.	St. Justin............*St. Irenæus.*
	26	St. John the Baptist.	Ovid.	St. Clement of Alexandria.
	27	Haroun-al-Raschid..*Abderrahman*	Lucan.	Origen................*Tertullian.*
	28	MAHOMET. [*III.*	VIRGIL.	PLATO.

		EIGHTH MONTH. DANTE. MODERN EPIC POETRY.	NINTH MONTH. GUTENBERG. MODERN INDUSTRY.	TENTH MONTH. SHAKESPEARE. THE MODERN DRAMA.
Monday...	1	The Troubadours.	Marco Polo.............*Chardin.*	Lope de Vega.........*Montalvan.*
Tuesday...	2	Boccaccio............*Chaucer.*	Jacques Cœur..........*Gresham.*	Moreto........*Guillem de Castro.*
Wednesday	3	Rabelais..................*Swift.*	Vasco de Gama.........*Magellan.*	Rojas...............*Guevara.*
Thursday..	4	Cervantes.	Napier...................*Briggs.*	Otway.
Friday	5	La Fontaine.............*Burns.*	Lacaille...............*Delambre.*	Lessing.
Saturday ..	6	De Foe ....*Goldsmith.*	Cook...................*Tasman.*	Goethe.
Sunday	7	ARIOSTO.	COLUMBUS.	CALDERON.
	8	Leonardo da Vinci..... ...*Titian.*	Benvenuto Cellini.	Tirso.
	9	Michael Angelo....*Paul Veronese.*	Amontons............*Wheatstone.*	Vondel.
	10	Holbein ....*Rembrandt.*	Harrison ....*Pierre Leroy.*	Racine.
	11	Poussin................*Lesueuer.*	Dollond................*Graham.*	Voltaire.
	12	Velasquez...............*Murillo.*	Arkwright ....*Jacquard.*	Metastasio.................*Alfieri.*
	13	Teniers..................*Rubens.*	Conté.	Schiller.
	14	RAPHAEL.	VAUCANSON.	CORNEILLE.
	15	Froissart...............*Joinville.*	Stevin...............*Torricelli.*	Alarcon.
	16	Camoens ....*Spenser.*	Mariotte...................*Boyle.*	Mme. de Motteville..*Mme. Roland.*
	17	The Spanish Romancers.	Papin................*Worcester.*	Mme. de Sévigné..*Lady Montagu.*
	18	Chateaubriand.	Black.	Lesage...................*Sterne.*
	19	Walter Scott.............*Cooper.*	Jouffroy ....*Fulton.*	Mme. de Staël..*Miss Edgeworth.*
	20	Manzoni.	Dalton...............*Thilorier.*	Fielding............*Richardson.*
	21	TASSO.	WATT.	MOLIERE.
	22	Petrarca. [*and Bunyan.*	Bernard de Palissy.	Pergolese.............*Palestrina.*
	23	Thomas à Kempis *Louis of Granada*	Guglielmini...............*Riquet.*	Sacchini ....*Grétry.*
	24	Mme. de Lafayette..*Mme. de Staël.*	Duhamel (du Monceau) *Bourgelat.*	Gluck....................*Lully.*
	25	Fénélon..:....*St. Francis of Sales.*	Saussure ....*Bouguer.*	Beethoven..............*Handel.*
	26	Klopstock...............*Gessner.*	Coulomb ....*Borda.*	Rossini....................*Weber.*
	27	Byron.*Elisa Mercœur and Shelley.*	Carnot..................*Vauban.*	Bellini................*Donizetti.*
	28	MILTON.	MONTGOLFIER.	MOZART.

Seventh Edition, Aug. 1855, in *Appel aux Conservateurs,* p. 115. Paris, Monday, 22 Charlemagne 67 (9th July 1855).
Positivist Catechism, p. 259.
To face p. 300.

D.

CALENDAR,

YEARS EQUALLY ; OR,

PERIOD OF MAN'S HISTORY,

HAS TO PASS : THE REPUBLIC WHICH, SINCE CHARLEMAGNE, HAS BEEN FORMED BY THE FREE COHESION
ITALIAN, SPANISH, BRITISH, AND GERMAN.

FOURTH MONTH. ARCHIMEDES. ANCIENT SCIENCE.	FIFTH MONTH. CÆSAR. MILITARY CIVILISATION.	SIXTH MONTH. ST. PAUL. CATHOLICISM.	SEVENTH MONTH. CHARLEMAGNE. FEUDAL CIVILISATION.
Theophrastus. Herophilus. Erasistratus. Celsus. Galen. Avicenna..............*Averrhoes.* HIPPOCRATES	Miltiades. Leonidas. Aristides. Cimon. Xenophon. Phocion...........*Epaminondas.* THEMISTOCLES.	St. Luke..............*St. James.* St. Cyprian St. Athanasius. St. Jerome. St. Ambrose. St. Monica. ST. AUGUSTIN.	Theodoric the Great. Pelayo. Otho the Great..*Henry the Fowler.* St. Henry. Villiers..............*La Valette.* Don John of Austria.*John Sobieski.* ALFRED.
Euclid. Aristæus. Theodosius of Bithynia. Hero...................*Ctesibius.* Pappus. Diophantus. APOLLONIUS.	Pericles. Philip. Demosthenes. Ptolemy Lagus. Philopœmen. Polybius. ALEXANDER.	Constantine. Theodosius. St. Chrysostom..........*St. Basil.* St. Pulcheria............*Marcian.* St. Genevieve of Paris. St. Gregory the Great. HILDEBRAND.	Charles Martel. The Cid.................*Tancred.* Richard I...............*Saladin.* Joan of Arc..............*Marina.* Albuquerque......*Sir W. Raleigh.* Bayard. GODFREY.
Eudoxus.................*Aratus.* Pytheas................*Nearchus.* Aristarchus............*Berosus.* Eratosthenes...........*Sosigenes.* Ptolemy. Albategnius........*Nasir-Eddin.* HIPPARCHUS.	Junius Brutus. Camillus ....*Cincinnatus.* Fabricius.............*Regulus.* Hannibal. Paulus Æmilius. Marius.............*The Gracchi.* SCIPIO.	St. Benedict..........*St. Antony.* St. Boniface.............*St. Austin.* St. Isidore of Seville...*St. Bruno.* Lanfranc...............*St. Anselm.* Heloise................*Beatrice.* The Arch'ts of Mid. Ages.*St. Benezet.* ST. BERNARD.	St. Leo the Great.........*Leo IV.* Gerbert................*Peter Damian.* Peter the Hermit. Suger...................*St. Eligius.* Alexander III.............*Becket.* St. Francis of Assisi..*St. Dominic.* INNOCENT III.
Varro. Columella. Vitruvius. Strabo. Frontinus. Plutarch. PLINY THE ELDER.	Augustus...............*Mœcenas.* Vespasian..................*Titus.* Hadrian...................*Nerva.* Antoninus......*Marcus Aurelius.* Papinian.................*Ulpian.* Alexander Severus ....*Aëtius.* TRAJAN.	St. Francis Xavier.*Ignatius Loyola.* St. Ch. Borromeo.*Fredk. Borromeo.* St. Theresa..*St. Catharine of Siena.* St.Vinc't de Paul *The Abbé de l'Epée.* Bourdaloue.........*Claude Fleury.* W. Penn.................*G. Fox.* BOSSUET.	St. Clotilde. [*cany.* St. Bathilda..*St. Mathilda of Tus-* St.Stephen of Hungary.*MathiasCor-* St. Elizabeth of Hungary. [*vinus.* Blanche of Castile. St. Ferdinand III......*Alfonso X.* ST. LOUIS.

ELEVENTH MONTH. DESCARTES. MODERN PHILOSOPHY.	TWELFTH MONTH. FREDERIC II. MODERN POLICY.	THIRTEENTH MONTH. BICHAT. MODERN SCIENCE.	Festival of all THE DEAD.	Festival of HOLY WOMEN.
Albertus Magnus.*John of Salisbury.* Roger Bacon.....*Raymond Lully.* St. Bonaventura.........*Joachim.* Ramus......*The Cardinal of Cusa.* Montaigne..............*Erasmus.* Campanella.....*Sir Thomas More.* ST. THOMAS AQUINAS.	Marie de Molina. Cosmo de Medici the Elder. Philippe de Comines..*Guicciardini.* Isabella of Castille. Charles V.............*Sixtus V.* Henry IV. LOUIS XI.	Copernicus..........*Tycho Brahé.* Kepler.................*Halley.* Huyghens..............*Varignon.* James Bernouilli. *John Bernouilli.* Bradley..................*Römer.* Volta...................*Sauveur.* GALILEO.		
Hobbes...............*Spinosa.* Pascal..........*Giordano Bruno.* Locke.............*Malebranche.* Vauvenargues..*Mme. de Lambert.* Diderot...................*Duclos.* Cabanis............*George Leroy.* LORD BACON.	L' Hôpital. Barneveldt. Gustavus Adolphus. De Witt. Ruyter. William III. WILLIAM THE SILENT.	Vieta...................*Harriott.* Wallis.................*Fermat.* Clairaut.................*Poinsot.* Euler...................*Monge.* D'Alembert.....*Daniel Bernouilli.* Lagrange..........*Joseph Fourier.* NEWTON.		
Grotius ....*Cujas.* Fontenelle...........*Maupertuis.* Vico...................*Herder.* Fréret.............*Winckelmann.* Montesquieu........*D'Aguesseau.* Buffon.....................*Oken.* LEIBNITZ.	Ximenes. Sully.................*Oxenstiern.* Mazarin................*Walpole.* Colbert...............*Louis XIV.* D'Aranda ....*Pombal.* Turgot...............*Campomanes.* RICHELIEU.	Bergmann..............*Scheele.* Priestley..................*Davy.* Cavendish. Guyton Morveau..........*Geoffroy.* Berthollet. Berzelius ....*Ritter.* LAVOISIER.		
Robertson ....*Gibbon.* Adam Smith............*Dunoyer.* Kant......................*Fichte.* Condorcet..............*Ferguson.* Joseph de Maistre........*Bonald.* Hegel...........*Sophie Germain.* HUME.	Sidney ....*Lambert.* Franklin................*Hampden.* Washington...........*Kosciusko.* Jefferson................*Madison.* Bolivar....*Toussaint-L'Ouverture.* Francia. CROMWELL.	Harvey..................*Ch. Bell.* Boërhaave..........*Stahl. Barthez.* Linnæus......*Bernard de Jussieu.* Haller..............*Vicq-d'Azyr.* Lamarck..............*Blainville.* Broussais ....*Morgagni.* GALL.	Complementary Day..............	Additional Day in Leap-years........

The provisional era begins January 1, 1789 (see *Pos. Pol.* iv., Eng. trans., p. 347).
The names in Italics are those of the persons who in Leap-years take the place of their principals.